The Scroll of Obadiah

The Life of a Norman Convert to Judaism in the First Crusade

Frank Riess

Helion & Company

To Norman Golb
who saw more

Helion & Company Limited
Unit 8 Amherst Business Centre
Budbrooke Road
Warwick
CV34 5WE
England
Tel. 01926 499 619
Email: info@helion.co.uk
Website: www.helion.co.uk
Twitter: @helionbooks
Visit our blog https://helionbooks.wordpress.com/

Published by Helion & Company 2025
Designed and typeset by Mach 3 Solutions (www.mach3solutions.co.uk)
Cover designed by Paul Hewitt, Battlefield Design (www.battlefield-design.co.uk)

Text © Frank Riess 2025
Photographs and illustrations as individually credited
Maps by George Anderson © Helion & Company 2025

Every reasonable effort has been made to trace copyright holders and to obtain their permission for the use of copyright material. The author and publisher apologise for any errors or omissions in this work and would be grateful if notified of any corrections that should be incorporated in future reprints or editions of this book.

ISBN 978-1-804518-31-1

British Library Cataloguing-in-Publication Data.
A catalogue record for this book is available from the British Library.

All rights reserved. No part of this publication may be reproduced, stored in a retrieval system, or transmitted, in any form, or by any means, electronic, mechanical, photocopying, recording or otherwise, without the express written consent of Helion & Company Limited.

For details of other military history titles published by Helion & Company Limited contact the above address or visit our website: http://www.helion.co.uk.

We always welcome receiving book proposals from prospective authors.Contents

Contents

Illustrations		iv
Maps		v
Acknowledgements		vi
Permissions		viii
List of Abbreviations		ix
1	The Dust of Centuries	11
2	Jacob and Esau	24
3	Call of the Crusade	42
4	Letter of Safe Conduct	54
5	Baghdad: City of Renown	69
6	Awaiting the Messiah	80
7	Siege of Aleppo	93
8	The Gift of the Nile	107
9	The Sound of Music	118
Bibliography		131
Index		141

Illustrations

1. Solomon Schechter in the Cairo room.   18
2. Norman Golb in his study.   22
3. Musical scores of Obadiah.   126

Maps

1. Obadiah's homeland in southern Italy. 29
2. The Levant and the world of Islam, 750–1150 CE. 88

Acknowledgements

The story of Obadiah, a twelfth-century Christian convert to Judaism, was originally to be published by Iradj Bagherzade. His untimely death in January 2023 was a great blow and a setback. I revere his memory and steadfast support. The draft of the manuscript had been written in 2019–2021, at a time that precluded me from travelling to southern Italy, the birthplace of Obadiah. The book is warmly dedicated to Norman Golb (1928-2020), whose work on Jewish proselytism has proved a guiding influence. More particularly, his translation of Obadiah's fragmentary account of his life is the main source. My work does not hope to provide new answers but offer a biography of a little-known person for general readers, who like me, are not conversant with Hebrew: modern or classical. My heart-felt thanks to Raphael Golb for permission to cite extracts from his late father's translation of the *Autograph Memoirs* of Obadiah. My work is also heavily dependent on the work of others, and I here offer thanks to them. Esther Yadgar provided translations from Hebrew articles, especially various publications of Norman Golb. Avshalom Caspi supplied an important English version of a medieval Hebrew poem. Holger Auffenberg clarified a valuable German text. Helga di Giuseppe informed me on points of regional Italian archaeology. Hope Doherty-Harrison, at an early stage, read a draft of the entire manuscript, offering illuminating insights: some were gratefully taken up. Anthony Bale gave encouraging support and suggestions. Richard Blackford read the chapter on music and notation, giving expert comments. Many of these offered suggestions, both general and particular, that saved me from egregious errors. All lapses that remain, factual or stylistic, are my sole responsibility. Paul O'Prey, at a crucial moment, offered important advice that opened up a new path.

The transcription of Arabic and Hebrew names betrays a lack of uniformity, given the many names and sources. However, I have relied as much as possible on Moshe Gil and his invaluable work, which cites many of these. I hope this will be accepted with a degree of tolerance and not considered a breach of scholarly usage. Quotations in American English have been left unchanged. I would also like to acknowledge the libraries that greatly assisted me in writing this work at a time of difficult access. The London Library, above all, posted numbers of books, and the Warburg Institute sent articles by email. The same was generously done by the British Library and the Institute of Historical Research. My greatest debt as always is to Lucia, a matchless reader and editor. Her work has improved the book to such an extent it is now her work as much as mine.

The book has found a good home at Helion. I am grateful to Duncan Rogers for enabling this to happen and to Charles Singleton for his wise tutelage in the production and editing. Kristi Snodgrass has proved a meticulous copy editor and George Anderson a clear-eyed cartographer. Kim McSweeney handled the typesetting, and Paul Hewitt designed the book cover. My thanks to all of them.

Permissions

The author wishes to thank the following for the kind permission to reproduce text and translations. Some are mentioned in the acknowledgements.

Oxford University Press © *The Song of the Distant Dove* by Raymond Scheindlin (2008) for permission to cite a poem by Judah Halevi.
Garnet Publishing © *The Best Divisions for Knowledge of the Regions* translated by Basil Collins (2001) for permission to cite an extract of Al-Muqaddasī.
Syndics of the Cambridge University Library © for permission to reproduce an image of Solomon Schechter and two folios of a musical score by Obadiah, T-S K5.41.
University of Chicago © for permission to reproduce a photo of Norman Golb.
Hackett Publishing © *Satires* translated by J. Svarlien (2012) for permission to cite extracts from a poem by Horace.
Edinburgh University Press © *The Crusades: Islamic Perspectives* by Carole Hillenbrand (2018) for permission to cite lines from Al-Mas'udi.
Penguin Classics © *The Alexiad* by Anna Komnene, translated by E. R. A. Sewter and revised by P. Frankopan (2009) for permission to cite short extracts.

List of Abbreviations

Autobiography/Autograph Memoirs – *The Autograph Memoirs of Obadiah the Proselyte of Oppido Lucano*
Itinerary – *The Itinerary of Benjamin of Tudela*
JJS – *Journal of Jewish Studies*
JQR – *Jewish Quarterly Review*
MS – S. D. Goitein, *A Mediterranean Society*, vols 1–6
REJ – *Revues des Études Juives*
T-S – Taylor-Schechter

Chapter 1

The Dust of Centuries

When the Suez Canal opened in 1869 with ostentatious ceremony, it marked a defining moment in the Mediterranean world. The passage from western Europe to India and the Far East had been cut by one-half both in time and distance, and the canal took on a game-changing role as a driver of the British Empire's aggrandisement, supporting its political influence and trade with India. On the morning of 17 November of that year, the inauguration of the canal was blessed by Moslem, Greek Orthodox, Coptic and Roman Catholic priests, with guns and cannon fired and 20 military bands striking up martial airs. A new Verdi opera *Aida* was specially commissioned.[1] Six years after its opening, Prime Minister Benjamin Disraeli turned all this to British advantage by master-minding the purchase of the shares in the canal company held by the Khedive, the Viceroy of Egypt. As a result of this bold move, carried out with a £4,000,000 loan from Baron Rothschild, the Prime Minister had called on his personal contacts with the owner of a major bank to initiate the virtual occupation of Egypt as a British possession.[2] The British invaded in 1882 and, after routing an Egyptian rebellion, seized Cairo and established a British protectorate over Egypt. This was never officially proclaimed, and, until 1914, the facade of Ottoman sovereignty was maintained. Despite this, the country was run by Britain, to safeguard its influence and its links with India. Evelyn Baring – later 1st Earl of Cromer – who had been appointed British commissioner for the finances of Egypt in 1877, managed the Egyptian government from 1883 till 1907, as Consul General and Adviser to the Khedive.[3]

A Jewish synagogue in old Cairo

Whilst the Suez Canal was being built with the fanfare of modern engineering, accompanied by high imperial grandeur, other events concerning a far older project

---

1 Alan Moorehead, *The White Nile* (London: Penguin, 1963), pp.145–48.
2 Robert Blake, *Disraeli* (London: Routledge, 1969), pp.581–87.
3 Jeremy Black, 'The Mediterranean as a Battleground of the European Powers: 1700–1900', in D. Abulafia (ed.), *The Mediterranean in History* (London: Thames & Hudson, 2016), pp.264–66.

were slowly unfolding at the centre of our story. In the slums of Old Cairo, the ancient synagogue of Ben Ezra had stood for centuries and acquired many traditions associated with religious worship and old age. The Jews of Old Cairo – originally called Fustāt – had looked to the Ben Ezra synagogue as a place for congregation, celebration, prayer and study for nearly 1,000 years. Now, although some of the communal leadership remained on the site of the synagogue, most of the population had moved north to the more modern city of Cairo. At the outset, the synagogue had been badly damaged by al-Ḥâkim, a hostile caliph, and was rebuilt between 1039 and 1041. A further restoration had been undertaken in 1892. Local legend always had it that, on this very site, Moses had appealed to God to bring one of the plagues before the Exodus to an end and that the prophet Jeremiah, in exile in 586 BCE, had recited his laments in this synagogue over the destruction of Jerusalem and the First Temple. Ezra the scribe was also said to have proved to the Egyptian Jews that he transcribed a Torah scroll with magical powers and placed it in the synagogue. His name was attached to this Torah scroll, said to have been kept in a special ark until 1899, high on the east wall of the ground-floor chamber.[4] Apparently, such a tale was the explanation for the name 'Ben Ezra' given to the synagogue in the nineteenth century. These legends would soon be trumped by new stories that began to seep out into the light of day connected with a room in the old synagogue.

Hidden books and manuscripts

The Ben Ezra synagogue might have slumbered on with its old stories, but, in the summer of 1864, as the canal was progressing, a visit first brought it to the attention of the outside world. A visiting Lithuanian scholar and collector of Judaic antiquities named Jacob Saphir went to the synagogue, as travellers were often directed there as a place of pilgrimage. Somewhere in the synagogue, it was pointed out to him that there was a room containing many worn and old books, and Saphir's curiosity was aroused. Upon asking the officials permission to enter the chamber where these lay, he was not allowed in, for it was claimed, they said, that there was a snake coiled up at the entrance. Saphir was now thoroughly emboldened and managed to obtain authorisation from higher officials of the Rabbinical court. What he found when he managed to get in was a space, two-and-a-half storeys high, open to the sky due to a recent roof collapse and apparently piled high with old papers under the rubble and debris. He left taking 'several sheets of different old scrolls and manuscripts', as he stated two years later.[5] But he had barely scratched the surface.

---

[4] Charles Le Quesne, 'Legend and Tradition at the Ben Ezra Synagogue', in P. Lambert (ed.), *Fortifications and the Synagogue: The Fortress of Babylon and the Ben Ezra Synagogue, Cairo* (Montreal: Canadian Centre for Architecture, 1994), pp.197–99.

[5] Adina Hoffman and Peter Cole, *Sacred Trash: The Lost and Found World of the Cairo Geniza* (New York: Schocken, 2011), pp.20–22; Rebecca J. W. Jefferson, *The Cairo Geniza and the Age of Discovery in Egypt: The History and Provenance of a Jewish Archive* (London: I. B. Tauris, 2022), p.25; Saphir account in Charles Le Quesne, 'Descriptions of the Ben Ezra Synagogue

This was the only description of the Ben Ezra synagogue before it was rebuilt. In truth, news was beginning to circulate amongst antiquarians and dealers: the synagogue was soon visited by Abraham Firkovitch, a Crimean Jew and an avid collector who, over the years, was to assemble an enormous collection of manuscripts and fragments gathered in Crimea and other parts. The Ben Ezra synagogue may have been the source of some of these items, today in the State Public Library of St Petersburg, but Firkovitch had found many himself elsewhere or purchased others from Cairo dealers with links to synagogue officials.[6] Over the next two decades, the pace quickened; more fragments appeared, especially in the years of the reconstruction of the Ben Ezra synagogue between 1889 and 1892. Earlier, starting in 1869, Moses Shapira, an energetic dealer established in Jerusalem, was offering scrolls and other antiquities to European buyers from other sources. He sold 40 Yemenite manuscripts to the British Museum in 1877.[7] New figures played an important role: Elkan Nathan Adler, brother of Hermann Adler, the future Chief Rabbi of the United Kingdom (or, to give him his full title, Chief Rabbi of the United Hebrew Congregations of the British Empire), appeared to have visited the Cairo chamber of the Ben Ezra synagogue and come away with a sack containing paper and parchment.[8] Another figure was the enterprising Jerusalem Rabbi, Solomon Aaron Wertheimer, who dispatched agents to Egypt in order to set up a supply chain of transactions from sites other than the Cairo synagogue, some of which ended up being shown to university librarians at Oxford and Cambridge. From 1894 to 1896, Wertheimer sold 62 manuscripts to Cambridge and another 29 to Oxford. In 1893, Wertheimer had publicly mentioned that a manuscript on which he was working 'comes from the old Geniza ... in the land of Egypt'.[9] This was a term familiar to all Judaic antiquarians, scholars and collectors.

A lost world that was found

The word 'geniza' is thought to have come into Hebrew from 'ganj', a Persian root meaning 'storehouse'. But it is not certain that the origin is only Persian, for the root of this term is also attested in Aramaic, Arabic, Ethiopic and late Babylonian with the meanings of 'hide', 'cover' and 'bury'. Nevertheless, the Persian root of the word is most often mentioned. Some later Biblical books written under the influence of Persian rule contain related meanings: *ginzei hamelekh* (Esther 3:9) and *ginzei malka* translated respectively as 'the king's treasuries' and the 'royal archives' or 'house of the rolls' (Ezra 6:1). Thus, one central area of meaning was the idea of storage and

---

from the Nineteenth and Early Twentieth Centuries', in P. Lambert (ed.), *Fortifications and the Synagogue: The Fortress of Babylon and the Ben Ezra Synagogue, Cairo* (Montreal: Canadian Centre for Architecture, 1994), p.245.
6   Jefferson, *Cairo Geniza*, pp.15–26.
7   Jefferson, *Cairo Geniza*, pp.39–47.
8   Jefferson, *Cairo Geniza*, p.114.
9   Hoffman and Cole, *Sacred Trash*, pp.33–35; Jefferson, *Cairo Geniza*, pp.97–100.

even concealment of objects that were of value or even sacred. In a similar manner, religious manuscripts, even secular texts that had been rendered unfit for use and contained sacred words like the written name of God, were precluded from being thrown out as refuse. All such things had to be protected from contact or contamination and preserved, as Hebrew was considered to be the language of God. Most interestingly, the word '*geniza*' morphed from being a process to signify a place. The location could be a burial plot, a storage chamber or a cabinet where such sacred writings could be entombed. Not all Jewish communities followed the same procedure, but undoubtedly there were other *geniza* (pl *genizot*). For many generations, texts that no longer circulated and needed to be discarded were consigned to the Cairo *Geniza*. Other synagogues and sites housing such artefacts contributed to the widening search by dealers and yielded more finds.[10]

It is difficult to generalise about this important custom, but it was widely understood by both the early and the later investigators and researchers attracted to the Ben Ezra synagogue in Cairo – or to any other synagogue – that there could be ancient and valuable texts piled up in these chambers. The mid-nineteenth century had opened up the Cairo synagogue and other sites to a rush for these manuscripts, fuelled by academic research and the expansion of libraries. It appeared that the opening of the Suez Canal had ushered in not only a passage of water but also a floodgate of competition. The Cairo Geniza (hereafter not italicised and often referred to simply as 'the Geniza'), which had been previously ignored for so many centuries, now assumes its place at the heart of this story.

The reader from Cambridge pays a visit

Solomon Schechter, a ginger-bearded and energetic Jewish scholar from Romania, had been appointed Reader in Talmudic and Rabbinic Literature at the University of Cambridge some years after his arrival in 1882. He was not unaware of the existence of the Cairo Geniza and, in the 1890s, had even handled some of the material shown by Wertheimer to the Cambridge library, advising them whether to buy some samples.[11] All was transformed when two Presbyterian twin sisters, now widowed and independently wealthy, approached Schechter. Frequent travellers in the Middle East, these ladies had gained a detailed knowledge of manuscripts and antiquities. Margaret Gibson and Agnes Lewis were well known to Schechter (amusingly referred to by him as 'the Giblews') and had brought back with them some documents and fragments from the Cairo Geniza, two of which they had picked out to show Schechter. Not considering them to be of importance, the Reader in Talmudic took them away, nonetheless, to pore over more closely. It proved to be a 'eureka' moment: one of the fragments was a piece of the original Hebrew of the book known in Christian circles as Ecclesiasticus. As he explained in an article later in the year,

---

10 Hoffman and Cole, *Sacred Trash*, pp.12–14, 248–49.
11 Jefferson, *Cairo Geniza*, p.122.

Schechter had stumbled on part of the original text of Ecclesiasticus (the Book of Wisdom) by Jesus Ben Sira, known to have been written around 200 BCE. But this original Hebrew text had been lost for centuries, and the book had only survived in a Greek translation. Now, with the original words at hand, it would be possible to study the details of the Hebrew in a particular idiom that would illuminate the years between this original text and the later books of the Old Testament and, more especially, any links with Rabbinic writings. What Schechter was looking at was an authentic chain of transmission from the original Hebrew through to the medieval period.[12] The last sighting of any part of the Hebrew original had been in the tenth century CE, and, by the time the Christian canon was formed, this text had become known as Ecclesiasticus, a term denoting 'Book of the Church'.

These important but learned musings were now overtaken in Schechter's mind by an urgent thought: were there more of such fragments, and could they lie hidden in the heaps of ancient material in the Cairo Geniza? Schechter was now possessed with an unstoppable urge to go to Egypt. In December 1896, he set off for Cairo armed with important support: a sealed and ornately prepared document from the Vice-Chancellor of Cambridge, addressed to the Jewish community of Cairo, and a letter for the Chief Rabbi of Cairo from Hermann Adler, the Chief Rabbi of the United Kingdom and British Empire, who had succeeded his father in 1891. His brother Elkan Nathan, who actually composed the letter, had already played a part in acquiring geniza fragments from Egypt. In fact, brother Elkan had helped enormously in preparing the ground for Schechter's arrival and reception in Cairo. Most importantly, prior to his trip, Schechter had obtained financial help from Charles Taylor, the master of St John's College, for funds to pay for the expedition and had also enlisted the support of the University. Taylor was a great admirer of Schechter and had studied under him.

Upon arrival in Cairo, Schechter devoted some time to a charm offensive on the Chief Rabbi Ben Shimon and on the leader of the Jewish community, Moise Cattaui. These two were not only impressed with his erudition but also won over by Schechter's engagement and enthusiasm and eager to forge links with a representative from one of Britain's top institutions. Soon, the Chief Rabbi escorted him to the Cairo Geniza and placed him in the hands of the synagogue beadles, giving him the green light to take whatever he wanted. Schechter's complete access and carte blanche to remove anything he wished was heavily underpinned by the interest that the virtual ruler of Egypt, Evelyn Baring, took in the project. Baring's first secretary had visited him soon after his arrival, and, during his stay, Schechter met several times with Harry Boyle, Baring's private secretary, who was a key aide to the Consul General. It was said that he had passed a letter from the University to the great man. Through Baring's offices, especially with the support of Boyle, Schechter would

---

12 Stefan C. Reif, *A Jewish Archive from Old Cairo: The History of Cambridge University's Genizah Collection* (Richmond: Curzon, 2000), pp.112–13; Jefferson, *Cairo Geniza*, pp.119–21; Hoffman and Cole, *Sacred Trash*, pp.46–54.

obtain the necessary export orders for any goods he eventually shipped. All this careful preparation would lead to a spectacular result.[13]

A hoard of Hebrew manuscripts

At this time, the Geniza chamber could be approached up a ladder from the women's gallery, and, in a description that became famous, Schechter was confronted with what he called 'a battlefield of books' that, as he went on to say, seemed to have struggled against each other for many centuries, breaking into many amputated pieces and strewn over the chamber. Some of these, he added, had been ground to dust while others had been pressed into large, distorted lumps. Different pages and leaves were stuck together: a printed work here, and a handwritten letter there. The room he had entered was dark, filled with dust and dirt, which clung to his throat, and was full of insects – *Genizaschmutz*, as he called it. Schechter had to work in such forbidding conditions and make quick decisions. As far as he could, he decided to take all the older manuscripts and leave behind the later printed work. By 20 January 1897, after four weeks, he had filled 30 sacks of fragments, which, with the help of the British authorities, especially Boyle, were shipped and spirited off to Cambridge. The dust of centuries had nearly suffocated and blinded him, but he had pulled off what would become one of the greatest coups in the history of Judaic studies, possibly only eclipsed by the find of the Dead Sea Scrolls five decades later.[14] It was a tale that would be told and retold many times, perhaps acquiring not a few embellishments, and the story was not quite as he recorded it. With the earlier demolition and rebuilding of the synagogue between 1889 and 1892, the Geniza chamber had actually been emptied of its contents, which were then put back in the new chamber, the one actually described by Solomon Schechter. What he saw was certainly old, but it had been disturbed, removed and then reinstated. It also seemed, when he arrived, that some of the contents had remained unreturned or buried in the ground during the building work. Other material was scattered around the synagogue, and items may also have been interred in the tombs of the Jewish cemetery at Basâtīn, on the right bank of the Nile. Later, it became clearer that Schechter might have even asked his assistants to empty out this new Geniza chamber and pile the contents on the ground outside to better examine them. This seems to have left further piles of fragments and documents remaining outside that became mixed up with rubbish. Much of this material was also eventually examined and passed into the hands of traders, collectors and buyers. After Schechter's departure with his haul of 30 sacks, the mound he had left behind was also the object of a thorough search by

---

13 Hoffman and Cole, *Sacred Trash*, pp.64–69; on Schechter's dealings with Baring's staff, see Jefferson, *Cairo Geniza*, pp.131-132, 141.
14 Hoffman and Cole, *Sacred Trash*, pp.69–74. The description of what he saw, 'A hoard of Hebrew manuscripts', appeared in *The Times* on 3 August 1897; also Reif, *Jewish Archive*, pp.80–81, and Hoffman and Cole, *Sacred Trash*, p.70, quote parts of the account.

Schechter's Cairo friend, one Reginald Henriques, a Cairene businessman who had originally introduced him to Boyle and who succeeded in shipping another six sacks to Cambridge.

The final count of how many items were removed from this chamber or from outside by Schechter or by others has been estimated to be between 140,000 and 300,000 manuscript fragments, suggesting, according to some, a total of three times that number in discrete leaves. But any number is now difficult to calculate precisely, as all these other items, removed from different sources at different times, eventually made up the collection stored at Cambridge. As the story has unfolded, we learn that not all the contents of the Cairo Geniza were removed by Schechter at the time and that other expeditions continued to take further consignments. How much of today's Geniza manuscript collection came from Henriques's later haul of six sacks remains unknown.[15] Meanwhile, in Cambridge, the classification of all this would take many years, with Schechter's find and the other acquisitions becoming named the Taylor-Schechter (T-S) Collection in honour of the two men who had done so much to make it possible.

Over the next decades, the sacks were to reveal an unknown Jewish world, a Mediterranean society illuminating not only Jewish but also other groups, notably Arab, Christian and many more. In the years to come, the task of sorting, cleaning, archiving and publishing the contents of what had been brought back to Cambridge spawned an industry of research and investigation driven by a multitude of scholars. The enormous task was vividly captured in a now famous photograph of Schechter, doubtless somewhat posed, soon after his return. It was taken in what was called the 'Cairo room' at Cambridge and shows him hard at work examining an item, surrounded by mountains of scraps and fragments brought back from Cairo.

But this was beyond the work of one man. As the months and years passed, an enormous jumble and variety of learned and customary documents, many in tattered and indecipherable pieces, came to light: scriptural texts, biblical manuscripts, correspondence, bills, contracts and marriage deeds. Letters written by women showed the high level of literacy and the feelings and opinions they held about men, marriage and their own wealth. Indeed, commerce, banking and industry were extensively represented in accounts, inventories, shipping documents and orders of payment. All this content was mainly concentrated on the communities that existed in and around Cairo from the tenth to the thirteenth centuries, although much would pre-date this period and go beyond into a later date.[16] The dust would not settle on this hoard for some time.

---

15 Rebecca J. W. Jefferson, 'Dangerous Liaisons in Cairo: Reginald Q. Henriques and the Taylor-Schechter Geniza Manuscript Collection', *Judaica Librarianship*, 20 (2017), pp.32–42; Charles Le Quesne, 'The Geniza and the Scholarly Community', in P. Lambert (ed.), *Fortifications and the Synagogue: The Fortress of Babylon and the Ben Ezra Synagogue, Cairo* (Montreal: Canadian Centre for Architecture, 1994), p.240, for the material left behind. Reif, *Jewish Archive*, p.151, for manuscript fragments and number of discrete leaves.

16 S. D. Goitein, *A Mediterranean Society* [MS]: *The Jewish Communities of the Arab World as Portrayed in the Documents of the Cairo Geniza* (Berkeley: University of California Press,

Solomon Schechter in the Cairo room. (Cambridge University Library)

A story of one Norman cleric

It would not be long before the documents uncovered in the Cairo Geniza began to reveal hidden stories of extraordinary forgotten people. One of the most impressive lives, which we now proceed to tell, is the tale of a Norman cleric called Johannes who, sometime in the twelfth century, had converted to Judaism and taken the name 'Obadiah'. Eventually, when the full details of his life were known, these would record the dangers to which he was exposed and describe his travels among the Jewish communities in the Middle East at the time of the Crusades. It would take more than half a century for the whole account of his life to become clear, as research and publication of any findings were carefully noted by scholars in different locations, because these details were written down on fragments that had become dispersed – after the extraction of so much material – to collections in Oxford, Cambridge, New York, London, St Petersburg, Manchester, Budapest and other places. All in all, 50 institutions and around 18 private names are said today to hold collections or fragments that originate from the Cairo Geniza.[17]

1967–1993), vol. 1, pp.9–13.
17 Jefferson, *Cairo Geniza*, pp.189–90. An appendix lists the largest collections.

Moments of the life of Johannes began to emerge in a haphazard manner with gaps in the story. Solomon Wertheimer, mentioned earlier, was the first to name him in a collection of manuscripts compiled in 1901, not long after Schechter's famous finds in the Cairo Geniza. This referred to only part of a medieval Hebrew text appearing to be written by one Rabbi Barukh son of Isaac to Obadiah the Proselyte (*Obadiah ha-Ger*) as a reference or testimonial to carry with him when visiting communities of Israelites. The other side of the manuscript contained the first part of Barukh's recommendation.[18] In 1921, Jacob Mann, another notable scholar of these early years, published the other half of this letter, showing that this Norman person had been perhaps connected with a messianic sect or movement. This had been further amplified by Mann in a later article, written in 1930, where he set out some fragments from what appeared to be a chronicle, one page of which had been published by E. N. Adler in 1919.[19] Mann also enlarged on these findings after coming across the final leaf and the colophon of a Sabbath prayer book (*siddur*) that Obadiah appeared to have written for his own use and that seemed to confirm that he was from Normandy and that he had converted in 1102. It also stated, most importantly, that the leaf had been written in his hand. The other side of this manuscript provided an Arabic title – seeming to suggest that this Norman convert had learned Arabic as well as Hebrew – and a prayer in Hebrew for the eve of the Sabbath to be recited privately. However, his Christian name was not given. Mann mentioned that he had purchased a bundle of these fragments in Cairo, which he said came from the Geniza, in the summer of 1924.

A big advance on more moments of this Norman's life was provided in 1953 by Shelomo Goitein's discovery of an important new fragment that clarified some of the assertions proposed by Mann. Goitein had come across a manuscript in the Cambridge collection – part of the material brought back by Schechter – which clearly referred to the persecution of Jews in western Europe on the eve of the First Crusade and unusually contained some lines in Hebrew characters transcribing a passage in Latin from the Vulgate text. The entire manuscript was badly damaged, with pages torn away, and what remained of the writing was either partly or entirely disfigured. In the reconstruction of the life of Obadiah, the difficult state of the manuscripts was to prove at times an insurmountable challenge. Goitein, a tireless investigator and renowned scholar who performed a major role in categorising and examining all manner of geniza documents, was here able to establish for the first time that this Obadiah was born with the name of John and that, although writing in his own hand, he referred to himself in the third person. There were four pages

---

18   Solomon A. Wertheimer, *Ginze Yerushalem* (Jerusalem: Publisher unknown, 1901), vol. 2, pp.16a–17a.
19   J. Mann, 'Obadya le Prosélyte', *REJ*, 71 (1921), pp.88–93 (also to be found in Jacob Mann, *The Collected Articles of Jacob Mann* (Israel: M. Shalom, 1971), vol. 1, pp.113–17), and 'Obadya, Prosélyte Normand converti au Judaïsme, et sa Meguilla, décrivant des événements survenus en Orient au temps des Croisades', *REJ*, 89 (1930), pp.245–59 (also to be found in Jacob Mann, *The Collected Articles of Jacob Mann* (Israel: M. Shalom, 1971), vol. 1, pp.118–32); E. N. Adler, 'Ovadiah le Prosélyte', *REJ*, 69 (1919), pp.129–34.

or sides that Goitein examined, and, between the first two (a–b) and the next (c–d), they suggested a gap of many years that placed Obadiah in Baghdad. This appeared to precede the account of the messianic encounter described by Mann in 1930.[20]

A most important fact now highlighted by Goitein was that the so-called scroll must have been written as a codex, for, between the lines 9–10 and 15–16, he remarked on the holes he had noticed for the binding of the leaves. This suggested that these pages, however difficult to decipher, were part of a book and not a scroll. Today, the evidence shows that many loose fragments from the Cairo Geniza originally belonged to codices. This observation dovetailed with the theory that, after the second century CE, many scrolls began to be copied into bound volumes, denoting a general shift from scroll to codex, so, by the time Obadiah was committing his life to writing, this was a common practice. The Hebrew codex made its full appearance in the eighth century, probably under the influence of Islam, which had taken up the form from the Christian and Classical worlds. The scroll continued to be used by the Jews for religious and ritual texts such as the Torah, read ceremoniously in the synagogue. Nevertheless, by the 1950s, the growing evidence of this material on Obadiah (also written as 'Obadyah') was labelled in scholarly parlance a 'scroll', a descriptive term that denoted it was ancient and seemed to exist in separate fragments. It is also relevant to note that, with copious material now appearing from the Geniza, the scroll or *megilloth* (sing. *megillah*) was also put forward as a genre, akin to the biblical rolls of Ruth or Esther that described happenings in the life of a person, a family or community.[21] Another case in point was the scroll or genealogy of Ahimaaz Ben Paltiel composed in 1054 CE and found in Toledo, which will be mentioned later. Like the account of Obadiah, all these so-called biographies are written in Hebrew and intended to be read as works of literature. This instance of an autobiography written by a Jew, Obadiah, in the Middle Ages takes a notable place as one of the first examples of such a literary genre.

The fragmentary details known up to then had first been unearthed by Wertheimer in 1901, Adler in 1919 and Mann in 1921 and 1930. Now, Goitein, in 1953, had come up with a fourth fragment. The early Adler piece examined was written in an unvocalised Hebrew, whilst the Cambridge fragments were provided with vowels, and this meant that the scroll seemingly existed in two different manuscripts, although both were written in the same script. The question remained: were there any more fragments? A year later, in 1954, Alexander Scheiber – a rabbi and noted Jewish

---

20   S. D. Goitein, 'Obadyah, a Norman Proselyte: A Propos the Discovery of a New Fragment of His "Scroll"', *JJS*, 4:2 (1953), pp.76–84; Golb (trans.), 'Autograph Memoirs', Document IV: Cambridge: Taylor-Schechter Genizah Collection, MS 8.271, fol. 1, *recto*, and Document V: Cambridge: Taylor-Schechter MS 8.271, fol. 1 *verso*, for manuscript.

21   Goitein, *MS*, vol. 1, p.14; On scroll to codex, see Reif, *Jewish Archive*, pp.210–14; Judith Olszowy-Schlanger, 'The Anatomy of Non-Biblical Scrolls from the Cairo Geniza', in I. Wardrey (ed.), *Jewish Manuscripts: New Cultures* (Berlin: De Gruyter, 2017), pp.49–88. On literary genre, see Joshua Prawer, 'The Autobiography of Obadyah the Norman, a Convert to Judaism at the Time of the First Crusade', in I. Twersky (ed.), *Studies in Medieval Jewish History and Literature* (Cambridge: Harvard University Press, 1979), pp.110–11.

scholar who was director of the Rabbinical Seminary in Budapest – came up with the answer when he discovered another piece of the puzzle in the Kaufmann Geniza Collection in Budapest. This became known as the 'Budapest fragment', the writing being identical to that of the colophon giving Obadiah's statement of the date of his conversion and penned, as he asserted, in his own hand. All the pieces of the scroll now proved to be written in this same hand. Like the four pages found by Goitein, Scheiber noted that the two pages found in Budapest were very badly preserved. The deciphering of this fragment presented a big obstacle, but it clearly complemented the example published by Goitein the year before.[22] Notable new information found in the Budapest fragment was a description of Obadiah's descent and place of birth: it revealed that he was born in Oppido in southern Italy, not in Normandy. The names of his mother and father were given for the first time and the fact that he was the younger of twins, calling himself Johannes or Guiàn. In the second folio, apparently speaking of events taking place years later, he described his experiences in Baghdad, where he appears to have been instructed in Hebrew writing and language. There were also unknown facts about Jews in Baghdad, providing a valuable source that added to our knowledge of this community. Scheiber concluded his important article by giving the Hebrew text accompanied by an English translation.

With these findings, the life and travels of Obadiah appeared to be more complete, if not better known, but the damaged state of the manuscripts and the difficulty even for specialists to read them made some parts impossible to interpret. Besides, the context in which these texts were discovered precluded at times any certainty of a clear chronological sequence. Finally, the whole picture risked being changed or challenged if more fragments should turn up. The next breakthrough was achieved by Norman Golb, an American scholar who had studied under Goitein. He was inspired by Goitein's achievements to look more closely at the work already done on the uncertain state of the passages uncovered on the life of the Norman from Italy. He saw the importance of returning to the work of Mann, Goitein and Scheiber to conduct detailed palaeographic analysis. Golb trusted himself to look carefully at the worn manuscripts in a natural bright light with a good magnifying glass, at times even eschewing ultraviolet photography.

Sometimes, he asserted, a word or a phrase or just the mark of a letter could be better seen in the sunlight with a magnifying glass than in the artificial light shining directly on the fragment. In 1980–1981, Golb brought out a lengthy study of the work he had done so far, where he proceeded to carefully revise some of the readings carried out by all these previous scholars, acknowledging that some interpretations of his own remained contentious.[23] His work established him as the maximum authority on the evolving life of the Norman convert.

---

22 A. Scheiber, 'Fragment from the Chronicle of Obadyah, the Norman Proselyte: From the Kaufmann Geniza', *Acta Orientalia Academiae Scientarium Hungaricae*, 4:1/3 (1954), pp.271–96.
23 Norman Golb, 'Megillat Obadiah Hager', in S. Morag, I. Ben-Ami, and N. A. Stillman (eds), *Studies in Geniza and Sepharadi Heritage: Presented to Shelomo Dov Goitein on the Occasion of His Eightieth Birthday by His Students, Colleagues and Friends* (Jerusalem: Magnes Press, 1981), pp.77–107.

Norman Golb in his study. (University of Chicago)

One example illustrates how his approach changed a reading. This can be found at the end of Folio 1a of the Budapest fragment examined by Scheiber, which raised a problem of interpretation and continuity. An episode of a dream that Obadiah had at the house of his father seemed to describe him receiving orders from the 'Princes of the Night', priests perhaps, with a voice crying out his name. The folio of the Budapest fragment broke off at this point. In the Cambridge fragment, now discovered, where the story seemed to continue, he awoke from a dream, but it is not clear if this refers to a new dream or the previous dream mentioned in the last folio of the Budapest fragment. Scheiber had read the Hebrew in the passage as *sarey layla*, implying 'priests of the night' that, Scheiber suggested, perhaps had contaminated Obadiah by teaching him the principles of Christianity. After Golb read this passage again with his trusty magnifying glass, he was able to clearly see '*mikrey layla*' (ירקמ הליל), which gave the meaning 'nocturnal emission'.[24] This was not the princes of the night or the priests as advanced by Scheiber. Such a reading of Golb's might be more accurate, even more personal, but still remained partly unexplained, as it was now held to mean that the young Norman had experienced a wet dream. The two areas of meaning could possibly be combined: Johannes implying that his association with Christianity was polluting him. Golb further suggested that the account was modelled on a passage in Deuteronomy 23:10–11 where a similar Hebrew expression occurs to indicate a nocturnal 'uncleanness' (as it is given in the King James

---

24   Golb, 'Megillat Obadiah Hager', pp.78–79.

version).²⁵ With many such instances of these rereadings, Golb's work seemed to clarify some passages, while others remained unresolved with extensive gaps in the reading. The main thrust of the work on the Norman convert had naturally been to find the fragments of his life and to understand what they said. But, as is shown later, Obadiah was also drawn to the beauty of the Hebrew script and language, and it seemed to Golb that he strove to emulate the tone and cadence of the Hebrew bible in his own writing. But any enlargement on this important topic is beyond the subject of this enquiry.

The creation of an autobiography

The real value of this close reading of the extant parts that had been found climaxed in the most important synthesis of all the manuscripts so far discovered. Published in 2004, this was Golb's own translation of all the different fragments found by others, taking into account the places where no clear reading could be elicited but giving explanatory additions and even suggestions that provided some sense where there were gaps in phrases and words – always warranted by a reasonable use of existing letters or sentences that made it possible to read passages in their entirety. Golb called this *The Autograph Memoirs of Obadiah the Proselyte of Oppido Lucano*. The fragments numbered seven folios or 14 pages, which were helpfully displayed by other scholars on a later website.²⁶ Golb wanted to stress by this title that the account had been written by the Norman himself. We refer to this translation throughout as the *Autobiography* or as Obadiah's *Autograph Memoirs*. The tale of this man's life as told by the Norman himself could now, for the first time, be read as a continuous biography, and, by looking back, the past became a story. The memorable story that had begun with the finding of long-forgotten dirty and dusty fragments in a chamber room of a Cairo synagogue had finally been told: after more than half a century of investigation and careful examination, the next story could commence. We now remain silent as we hear, in his own words, the life of Johannes/Obadiah.

---

25 Norman Golb, 'The Music of Obadiah the Proselyte and His Conversion', *JJS*, 18:1–4, (1967), p.46; Melonie Schmierer-Lee and Gary Rendsburg, 'Q&A Wednesday: From Monk to Jew in 1102 – Obadiah the Proselyte, with Gary Rendsburg', *Geniza Fragments* (2021), <https://www.lib.cam.ac.uk/genizah-fragments/posts/qa-wednesday-monk-jew-1102-obadiah-proselyte-gary-rendsburg>, accessed 2024.

26 Norman Golb (trans.), 'The Autograph Memoirs of Obadiah the Proselyte of Oppido Lucano and the Epistle of Barukh b. Isaac of Aleppo', prepared for the *Convegno internazionale di Studi Giovanni – Obadiah da Oppido: proselito, viaggiatore e musicista dell'età normanna, Oppido Lucano (Basilicata) 28-30 Marzo 2004*, <https://isac.uchicago.edu/sites/default/files/uploads/shared/docs/autograph_memoirs_obadiah.pdf>, accessed 2024, comprising: i–ix Introduction, translated text of *Autograph Memoirs*, also called the *Autobiography*, the epistle of Barukh of Aleppo and the music texts of Obadiah. All references to Obadiah hereafter are from this work. See the website compiled by Gary A. Rendsburg and Peter M. Shamah, *Johannes of Oppido = Obadiah the Proselyte* (2018), <https://johannes-obadiah.org>, accessed 2024, for images of Obadiah texts and manuscripts.

Chapter 2

Jacob and Esau

In his visionary imagination and recollection, Johannes of Dreux tells, in his own words, the story of his birth in southern Italy. Many years after the event, in a unique autobiography written down in Egypt, he recalls a tale told to him of his entry into life. This was after an enormous journey across the Mediterranean, traversing the Arab world of Iraq, Palestine and Syria in the twelfth century. We cannot follow him just yet into that later world until he recounts his arrival and early years in the town of Oppido, situated in the region of Basilicata, known as Lucania in Roman times.

A significant birth

As he tells it, he came crying into life after a difficult passage out of the womb of his mother, Maria, as the second-born of twins. The fragment begins abruptly with the name of the town:

> whose name is Oppido. He took a wife named Maria, and Maria conceived and bore unto Dreux her husband two sons on the same day —
> the first (born) according to the usual manner of women as to their children, to whom they gave the name
> Rogerius, that is, Rogier, (As for) the second, his lower [parts] came (out) first, his mother bearing him with great pain; she gave
> him the name Joha[nnes], that is, Giovan.[1]

---

1 All references hereafter of Obadiah's memoir to what we term the *Autobiography* are to Golb (trans.), 'Autograph Memoirs'; in this case, Golb (trans.), 'Autograph Memoirs', Document II: Budapest: Kaufmann Genizah Collection, MS 134, fol. 1. *Recto*, lines 1–6. The parentheses ( ) used throughout the *Autobiography* are Golb's likely explanatory additions, and square brackets [ ] also his probable restorations of missing phrases or words. This entire translation is available online. Discussion on the language of Johannes's name in the passage above in Ciryl Aslanov, 'Ovadiah the Proselyte and His Linguistic Background', in A. De Rosa and M. Perani (eds), *Giovanni-Ovadiah da Oppido, proselito, viaggiatore e musicista dell'Età normanna. Atti del convegno internazionale Oppido Lucano 28–30 marzo 2004* (Florence: Casa Editrice Giuntina, 2005), p.94.

This must certainly have been a painful birth, with whatever aids existed at the time, probably helped by a midwife or some female member of the family. Johannes may also be implying that this troubled experience could have been a sign or portent for the apparitions and images that he later recounts and that appeared together with voices speaking to him. He believes that he was elected to follow a chosen path and that his actions were in some manner pre-ordained, peopled with incidents telling him of events to come, guiding his life. As he moved into the greater world, his overwhelming memories were of an early occupation of this prophetic space. The name given to this Johannes is in fact Giovan or Guiàn, a southern Italian form equivalent to the Tuscan Giovanni. This might also denote that the southern Italian dialect was influenced in some cases by the Old French dialect spoken by the Normans.

Normans in the south

The difficult birth of Johannes, recorded by him as having taken place in a southern Italian town, was evidence of the presence of Normans from France in the region. 'Norsemen', originally Vikings, had raided and plundered all over Europe then settled in the region of northern France to which they gave their name: Normandy. The grant of this land to Viking raiders was agreed so that they would stop carrying on raiding far upriver to Frankish Paris, urging them to defend this territory as their own from future attacks and remain as peaceful settlers. This was partly achieved but not before these new Normans had enlarged their initial conquests to include the Cotentin peninsula in 933.[2] The upstarts settled in this part of France, expanding their presence. Soon, another significant Norman movement spoke of their conquest of southern Italy and later Sicily, taken over from a number of different powers already established there: the Byzantines holding large tracts in Puglia and Calabria – overseen from their Italian headquarters at Bari but governed from their imperial capital at Constantinople – not to mention the Arab emirs in Sicily and various local lords, dukes and princes who owed allegiance to the Byzantines or the Lombards. Legend has it that this arrival might have started as early as 1013, when Norman pilgrims visiting Monte Gargano, the shrine of the Archangel Michael situated on a coastal spur in Apulia, were approached by the local Lombard leader for help in rebelling against Byzantine rule in Bari. Normans were thereby encouraged to migrate to this region, relentlessly insinuating themselves into unending local power struggles and politics. These Norman groups first arrived as willing warriors to be recruited, becoming effective mercenaries in continuing wars between

---

2   Kenneth B. Wolf (trans.), *The Deeds of Count Roger of Calabria and Sicily and of His Brother Duke Robert Guiscard* (Ann Arbor: University of Michigan Press, 2005), Book 1, Chapter 2; Peter Sawyer, 'The Age of the Vikings, and Before', in P. Sawyer (ed.), *The Oxford Illustrated History of the Vikings* (Oxford: Oxford University Press, 1999), pp.12–14; Janet L. Nelson, 'The Frankish Empire', in P. Sawyer (ed.), *The Oxford Illustrated History of the Vikings* (Oxford: Oxford University Press, 1999), pp.30–31; James Graham-Campbell (ed.), *Cultural Atlas of the Viking World* (Oxford: Checkmark Books, 1994), pp.142–46.

Lombards and Byzantines in the first years of the eleventh century. Gradually, the new Norman arrivals in southern Italy saw that there were promising opportunities to establish their own lordships. They upgraded from upstarts to conquerors, as was their usual course of action. In many respects, this mirrored the same process they had followed in Normandy.[3]

To begin with, a Norman power centre arose at Aversa, still ruled by the local duke of Naples. By the next decade, different Norman groups of fighters, set up as warlords and settlers, were expanding in numerous areas of the southern Italian mainland. One landmark episode proved a turning point: their victory over the army of Pope Leo IX at the coastal town of Civitate in 1053. This constituted a stunning upset and a vindication of Norman fighting prowess and superior willpower, even though they were sizeably outnumbered. The Papacy then had to change its policies: from trying to push the Normans out, they now were obliged to cooperate with their previous enemy and enlist them to assist in their own challenge to the presence of Greek Orthodox Byzantium. This devotion to the Catholic Papacy was an opportunity skilfully exploited by the Normans and helped to increase their influence so that, by the 1060s, most of the mainland of the southern Italian boot came under Norman domination. Cleverly, after the Pope's defeat at Civitate, the Normans had implored his forgiveness on bended knees whilst taking him captive, thereby underlining their support for the Papacy and defining their opposition to Byzantium and its presence in Italy.[4] Soon, the Pope would officially empower them in his name to undertake further expansion and conquest in Sicily from the Arabs. In 1058, Pope Nicholas II had made the Norman Robert Guiscard their most successful leader: the future Duke of Sicily. For the Normans, the support of the Pope legitimised their odyssey of conquest and rule.

A ruling family

Such a growing movement of mercenaries and irregular freelancers was presided over by certain members of the Hauteville family originating from a town of that name on Normandy's Cotentin peninsula. Around the year 1000, Tancred, their little-known and undistinguished patriarch (who would later lend his name to a famous crusader), had, by dint of two marriages, fathered 12 sons, who, through lack of money and land, had been encouraged to seek their fortune elsewhere: this, in short, proved the principal incentive for the story of the Norman move to Italy.[5] A son from Tancred's first marriage was an early arrival in Italy: Drogo

---

3   Wolf (trans.), *Deeds*, Book 1, Chapters 5–6; Chris Wickham, *Medieval Europe* (New Haven, CT: Yale University Press, 2016), pp.117–19; David Abulafia, *Frederick II: A Medieval Emperor* (London: Oxford University Press, 1992), pp.19–25.
4   Wolf (trans.), *Deeds*, Book 1, Chapter 14; John J. Norwich, *The Normans in the South, 1016–1130* (London: Faber & Faber, 2018), pp.90–96.
5   Robert Bartlett, *The Making of Europe: Conquest, Colonization and Cultural Change, 950–1350* (London: Allen Lane, 1993), pp.48–49.

de Hauteville spearheaded a series of raids in 1042, together with the Lombards. Along with his brother and other Norman warlords, they took Melfi and other towns such as Venosa, which was given to Drogo as a fiefdom. In 1046, Drogo was invested as Count of Apulia. While unending early wars and contests between the Holy Roman Emperor and the Papacy against Lombards and Greeks rumbled on, Drogo de Hauteville's career was cut short by his assassination and the rise of a new generation of Hauteville sons from Tancred's second marriage. Two younger half-brothers of Drogo greatly exceeded him: that same year, 1046, 31-year-old Robert Guiscard came to Italy with little achieved thus far, but he laid the groundwork for the Kingdom of the Two Sicilies to eventually comprise the island and the southern half of the Italian peninsula. Guiscard – this sobriquet stood for 'cunning' – was certainly that, and his later story blazed a famous trail, carried on in partnership with his brother Roger, who eventually assumed the title of Roger I of Sicily. Only part of this tumultuous story of arrival, settlement and conquest by the Hautevilles would be in place when Johannes came into the world a few years later.[6] At this time, few would have predicted that the dispersed Norman territories would eventually be welded into a single monarchy. By adapting to farming and turning to Christianity, these arrivals from France had mixed and intermarried with the local population in Italy, just as had happened in Normandy, and were now equally known as pious pilgrims and infamous mercenaries.[7] All these elements remained in their blood, traits partly retained in the Norman personality of Johannes of Dreux and in his later actions and travels.

Johannes's birth in Italy might be located in the mid to late 1060s, perhaps even a few years later in the early 1070s, and his father would also have been called Roger or Rogerius (the name given to the first-born of the twins), a small title holder with some land in Oppido. There is a significant reference that supports the autobiographical account given by Johannes. This is to be found in the *Catalogus Baronum*, a collection of military registers of obligations owed by barons of the Kingdom of Sicily. The list has had a troubled and patchy textual career, and the entry of one 'Rogerius of Oppido' is either a reference to Johannes's brother or to the father of the twins. The entry suggests that this Rogerius was a baron holding land of a Count Philip of Balbano, who assigned to him four guards and 10 servants.[8] Johannes's characterisation of his father as Roger 'of Dreux' suggests an intriguing family connection of this father of Oppido and his sons.[9] Dreux or 'Drogo' may have been a fairly

---

6   Wolf (trans.), *Deeds*, Book 1, Chapters 12–13; Christopher Tyerman, *God's War: A New History of the Crusades* (London: Penguin, 2007), pp.13–15.
7   Dirk Booms, 'The Normans', in D. Booms and P. Higgs (eds), *Sicily: Culture and Conquest* (London: British Museum Press, 2016), pp.173–74.
8   Evelyn Jamison (ed.), *Catalogus Baronum* (Rome: Istituto storico italiano per il Medio Evo, 1972), p.125.
9   Angelo Lancellotti, 'Nella cronaca di Giovanni-Abdia il proselita normanno la prima pagina di storia di Oppido della Lucania', in P. Borraro (ed.), *Antiche Civiltà Lucane. Atti del Convegno di Studi di Archeologia, Storia dell'Arte e del Folklore, Oppido Lucano, 5–8 Aprile 1970* (Galatina: Congedo, 1975), pp.254–55.

common name among the Normans, possibly deriving from the city of that name in Normandy, but the father of Johannes was certainly not that Dreux/Drogo of the Hauteville family named count of Apulia, assassinated in 1051. Even so, the associations of the name do licence us to speculate that there may have existed some more distant family connection to these Hautevilles. Such a family link remains an open question. At the very least, he was of minor noble lineage and could have boasted a more illustrious family background. Some further references in the account of his life on this matter come up later in the story of Johannes's wanderings in the East. A close examination of the surviving opening fragment of the autobiographical account indicates a previous folio or more now lost, where Johannes presumably describes earlier events in connection with the Normans. Fortunately, we can partly fill in these events from other sources, although, with reference to the provenance of his family, we cannot be sure of any other facts than those contained in this important autobiographical source and in the *Catalogus Baronum*. One scholar hazards that the family may have arrived in Italy 30 or 40 years before the birth of Johannes. This could place their arrival in the 1020s. It is not impossible that Roger of Dreux had married Maria, a local woman, possibly Greek, as is suggested elsewhere. This arrival of the Dreux line could have even predated the birth of the father who would then also be born in Italy, taking a local wife in marriage to produce twin sons.[10]

The place of his birth

The region where Oppido is situated, called Lucania in Roman times and today known as Basilicata, lies between the towns of Tolve and Acerenza, near the River Bradano, the longest of the five rivers of the province flowing into the gulf of Taranto in the Ionian Sea – the instep of the Italian boot. Both the river and the important town of Potenza are recalled by Johannes in the *Autobiography*, along with Acerenza and Bari, a city to the east, the capital of the Byzantines in Italy until its takeover by the Normans in 1071.

The character of the landscape surrounding Oppido rendered communication difficult: the Lucanian Apennines bisected what is now Basilicata with many areas that had once been dotted with forest, even more widespread in ancient times but subjected to heavy deforestation in later centuries, starting with the Romans. Its classical name 'Lucania' (*lucus*, woodland) reflected perhaps such a former geographical condition of dense woods. Another explanation offered of the word's origin was linked to '*lux*', suggesting 'the land of light': the precise explanation remains disputed. The town of Oppido was on a rolling mountainous plateau with many valleys and ravines displaying extensive parts that now are somewhat bare and desolate. In some places, the eye can today sweep over an endless expanse in every direction, a lunar landscape like a sea of chalk soil, monotonous and without trees, showing villages dotted on the heights of mountains, white and far away. This

---

10   Prawer, 'Autobiography', pp.113–14.

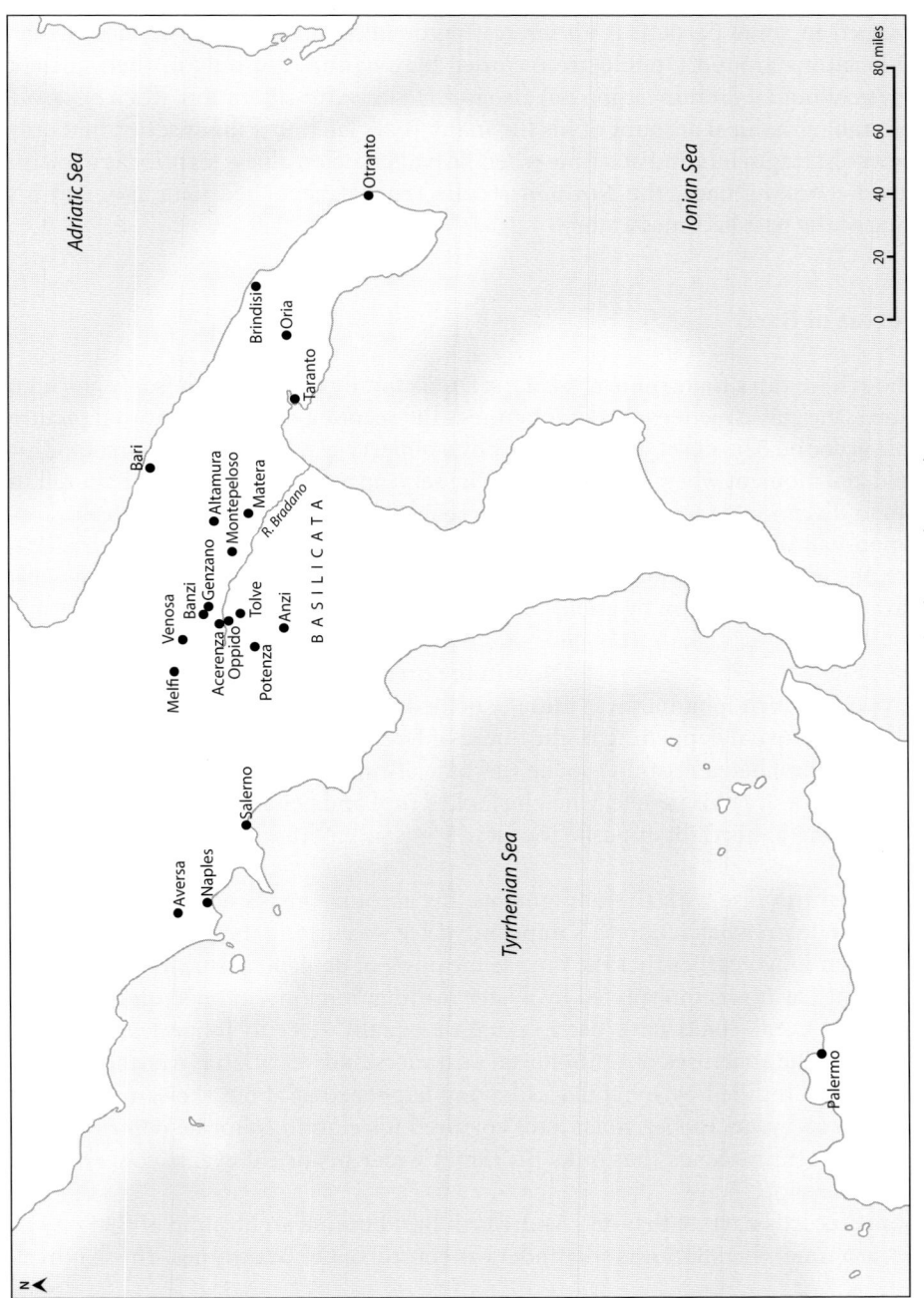

Map 1 Obadiah's homeland in southern Italy.

bare region only preserves a few bits of the wooded land that once included all of Lucania. But, at the time of Johannes, a plentiful number of trees would still have remained in some parts. It is an interesting detail that the names of these towns and locations around Oppido are recorded by Johannes not only in their ancient Italian colloquial pronunciation but also in a Hebrew transliteration, when he wrote the autobiographical account of his life many years later, in a manuscript that only survives in fragments and at a time when he had taken on a new identity as a Jewish convert. Looking back, the Norman recollects what happened long ago, and his telling of the past becomes a story.

Andreas of Bari

Although we can situate the arrival of the Dreux family in this recognisably Norman context, the subsequent events of Johannes's life record a distinctly unusual picture in his account. The onset of the young boy's puberty was marked by a dream. This is told at a moment when he was likely to be serving as an altar boy at the church in Oppido. Even if this was a dream, it is probable that, in real life, his path towards religion had in fact led him to take part in church services at the town's basilica. Here, the emotions of adolescence giving way to sexual urges were caught up with an awakening call to him by an unknown voice of authority:

> Now in the first
> year in which Johannes was initially defiled
> by a nocturnal happening in the house of Dreux his father, in that year
> [Johannes] had a dream — lo, he was officiating at the main church
> of Oppido [...] his people, when he looked (up) and beheld a man
> standing to his right opposite the altar. He [said] to him, "Johannes!"[11]

As is often the case with these fragments, his account breaks off here, and we are not able to learn what action this imposing voice was urging the young boy to take. It was mentioned earlier that the precise meaning of defilement due to 'a nocturnal happening', as it was interpreted by a later reading, remains an open question. The night-time event could have been sexual or equally refer to Johannes's growing reaction to the strictures of Catholicism as understood years later. Another historical incident recalled by Johannes as having happened at about the same time, or perhaps a few years earlier, must have coloured his emotions, for he describes it in a personal reminiscence that links his life to wider historical events concerning a local archbishop.

Some records narrate that one Andreas of Bari became archbishop of that city in 1062, at a time when Bari was still under the control of the Byzantines. This Andreas

---

11   Golb (trans.), 'Autograph Memoirs', Document III: Budapest: Kaufmann Genizah Collection, MS 134, fol. 1, *verso*, lines 14–19.

is additionally said by Johannes in his account to have converted to Judaism, having left for Constantinople to carry this out and moved to Egypt before his death. News of this conversion had seemingly made its way back to southern Italy, where Johannes was perhaps still a boy. The wider backstory was evidently somewhat more nuanced and disputed, but Johannes leaves us in no doubt that he heard of this and was deeply affected. At any rate, this is how he recalls it:

> It happened
> at that time regarding Archbishop Andreas the high
> priest in the city of Bari, that the Lord put the love of
> the Torah of Moses into his heart. He forsook the land, [his] priesthood [and a]ll
> his glory and came to the city of Constantinople, (where) he circumcised the flesh of his foreskin.
>
> The re[port] concerning Andreas reached
> unto the entire land of Lombardy and unto the sages of Greece and
> the sages of Rome, which is the place of the throne of the kingdom of Edom.[12]

The conversion of Andreas is presented by him as a powerful influence, a sign, a prefiguration of the future path eventually taken by Johannes himself: even a spiritual turning point. He also underlines the deep effect this action had on the Catholic and Greek Orthodox world of Rome and Byzantium. The 'sages', in this case, refer to the ecclesiastical and learned notables of the Greek and especially the Latin church of Rome, where the Papacy presided over Christendom, here called 'the kingdom of Edom'. The 'land of Lombardy', or Longobardia as it was called, in southern Italy, is a reference to a Byzantine theme, a word denoting a territorial term with political and military reference. But this sequence of events really tells another story: Andreas had in fact been consecrated archbishop by Pope Alexander II in 1063. This was a Catholic appointment in a Byzantine-controlled seat and may not have had the unanimous approval of the Greek Orthodox masters, due to a long-standing theological disagreement between the Orthodox and Catholic faiths.[13] The city of Bari was by now sharply divided into factions supporting either the Byzantine Empire or the rising influence and power of the Normans who stood behind the Catholic Papacy. This difficulty was reflected in the title given to Andreas in his appointment:

---

12 Golb (trans.), 'Autograph Memoirs', Document II: Budapest: Kaufmann Genizah Collection, MS 134, fol. 1. *Recto*, lines 8–13, 19, and Document III: Budapest: Kaufmann Genizah Collection, MS 134, fol. 1, *verso*, lines 1–2.
13 Cesare Colafemmina, 'La conversione al giudaismo di Andrea, arcivescovo di Bari: una suggestione per Giovanni-Ovadiah da Oppido', in A. De Rosa and M. Perani (eds), *Giovanni-Ovadiah da Oppido, proselito, viaggiatore e musicista dell'Età normanna. Atti del convegno internazionale Oppido Lucano 28–30 marzo 2004* (Florence: Casa Editrice Giuntina, 2005), pp.56–59.

he was actually named Archbishop of Canosa with 12 suffragan bishoprics of which Bari was the most important and where he was wont to reside.[14]

Rome and Constantinople

This confrontation between the Roman Catholic world and Orthodox Byzantium was both religious and political and deeply relevant to the appointment of Andreas. Relations between the Papacy and the Byzantine authorities were worsening in any case following the Great Schism in 1054. This sundering over Catholicism and Byzantine dogma had followed years of debate and confrontation over doctrinal beliefs, after three papal legates had notoriously stormed into Hagia Sophia, the Byzantine cathedral in the East, and excommunicated the patriarch of Constantinople. The story was a tortuous one: Greek Orthodox religion had from the onset manifested a fractured relation with any opinion held by the Catholics in respect of the nature of Jesus Christ and the Holy Ghost. The Byzantine Greek rite held that the Holy Ghost proceeded from, or emanated from, God the father alone: the Latins held that the Holy Ghost proceeded from God the Father *and* the Son. This became a crucial and critical distinction referred to thereafter as the *filioque* ('and from the Son') question. The original version of the Creed had said that the Holy Spirit proceeded from the Father. Now, the western version maintained that he proceeded from the Father and the Son. The ensuing disagreement reverberated over Christendom, clearly feeding the heightening conflict between the religions of East and West, so that, a few years later, any territorial rivalries over Bari manifested themselves in these ruptures and tensions over the appointment of Andreas as archbishop. The appointment of Andreas is certainly recorded, along with his departure to Constantinople in 1066.[15] His journey to Constantinople, also mentioned by Johannes, suggested this background and a conversion to Judaism that in fact may not have taken place at all, even if Johannes later saw it as a turning point in his own eventual path to Judaism. Following the death of Andreas, the see of Canosa/Bari had no new incumbent until 1079, when a certain Urso was appointed with the support of the Normans. The entire apostasy of Andreas recounted by Johannes, which appears to have caused such widespread consternation according to his account, might have happened when he was aged 10 years or perhaps even younger. But, even if this abandonment of Christianity is not clearly recorded anywhere else,

---

14   Colafemmina, 'La conversione', p.57; Hubert Houben, 'La Chiesa di Bari alla fine dell' XI secolo', in S. Palese and G. Locatelli (eds), *Il Concilio di Bari del 1098. Atti del Convegno Storico Internazionale e celebrazioni del IX Centenario del Concilio* (Bari: Edipuglia, 1999), p.91; Jean-Marie Martin, *La Pouille du VIe au XIIe siècle* (Rome: Ecole française de Rome, 1993), pp.502–03.
15   Prawer, 'Autobiography', p.115, n.28; Andreas's appointment: Ludovico A. Muratori, *Rerum Italicarum Scriptores* (Mediolani: Typographia Societatis Palatinae in Regia Curia, 1724), vol. 5, pp.152–53, records the appointment and move to Constantinople. This is a compilation of different sources made up of 25 volumes, put together by Ludovico Antonio Muratori.

what matters is the powerful memory Johannes claims to have vividly retained in recollecting the incident. Andreas's successor, Urso, was actually appointed to the see at the request of Robert Guiscard, for the city of Bari was by then dependent theologically on Rome and politically controlled by the Normans. A subsequent story, not generally attested, has it that Urso surprisingly ended his days at the court of the caliph in Cairo, having converted to Islam.[16]

So the historical evidence of Andreas's archbishopric is certain, but his conversion is not, or, at any rate, is still debated amongst scholars. The subsequent story of Urso might suggest that Johannes confused the two episodes, even if Urso is said to have embraced another faith. Nevertheless, this memory of Andreas's apostasy, true or not, was deemed decisive for Johannes regardless of its historicity. Even today, scholars are still equally divided as to whether the conversion of Andreas took place. Johannes's account of Andreas embracing Judaism has its supporters. Whatever the outcome, it is firmly linked to the unfolding of Johannes's biography.

Jews in southern Italy

The story of Andreas matters because it also tells us about the presence of Jewish communities in Bari and other Italian towns, going back to earlier centuries.[17] Jews were certainly attested in Europe as early as the Roman era, mainly along the Mediterranean coast – notably in Italy, the Balkan peninsula and Spain – and in smaller numbers farther north: in France and even in Germany. These communities underwent a reduction in size after the collapse of Roman power in the fifth century but grew in later years following migration from three important areas of settlement – Asia Minor, southern Italy and the Balkans – in the ninth and tenth centuries. There were also indirect influences of large waves of Jewish migration into the Muslim caliphates from Babylonia westward to North Africa and Spain. While no complete or exact information is available on the extent or course of these migrations, growth of Jewish migrants should not be seen as exceptional. The opening years of the eleventh century after the Fatimid rise to power in 969 witnessed the consolidation of Egypt, Tunisia and Sicily under one government in Egypt, bringing about a shift in economic power to Fustāt, the original capital of Arab Egypt, which now expanded to take in the adjoining city of Cairo. These developments mirrored

---

16 Prawer, 'Autobiography', p.118; Houben, 'La Chiesa di Bari', p.96; Colafemmina, 'La conversione', p.60, suggests that the Normans wished to discredit the pro-Byzantine Andreas; Joshua Holo, 'Jewish Communities and Personalities within Ovadiah's Chronicle', in A. De Rosa and M. Perani (eds), *Giovanni-Ovadiah da Oppido, proselito, viaggiatore e musicista dell'Età normanna. Atti del convegno internazionale Oppido Lucano 28–30 marzo 2004* (Florence: Casa Editrice Giuntina, 2005), pp.152–53, supports Obadiah's account; Golb, 'Megillat Obadiah Hager', p.81, stands by Obadiah and his account.

17 Shlomo Simonsohn, *The Jews of Italy: Antiquity* (Leiden: Brill, 2014), pp.94–102; Vera von Falkenhausen, 'The Jews in Byzantine Southern Italy', in R. Bonfil, O. Irshai, G. G. Stroumsa, and R. Talgam (eds), *Jews in Byzantium: Dialectics of Minority and Majority Cultures* (Leiden: Brill, 2012), pp.271–96.

a sustained economic boom, accompanied by a substantial population rise in the following years all over Europe and the Mediterranean. In Cairo and Alexandria, Jewish merchants provided a trading bridge between the western Mediterranean, East India and Asia, profiting from this growth in business and populations.[18]

The Jewish inhabitants of Bari and other Italian cities certainly benefited from all these developments, but growth and prosperity failed to dampen inter-religious tensions that the main religious powers saw fit to visit upon the Jews. In particular, the Byzantine government repeatedly instigated persecution of Jews in Bari and other cities. Under Emperor Romanus Lecapenus (920–944), for example, a campaign of book burning was instigated in Bari. As precious Hebrew manuscripts were thrown into the flames, Jewish notables warned their co-religionists at nearby Otranto of the danger. During the next century, in the spring of 1051, the Bari community saw its own quarter sacked and set alight by Byzantine extremists. Some 20 years later, when the Norman ascendancy had just been established in the city, the Norman leader gifted his new wife, Sikelgaita, all income arising from Jewish tax receipts. The Jewish community hastened to pass over to her control the property of their entire quarter next to the cathedral, perhaps seeking her protection. The outcome for the Jewish synagogue was an unhappy one: its later partial demolition would be replaced by a Christian church. For some, this was viewed as punishment inflicted upon the community for the supposed role they had played in Andreas's abandonment of Christianity a few years earlier.[19] When the Norman ruler Robert Guiscard died in 1085, his widow assigned all Jewish assets, including the population, to Urso, the new archbishop. But harassment and persecution of Hebrew communities was not limited to the Byzantines alone. This assignment of Jewish people and their tax revenues demonstrated how Jewish communities (*Judeca*) sometimes passed from the jurisdiction of the secular authorities into the arms of ecclesiastical ones. The whole process of ceding ownership of peoples to a queen or archbishop was part of a wider phenomenon: the 'protection' of the Jews that restricted their legal and political status. The Jews became 'Serfs of the chamber' (*servi camerae*). By this means, they became the property of a king, sometimes assigned to a queen or an archbishop. Generally, the king possessed the right of ownership over Jews and their property. This was supposed to be in exchange for a promise on his part to defend their lives and possessions. In reality, this offer of security was a means to obtain from the Hebrew community the assignment of its tax revenues that provided the king with a valuable source of income.

---

18   Wickham, *Medieval*, pp.119–40.
19   Von Falkenhausen, 'Jews', p.285; Vera von Falkenhausen, 'Identità religiose in una società multiculturale: l'Italia meridionale nell'epoca di Giovanni-Ovadiah', in A. De Rosa and M. Perani (eds), *Giovanni-Ovadiah da Oppido, proselito, viaggiatore e musicista dell'Età normanna. Atti del convegno internazionale Oppido Lucano 28–30 marzo 2004* (Florence: Casa Editrice Giuntina, 2005), p.40; G. Musca and F. Tateo, 'La comunità ebraica', in F. Tateo (ed.), *Storia di Bari. Dalla Preistoria al Mille* (Bari: Editori Laterza, 1989), vol. 1, pp.305–11; Martin, *La Pouille*, p.503, n.90, casts doubt on this punishment; Pierre Savy, 'Autour de la conversion d'Obadiah et de quelques autres (vers 1100)', *Archives de sciences sociales des religions*, 182 (2018), p.220, agrees with Martin.

The entire story of Andreas of Bari, told in Johannes's *Autobiography*, carries a wider political and religious resonance than has hitherto been thought to be the case. Its full significance within the hardening policies of Byzantine and Catholic attitudes to Jews served to point out how these Jewish populations within towns, large and prosperous though they appeared to be, were also losing influence to northern Europe and the states of France and Germany. Up to this period just before the birth of Johannes, the Jews of Byzantium and southern Italy could still be seen as influential, with relatively large populations boasting flourishing cadres of rabbinical scholars. Until then, as has been suggested, southern Italy had served as a bridge between the Christian and Muslim worlds, exemplified by the commercial activity of Italian Jewish traders in Sicily and the mainland with Alexandria, the towns of Egypt and the Middle East. Now, in the mid-eleventh century, the increase in population growth and trade created new pressures originating out of the towns of the Rhine region. A consequence of this noticeable change coupled with the rise of new markets caused the importance of such Jewish traders to be questioned by the northern populations and would eventually lead to serious repercussions in the last years of the eleventh century. This was the world that Johannes was growing into, and it was to come to a head with the proclamation of the First Crusade. The build-up to the Crusade crystallised the messianic and prophetic visions Johannes harboured in his mind, leading to profound consequences he carried with him in his later travels overseas.

Jewish towns and persecutions

The history of a Jewish presence in Italy is central to our story about Johannes, who must have been influenced by them and their writings whilst already predisposed and inclined to the faith of Abraham. Jewish inscriptions have been attested all over Italy, more in the southern than the northern region, especially in the coastal cities. It suggests that Jewish communities of some kind had predated by more than 500 years the onset of Justinian's Gothic wars in Italy from the late sixth century CE. The ruins of synagogues and other sites active between the second and sixth centuries have been excavated, and, in various medieval texts, there is a record of these Jewish arrivals from the time when Roman Emperor Titus brought prisoners of war back to Italy after the destruction of the Second Temple in Jerusalem in 70 CE. The largest of these communities, evidenced by about 600 inscriptions, must have been established in Rome and nearby ports at this early time. Later medieval Jewish works such as *Sepher Yuhasin* (also known as the *Scroll of Ahimaaz*) and some manuscripts of the *Sepher Yosippon*, to be looked at later, report that some 5,000 of these Jewish prisoners brought by Titus to Italy were settled in Oria, Otranto, Taranto and other Apulian cities.

With the emergence of Byzantine power and influence in Italy dating from the sixth century, the Jews had good reason to fear for their social and religious status: the anti-Jewish policies of the Byzantine rulers in the ninth and tenth centuries, like Basil I (866–886), were recorded and remembered, by southern Italian Jews, especially in Oria, as well as the aggressive efforts to convert them. This persecution is brought out in the above-mentioned *Scroll of Ahimaaz*.[20] The location of these communities remained largely unchanged with the arrival of the Normans in the second half of the eleventh century. Jews continued to reside in the major administrative centres such as Bari, or in the more important ports connecting these southern Italian provinces with Constantinople, such as Otranto and Taranto. But Norman sources also mention settlements in Melfi and Troia. Ahimaaz Ben Paltiel, author of the *Sepher Yuhasin*, considered Oria, Otranto, Taranto and Bari to be the four most important settlements in Apulia and called Bari 'the metropolis facing the sea' as it became the capital of Byzantine southern Italy.

From the ninth to the mid-eleventh century, Bari was the centre of Byzantine politics in Italy, shaping events like the aforementioned conversion of Andreas and the doubtless frequent anti-Jewish pogroms organised by the local Byzantine sympathisers – such as the book burnings under Emperor Romanus Lecapenus and the burning of the Jewish quarter in 1051. Later, we see how Bari played a crucial role in the mid-1080s, in the widening of power politics leading to the fashioning of the First Crusade. Some such details find their way into Johannes's story, an account of his experiences as he saw them. After this period, Bari was raided and destroyed in 1156 but soon restored. When Benjamin of Tudela travelled in this region in later years, recording Jewish populations in other towns, Bari was absent. His important descriptive panorama in the late 60s of the twelfth century, called *The Itinerary*, notes this omission but gives other neighbouring towns and the size of their Jewish population: Otranto (500), for example, is singled out as important and recalls the saying of a rabbi from Troyes of that time, 'For out of Bari shall go forth the law, and the word of the Lord from Otranto'.[21] This figure of 500 represents the highest number of Jewish inhabitants mentioned by Benjamin of Tudela in any town of the former Byzantine territories of southern Italy. However, it would seem that, in his study, he provided a count of households rather than of individuals, so the total figures are difficult to gauge accurately. The learning of the Jews in Otranto was well known in the Middle Ages, as was also the case with Bari, the capital of Byzantine Italy.

---

20   J. H. Chajes and Kenneth Stow (trans), 'The Scroll or Genealogy of Ahimaaz ben Paltiel: Jewish Learning, Myth, and Ideals in an Uncertain Salentine World (1054)', in K. Jansen, J. Drell, and F. Andrews (eds), *Medieval Italy: Texts in Translation* (Philadelphia: University of Pennsylvania Press, 2009), pp.508–13.

21   Youval Rotman, 'Converts in Byzantine Italy: Local Representation of Jewish-Christian Rivalry', in R. Bonfil, O. Irshai, G. G. Stroumsa, and R. Talgam (eds), *Jews in Byzantium: Dialectics of Minority and Majority Cultures* (Leiden: Brill, 2012), pp.912–14; von Falkenhausen, 'Jews', p.287; Marcus N. Adler (trans.), *The Itinerary of Benjamin of Tudela* (London: Oxford University Press, 1907), p.9, for Bari and Otranto.

The siege of Bari

In 1068, matters came to a head with regard to the fate of Bari. Pushing to conquer Palermo in Sicily, the Normans finally also moved to take Bari, capital of Byzantine Longobardia, as the province was called, headquarters of the Greek army and the great prize in order to achieve mastery of southern Italy. Bari was the largest, richest and best defended of all the Apulian cities. The old city stood on a narrow promontory facing northwards into the Adriatic. Robert Guiscard faced two challenges: the massive and heavily defended land walls that required penetration by a heavy siege and the successful implementation of a naval blockade. Both these issues were the important reasons why this siege and eventual conquest of Bari lasted from August 1068 to April 1071.[22] The Normans had to quickly gain naval expertise and the ships to match the unrivalled Greek knowledge and mastery of the sea. From the top of enormous fortifications, the inhabitants of Bari paraded along the ramparts, mocking the Normans below who were continually attacking the walls and unsuccessfully blockading the city from assistance by sea from nearby ports, whilst the Greeks sought reinforcements from Constantinople. The new Norman navy was virtually chained together to form a single barrier of vessels encircling the promontory around the old city, with the Norman army preventing any approaches by land. Dramatic ups and downs experienced by both sides took place, not least reflected in the constantly changing levels of support within the city. The Greek leader inside the city managed to evade land and sea encirclement and even reached Constantinople, where he urged urge the empress to send a relief force. In a first naval encounter, the Normans sank some of the Greek rescuers, but the main Greek force succeeded in breaking through into the harbour of Bari, bringing much needed arms and supplies. Even so, the siege dragged on despite the assassination of the Greek leader Byzantius in July 1069, and, according to another account, in 1070, Robert Guiscard narrowly escaped being assassinated by a poisoned javelin just outside the walls. This report states that a certain Amerino, a discontented ex-mercenary of Guiscard's, had penetrated the encampment and failed to land the killing blow. There was suffering and growing famine inside the city and an increasing tide of Norman support within from the non-Greek population. Finally, in 1071, Guiscard's brother arrived from Sicily with a fresh fleet and successfully routed a last desperate Byzantine naval force sent from the East. There was no obstacle remaining, and, on 16 April 1071, Robert Guiscard and his brother Roger entered the city in triumph. This victory was the culmination of 50 years of small-scale campaigns and raids that began as an intrusion and would rank in significance with that other victory at Hastings in 1066, when William Duke of Normandy had defeated the Anglo-Saxons and established a new Norman state. The taking of the ancient stronghold of the Byzantine Greeks was perhaps not as comprehensive a destruction as that of an Anglo-Saxon ruling class

---

22   Wolf (trans.), *Deeds*, Book 2, Chapters 40 and 43; Prescott N. Dunbar (trans.) and Graham A. Loud (rev.), *The History of the Normans by Amatus of Montecassino* (Woodbridge: Boydell Press, 2004), Book 5, pp.27–28; Norwich, *Normans*, pp.168–73.

and the building of a new English state in 1066, but this second date, only five years later, in 1071, set the Normans on a path to dominance in the Mediterranean: they were now a major player in European politics. The new Norman success was also partly due to an overextended Byzantine Empire having to fight Turkish invaders in the East, which spoke of a longer-term decline of the Eastern Roman Empire. The fall of Bari finally confirmed Guiscard's military and political supremacy, consolidating his military prowess and the empowerment of future plans to expand in Sicily and even take the challenge overseas to the Middle East.

Johannes enters a monastery

The Bari campaign in 1071 must have culminated around the time Johannes and his twin brother came into the world: Johannes would grow up in the shadow of this new political and religious context. These early years leading up to the end of the eleventh century covered the time of his religious studies and ordination in a monastery near the hometown of Oppido. The date and precise location of his religious education are not known with any precision, and not recorded in the *Autobiography*, but there are some strong conjectural details. It is probable that Johannes, educated by a local country priest in Oppido to begin with, passed afterwards into the Benedictine monastery of San Pietro located in the neighbouring town of Tolve. This would have taken place in his early teenage years or earlier, after hearing of the experience of Andreas and experiencing the earlier dream he recounts. In truth, the monastery of San Pietro di Tolve remains only a possibility. Some scholars, like Golb, have held that a line in the autobiography mentioning the abbot of Tolve is not universally endorsed as a correct reading of a difficult passage. As Golb asserted, there is no certain mention of the monastery of San Pietro di Tolve, even if other scholars propose this as the location of Johannes's monastic education and ordination.[23] There are indeed references to this monastery in local archival sources, where originally the institution professed an adherence to the Greco-Byzantine rite, and was later latinised, becoming part of the Benedictine order. This was a common development that took place over the region as control passed from Constantinople to Rome. But the passage from Greek Orthodoxy to Catholicism was overall a slow process on the ground, reflecting a shedding of many years of customary practice even if decrees from on high proclaimed such changes. It can be safely assumed that, if Johannes entered the monastery in Tolve, it would be as a practising Catholic. Records in the thirteenth century show the San Pietro monastery paying ecclesiastical tithes. Local histories do mention the connection of San Pietro with Johannes of Dreux, but this is based on this same disputed reading of the autobiography already mentioned. All evidence of a monastic education and ordination, whilst circumstantial, is universally endorsed by all scholars.

---

23   Golb, 'Megillat Obadiah Hager', p.83, questions Prawer, 'Autobiography', p.114.

The other religious location that has been put forward is the Benedictine abbey of the Most Holy Trinity in Venosa, not far from the important town of Melfi, an early centre of Norman influence. Venosa also had a long-standing flourishing Jewish community, one of the largest in southern Italy dating from Roman times, perhaps second only to Rome. The early record of Jewish burial sites testifies to this, and, to date, more than 75 Hebrew inscriptions have been discovered, together with a large number of graves. All three languages – Greek, Latin and Hebrew – are represented, this last becoming dominant in the Middle Ages. The cathedral of Venosa became part of the Benedictine abbey and thereby gained in influence. Today, the ruins of the abbey have become an epigraphical encyclopaedia, with inscriptions that were worked into the masonry, both in Latin and Hebrew, although the church still stands heavily restored.[24] The town is also associated with Horace, who was born there and was the author of a humorous piece in his work that already satirised the eager activities of Jews who sought out candidates for conversion to their religion. But Horace's poem told an interesting story. In the early days of the Roman Empire, there appeared to be numerous adherents attracted to the Jewish religion who were only sympathisers or fellow travellers, not complying with the conditions of full conversion. Nevertheless, around the first century CE and shortly afterwards, Judaism acquired a moral and spiritual prestige that drew in large numbers of Gentiles, and this appears to be behind the eagerness of Jews to seek out these Gentiles. Horace's humorous mention of God-fearing fellow travellers at an earlier period maintained its relevance.

> Should you not concede me this, the poets
> In battle groups, will rally to my aid.
> You see, there're more of us – and like the Jews,
> We'll make you yield your ground and join our mob.[25]

But the abbey at Venosa was by now a Norman centre of power: it is first mentioned in 942, a date that locates its foundation at approximately this time. Certainly, a papal bull promulgated in 1059 mentions the foundation, or its refounding, as well as the support of Drogo of Hauteville in its establishment. The abbey became largely associated with the domination of southern Italy by the Hauteville family. In 1085, the great trailblazer Robert Guiscard died, and his remains were brought back from Cephalonia to join members of his family lying at the abbey church of the Holy Trinity at Venosa. Corfu had been occupied temporarily by Robert Guiscard in 1083–1084 but was subsequently recovered by the Byzantine Emperor Alexios Komnenos (1081–1118) and his Venetian allies. Venosa had now become the shrine

---

24 Hubert Houben, *Il "libro del capitolo" del monastero della SS. Trinità di Venosa (Cod. Casin. 334): Una testimonianza del Mezzogiorno normanno* (Galatina: Congedo, 1984), pp.21–41, on abbey SS. Trinità di Venosa; Simonsohn, *Jews of Italy*, pp.96–97, on inscriptions in Venosa.
25 Horace and John Svarlien (trans.), *Satires* (Indianapolis: Hackett, 2012), *Satire* I, p.4.

and mausoleum of the ruling Norman dynasty. By this time in the 1080s, the entry of Johannes to commence his studies and be ordained a monk could have taken place within the most holy centre of Norman Catholicism. The abbot of Venosa from 1066 to 1094 was Berengarius, a monk who came from St Evroul in Normandy and presided over the many donations and the interment of the Hautevilles. He reformed the spiritual life of the abbey and oversaw the enlargement of inmates from 20 to 100.[26] Johannes could therefore have engaged with biblical studies at the heart of Catholic theological programmes that were closely allied with the new state developing in Apulia and now in Sicily. If Johannes was linked with this monastery, he was linked to a religious institution playing a key role in Norman Italy. By the end of the eleventh century, the centre of power would gravitate to Sicily following the death of Robert Guiscard. Palermo, the Sicilian capital, had fallen to the Normans in January 1072, one year after Bari. After Robert's death, his brother Roger became the driving force behind the Sicilian venture. By then, the centrality of power radiating from the abbey at Venosa was over, and Johannes was undergoing some profound changes in his upbringing and belief as a Christian.

Johannes's entry into a monastery may have taken place about the time of Robert Guiscard's death in 1085. His daily routine of psalms, mass and observance of the Benedictine rule continued his immersion in the study of the Scriptures and theological commentaries already begun with a local priest at his hometown. The 24 hours of daily life in the monastery were divided to allow some hours for meditative or private prayer, and some four to six hours for manual work (*opus manum*). Benedict's rule, dating from the sixth century, provided the essential context for the ordering and measurement of time in the early Christian world. A section of the rule had to be read aloud to the assembled monks every day, and the listeners could check that such an event was happening regularly at the appointed time and hour. The canonical hours were Matins, Lauds, Prime, Terce, Sext, None, Vespers and Compline, and the Psalms were also exactly prescribed by the rule, to be chanted every day of the week, at these eight moments of the day (*opus Dei*). With this daily programme, Benedict was able to fix hours of waking, eating and resting and to vary them according to the lengthening and shortening of the solar year and the changing hours of daylight. The life of the monastery thus centred on an intricate performance of chanted services punctuating every day of the year. This highly organised day had other specialisms added, such as training in writing manuscripts in the *scriptorium* and studies in music and plainsong. It is possible that Johannes advanced his studies in musical notation and was being prepared to become a cantor. There is no record of this, but evidence from his later years suggests that it may have been the case.[27]

---

26 Houben, *SS. Trinità di Venosa*, pp.30–31, on Berengarius.
27 Arno Borst, *The Ordering of Time: From the Ancient Computus to the Modern Computer* (Cambridge: Polity Press, 1993), pp.32–36; 'Rule of St. Benedict', *Christian Classics Ethereal Library*, <https://ccel.org/ccel/benedict/rule/rule.toc.html>, accessed 2024, Chapters 9–18 on psalms.

Although there is no evidence of any singing instruction received in the monastery during these years, it is relevant to the discovery of notated chants, which he transcribed in later times in the East. In one example, fragments of a Hebrew poem appear to bear twelfth-century Lombardic musical notations that could hark back to those early years in Italy. At some point, probably during these early years in Italy, he must have learned to record music notation. His deep penetration of the Bible in its Christian form became the object of continual meditation and interpretation for Johannes, forming part of the monastery's curriculum of study, but his Jewish rereading of this book, whether during the monastic years or later, was going to affect and change his entire life. After he had been linked to a monastery for a period of years, and probably ordained, Johannes would have attained the age of 25. He may even have been younger. Events outside his monk's life had moved swiftly to intensify his connection to Judaism.

Chapter 3

Call of the Crusade

In March 1088, Eudes de Châtillon, the Cardinal Bishop of Ostia, had been appointed the new Pope Urban II, but his position was precarious. There was an anti-Pope, Clement III, installed in Rome and strongly backed by the Holy Roman Emperor Henry IV. Pope Urban was forced to stay in Norman territory in southern Italy, supported by the former Viking intruders who were now masters of lower Italy and Sicily. Influenced by his time as Prior of Cluny, this new Pope sought to further his reform policies by propounding the idea that the Church of Rome was synonymous with the universal Church and that the Pope had temporal as well as spiritual jurisdiction on earth as the heir of St Peter. Urban was associated with this reform agenda, which included the eradication of simony (paying for church office) and the power to appoint bishops and archbishops over and above any secular authority, including the emperor. The power of the German kings rested on control of the Church. The papal reforms proposed otherwise.[1]

While the anti-Pope was in office in Rome, the northern emperor enforced the imperial policy by repeated incursions over the Alps. Urban needed a convincing theme to shore up his role as a reformer and appeal to a wider international audience that would overcome his exclusion from Rome: this is partly what led to the initiative of summoning a crusade, an agenda that would enable him to emphasise his actual leadership of Christendom worldwide free from any control of secular monarchs. The calling of the First Crusade outflanked any of the emperor's pretensions and even any Norman designs, giving him sole ownership of a project that combined rigorous principles with political realism: a winning idea. Another important aim was his attempted rapprochement with the Byzantine Emperor Alexius I. This policy had already begun at the Council of Melfi in 1089, where, in the presence of ambassadors from Constantinople, he lifted the ban of excommunication against Alexius. Now, such a crusade could be seen as an important instance of cooperation with the Eastern Roman Empire in its war with the Seljuk Turks.

The all-important announcement was made in an open field, outside the eastern gate of the city of Clermont on 27 November 1095. At the time that Urban made this

---

1 Steven Runciman, *A History of the Crusades* (London: Penguin, 1980–1981), vol. 1, pp.100–05; Thomas Asbridge, *The Crusades: The War for the Holy Land* (London: Simon & Schuster, 2020), pp.33–35.

crucial declaration, it was not defined by him as a crusade: rather, he stressed the holiness of Jerusalem and dwelt on the sufferings of pilgrims who journeyed there. Christendom's enormous undertaking, he said, was to be a pilgrimage and journey to rescue the Holy City from the domination of Islam by fighting a just war, carrying out the work of God. For those who died in battle, there would be absolution and the remission of sins. This 'journey to Jerusalem', as it initially became known, brought forth an explosion of energy that seized the imagination of large parts of Europe.[2]

Massacre of Jews

Nor was the effect on Johannes of Dreux negligible, as he later recounts in his autobiography. To begin with, he heard, and probably witnessed, an outpouring of violence against Jews, unlike anything that had occurred in recent memory. The call for journeying to Jerusalem unleashed unforeseen emotions that seemed to lie beyond the control of bishops and rulers. It was often said that this was a popular insurgence, but, at times, emotions were also spearheaded by local counts and other notables.[3] The proclamation made by Urban II in 1095 seemed to licence crowds and mobs to kill and plunder Jewish communities at will. One source, the *Anonymous of Mainz*, describes the murder of men and women, infants and new-born babies who were trampled like dust, with pregnant women ripped open. In the course of this massacre at Mainz, in May 1096, about 1,000 Jews had perished. Emicho of Leiningen (also known as Emich of Flonheim), who led the massacre, was a notorious lawbreaker who now claimed to have a cross miraculously branded on his flesh.[4] This rise in violence, just before the year 1100, was linked with millennial anxieties, a potent mix that is also reflected in the mind of Johannes. But there were other factors. As the European and Arab economies boomed and populations rose in the tenth to twelfth centuries, the dependence on Jewish knowledge seemed to falter, leading to a denunciation of the heretofore special and protected position of Judaism. There was now renewed pressure to secure Jewish conversion to Christianity, a process emerging at the intellectual centre of Christian religious leadership. But this insurgency at the onset of the First Crusade awakened the demand for mass conversion at the point of a sword. Europe was emerging from the low point of population and economic decline after the demise of the Roman Empire and was now looking to expand by challenging Islam and regaining its holy site of Jerusalem. The Jews were now seen in the popular mind as the clear killers of Christ in Jerusalem, leading

---

2   Tyerman, *God's War*, pp.58–70.
3   R. I. Moore, *The Formation of a Persecuting Society* (Oxford: Wiley, 1990), p.30.
4   Runciman, *History*, vol. 1, pp.134–41; Tyerman, *God's War*, pp.100–06; Jacob R. Marcus, *The Jew in the Medieval World: A Sourcebook, 315–1791* (Cincinnati: Hebrew Union College Press, 1938), pp.115–20, for text of the Mainz massacres; see also Shlomo Eidelberg (trans.), 'The Narrative of the Old Persecutions, or Mainz Anonymous', in *The Jews and the Crusaders: The Hebrew Chronicles of the First and Second Crusade* (Madison: University of Wisconsin Press, 1977), p.107.

to a drastic change in Jewish–Christian relations within the West. The pogroms of 1096 testified to a new persecuting attitude that soon took hold throughout Europe.[5] Johannes captures this dark mood, picking up the detail of the cross on someone like Emicho, when in his *Autobiography* he recalls members of the First Crusade prepared to march to Jerusalem:

> [. . . . .] and they put the crosses
> [each and every one o]n his clothing and on his shoulder.
> [. . . . .] to go to Jerusalem.
> [Then said they one to ano]ther: Why is that we
> [are going to fight against] our enemies, when, behold, in our (own) lands
> [. . . . . .reside] our enemies and those who hate
> [. . . . . Why should we lea]ve them with our women
> [. . . . . This was the talk in all] the camps of the Franks.[6]

Johannes had reason to be in such a dark mood. Jews had no collective civil rights: both lay and ecclesiastical authorities occasionally gave special protection to specific merchants and other members of Jewish communities but only when it suited them. There were no general laws to safeguard entire populations. Crusaders requiring money to fund their expeditions or simply for private gain exploited this wild anti-Jewish fervour by allowing some of the petty lords who could not be controlled to issue threats. The Jewish communities of Mainz and Cologne each offered Count Godfrey of Bouillon 500 pieces of silver, even though the Jews of the Rhineland had already asked the Chief Rabbi of Mainz to write to Godfrey's overlord – Emperor Henry IV – and ask him to stop any persecution. But the issuing of these threats by some crusaders was largely ignored by the rulers. In May 1096, a massacre occurred at Spier, followed by the terrible one at Mainz already mentioned. Another outbreak of killings took place at Worms and other towns, spreading panic and desperate offers of money to halt it. The incidence of killings followed the progress of some of these crusading armies as they advanced towards the East, and, in June that year, more massacres took place in Prague.

The visions of Johannes

An eclipse that occurred on 9 February 1095 not only darkened the skies further but also clouded the mind of Johannes, who, when recollecting this event many years later, seems to have been profoundly affected by such heavenly signs, together with the man-made horrors he describes. In fact, there were two eclipses recorded, one in February 1095 and another a year later also in February. Either of these eclipses

---

5   Moore, *Formation*, pp.30–39.
6   Golb (trans.), 'Autograph Memoirs', Document V: Cambridge: Taylor-Schechter MS 8.271, fol. 1 *verso*, lines 7–14.

can be dated to the sixth month of *Adar* in the Jewish calendar, which began on 9 February in 1095. This may explain the reference to 'six' in the *Autobiography*, in what is a difficult passage. Some lines further down, this dating seems to be reinforced by a mention of Pope Urban II and his journey to Clermont in 1095.[7] The eclipse mentioned is also compared by Johannes to a biblical eclipse described in the Old Testament Book of Joel, which he sets out in his autobiography in the original Latin Vulgate of the Bible, or, as Johannes terms Latin: the language of the Edomites. 'And I will shew wonders in the heavens and in the earth, blood, and fire, and pillars of smoke / The sun shall be turned into darkness, and the moon into blood, before the great and the terrible day of the Lord come' (Joel 2:30–31). This short prophetic book of only four chapters, which proved so powerful in Johannes's imagination, falls into two distinct parts. In the first part, the land is ravaged by a locust swarm, regarded by the prophet as heralding 'the day of the Lord' climaxed by the eclipse. The last two chapters of this brief book allude to the judgement executed against enemy nations on that day. The powerfully described locust swarm suggests armies of Christian crusaders slaughtering Jews and advancing to the Holy Land, invading the city. The mind of Johannes is here moving away decisively from a Christian reading of the Bible that had been his formation to another one shaped by Judaism. This ecological disaster of the locusts, an allegory for conquering armies, is reversed in the final chapters of Joel to a restoration that will return Judah and Jerusalem to the people of Israel. The persecution of the Jews before the First Crusade and the eschatological tone of this short Book of Joel provides an explanation that foretells the liberation of Jerusalem and the awakening of Zion, all of which may have fed Johannes's decision to forsake Christianity for Judaism. The doubts engendered by these two events seemed to take root in the centre of his being along with other thoughts, which will shortly be examined. His journey to Jerusalem would eventually prove to be guided by very different goals from those preached by Pope Urban II at Clermont.

The Council of Bari

In the intervening years after his proclamation and the departure of crusading armies, Pope Urban sought to cement his authority over the Catholic Church by asserting the primacy of Rome over Constantinople in the Norman south. The Council of Bari, held in that city between 3 and 10 October 1098, was a highly symbolic event that touched on several practical and political matters. The local bishops who still practised the Greek Orthodox rite of Byzantium needed to be reined back in some manner from any binding allegiance to Constantinople. The aim was partly achieved at Bari: the Greek churchmen acknowledged the authority

---

7 Golb (trans.), 'Autograph Memoirs', Document IV: Cambridge: Taylor-Schechter Genizah Collection, MS 8.271, fol. 1, *recto*, lines 6, 14, for 'sixth' month and mention of Pope Urban; reference to Urban also discussed in Golb, 'Megillat Obadiah Hager', p.83.

of the Catholic Church in Italy but failed to fall into line with Rome on the *filioque* question. One source speaks of an attendance of 185 bishops, all told. The council or synod took place in the basilica of St Nicholas in Bari presided over by Archbishop Elias. In 1087, sailors from Bari had brought back to their city the relic of St Nicholas of Myra, an early Christian bishop of Asia Minor, in whose honour a basilica consecrated by Urban was built two years later. This consecration of relics of an eastern bishop highlighted Urban's policy of building up the Catholic influence in Bari over the Byzantine church. Pope Urban had also enlisted Anselm, the Italian exiled Archbishop of Canterbury, who was seeking Urban's support in his stand against the English King William Rufus concerning his investiture. Urban also asked Anselm to pen a rebuttal of the theological arguments against eastern Greeks attending the Council of Bari. The importance of these theological arguments went far beyond the nature of the Trinity, the original cause of the dispute that had rumbled on. The origin of the schism mentioned earlier reflected in some measure other claims of the Pope, as Bishop of Rome, to primacy over the four patriarchs of the East: Constantinople, Jerusalem, Antioch and Alexandria. Meanwhile, despite a compromise reached with the Greeks attending at Bari, the question of the *filioque* remained. But the Council did produce an opening and expansion of the West towards the East that had been signalled by the calling of the Crusade, and, for a while, Bari was the epicentre of this encounter of East and West.[8]

Crusaders sail to the East

The gathering of bishops and the presence of the Pope had been preceded by the departure of a large contingent of Normans from southern Italy for the journey to the Levant. The most obvious leader of this expedition was Bohemond of Taranto. Fired by the zeal engendered by Urban's call, he tore up his cloak in front of his army to make crosses with it for his captains. Despite the fact that Bohemond was the eldest son of Robert Guiscard, that great trailblazer who had conquered southern Italy, his inheritance of the duchy of Apulia had been claimed by the son of Guiscard's second wife because Guiscard had divorced Bohemond's mother on the grounds of consanguinity. Now disinherited, the prize of military glory and a lordship overseas in compensation was a powerful lure. Bohemond was accompanied on his pilgrimage to the Levant by his 20-year-old nephew Tancred of Hauteville, named after the patriarch of the dynasty. This army of 7,000, assembled in part from vassals or adherents of the Hauteville family, set sail from Bari in October 1096.[9] The gathering of ecclesiastics two years later in Bari, which had followed this departure,

---

8   C. D. Fonseca, 'L'apertura "trinitaria" del Concilio di Bari', in S. Palese and G. Locatelli (eds), *Il Concilio di Bari del 1098. Atti del Convegno Storico Internazionale e celebrazioni del IX Centenario del Concilio* (Bari: Edipuglia, 1999), pp.39–54; G. R. Evans (ed.), *The Medieval Theologians* (Oxford: Wiley-Blackwell, 2001), pp.94–101, on Anselm.

9   Runciman, *History*, vol. 1, p.155.

so redolent with theological issues and Church politics, was also to set the seal for the arrival of the Normans on the world stage, even if events seemed to be managed largely by churchmen. Indeed, Urban's authority was ultimately underpinned by these Normans whose story we have told, for they were anxious to repeat their previous exploits in Normandy, England and Italy, now sanctioned by the Pope's call to regain Jerusalem for Christendom. Johannes soon made a similar choice to depart on what would be a different type of pilgrimage, though brought about by the same events.

The path that he took can be inferred from the fragment that was found, written in his own handwriting, on the final leaf of a prayer book. As yet we cannot go into this part of the story in detail, for that belongs to the next chapter, but we may elucidate some of what must have taken place in his homeland. This fragment has one of the two precise dates of Johannes's life story: it records the date of his conversion to Judaism in August or September 1102 at an unnamed place. His adoption of a new religion has to be considered together with a revealing fragment of a letter written by Rabbi Barukh of Aleppo at a later date. Scholars have read and transcribed some sections of this letter with great difficulty, by reconstructing lines that are only partly extant. The content of the letter is in fact a recommendation by Barukh, head of the Talmudic Academy in Aleppo, whom we meet later, describing Johannes and his suitability to be received by all Jewish communities in Syria and the Middle East.

The conversion of Johannes

The letter, examined in due course, speaks unequivocally of some formal ceremony of conversion to Judaism probably taking place in Italy. The letter also describes the ceremony with the proper questions and answers for conversion that take place as set out in the Talmud. Johannes, as will be seen later, had evidently carried with him from Italy a letter from the Jewish scholar-sages – *haverim* as they are known – giving a full description of this ceremony that Barukh, the rabbi in Aleppo, judged to be valid and now reconfirmed, rubber-stamping it, if you like, in his own letter and quoting in detail parts of this Italian account. Johannes was therefore properly, but secretly, Jewish before his departure and arrival overseas in Syria sometime after 1102, having undergone a ceremony in accordance with the orthodox conversion rite prescribed in the Talmud. We shall see how important this was to prove. In short, Johannes became Jewish somewhere in Italy, most probably in a city of Apulia where there was a community of sages authorised to carry out this official ceremony. The most informed guesses of the locale would be Taranto, Brindisi, Bari or Otranto, all situated near his hometown of Oppido. More likely would be the presence of a strong Jewish community situated in a busy port like Bari that was already growing active in transport and trade to the Middle East because of the Crusade. Johannes might even have set sail from the same point of departure, as Bohemond did a few years earlier. But Johannes could not have felt entirely safe to publicly announce his apostasy, a renunciation of Christianity, so he would have concealed this, waiting to reveal his new faith only when securely away from his homeland. He probably booked his passage immediately after the ceremony, which is why it is deemed more likely to have happened in a port, ready for a quick embarkation, a getaway in fact.

Jacob reborn

But by now we may be able to see, if we look attentively, that, before his departure, Johannes had interpreted or reimagined the circumstances of his birth, as mentioned earlier, in order to explain a prophetic significance at the heart of his espousal of Judaism. In medieval times, it was not frequent to record such moments of birth in quite the manner Johannes did in his *Autobiography*. Modern scholarship has at times succeeded in unearthing some revisionism and hidden details about such events and dates, as in the more famous case of Charlemagne's birthdate in the eighth century, for example. In such documents, intimate details about birth and adolescence were often left unsaid. This is what makes a fifth-century autobiographical testimony, such as that of Augustine of Hippo, so exceptional. Details or exact dates of a person's birth or childhood, even with Augustine, are almost never given. Einhard, the medieval courtier who had recorded Charlemagne's life, knew the year of his death but stated that he had died in his seventy-second year because he may have wished to equate the span of his life with that of the Roman Emperor Augustus: a fact he took from the account given by Suetonius.[10] In source-poor times, the very unusual manner of Johannes's own recording of the manner of his birth indicated something of equal importance, an analogy imbued with meaning that takes us right to the heart of his personal convictions. In the light of his visionary remembrance, his arrival in the world and the difficult birth of twins recall the cadences of the Old Testament that he would have studied so deeply from an early age and pored over during his years in the monastery.

Johannes associates his entry into the world and that of his brother, Rogerius, with the primordial story of the birth of Jacob and Esau told in Genesis. The opposition between the elder Rogerius, who became a soldier, and Johannes, directed to be the student of religious texts, is derived from the same Biblical contrast when Rebekah, Isaac's wife, conceived:

> And the children struggled together within her; and she said, If it be so, why am I thus? And she went to enquire of the Lord.
>
> And the Lord said unto her, Two nations are in thy womb, and two manner of people shall be separated from thy bowels; and the one people shall be stronger than the other people; and the elder shall serve the younger. (Genesis 25:22–23)

---

10 Janet L. Nelson, *King and Emperor: A New Life of Charlemagne* (London: University of California Press, 2019), pp.28–29.

Esau, the first-born, we are famously told, was covered with red hair. He grew up to be a hunter and a favourite of his father. Jacob came out of the womb second, clutching his brother's heel (Genesis 25:26), and the Hebrew name '*Ya'acov*' is said to be derived from '*ekev*', 'the heel of the foot'. Jacob would eventually be known by another reading of his name, suggesting the 'supplanter', from '*aqab*', 'to supplant' (Genesis 27:36). Years later, in his encounter at the River Jabbok with a stranger, Jacob was told after a night of struggle with this stranger that he would henceforth be known as 'Israel'. In fact, the 12 tribes that eventually occupied Canaan traced their descent and their names from the House of Jacob or the Children of Israel.

This story of Jacob, with these details of birth and genealogies, occupies a pivotal place in Hebrew history, and the account was appropriated by Johannes to lend a special meaning to the circumstances of his own birth: it came to inhabit the very core of his identity. The theme of the younger son, of course, dominates the stories of the four generations of patriarchs in Genesis.[11] This parallel is also carried over with Esau, the older brother, who is implicitly compared with Rogerius: in each case, two first-born are subverted or supplanted by younger siblings who are cast as the chosen ones. We are unaware of the later relationship of Johannes of Dreux and his older brother, but the norms of primogeniture destined the first-born to inherit the father's title and serve as a soldier. The famous deceit carried out by Jacob on his brother, Esau, permitted him to obtain his father's blessing when he was old and blind, pretending to be the elder Esau and thereby fulfilling the prediction that 'the elder shall serve the younger'. The continuation of this deceit, by converting to Judaism, became an uncontrollable echo in the visionary belief of Johannes, enabling him to imagine the inheritance of the title to rule over the Norman family of his birth in a very particular fashion. His conversion was a new birth that became confirmed through his adoption of Judaism. This had to do with the way these roles of Jacob and Esau were understood and interpreted in opposing ways by Judaism and then Christianity. In the foundational text in Genesis, Esau is equated with Edom, a region situated to the south of Palestine, below the Dead Sea. This rugged country was the semi-desert terrain of Seir or Edom. The story in the opening book of the Bible lists the '… Generations of Esau who is Edom … Thus dwelt Esau in mount Seir: Esau is Edom' (Genesis 36:1, 8). The biblical story recognises the community of Edom as older than Israel, a group that seemed to alternate as an enemy or ally of Judah, the nascent Hebrew state. At times, Edom is vilified for attacks upon the Jews, and its speedy destruction is foretold in certain prophetic passages of the Old Testament. These attacks, sometimes linked to the desecration of Jerusalem by the Babylonians in 587/586 BCE, may even imply conditions after the restoration and exile in Babylon. The slant taken in this interpretation was that the nation of Israel was in a state of enmity with Edom, which was presented as a continuation of the struggle in Rebekah's womb between the brothers-to-be-born. This contest between Israel and Edom,

---

11 Holo, 'Jewish Communities', pp.150–51; Gary A. Rendsburg, *How the Bible Is Written* (Peabody, MA: Hendrickson Publishers, 2019), pp.452–53.

the contentious southern neighbour, had an economic wellspring: the perennial contest to control the southern Negev and the trade routes from Petra, in the interior, to the coast and Arabia. But it continues to be manifested in the tales of fraternal rivalry between Jacob–Israel and Esau–Edom, where Edom has become the archetypal adversary. Such an adversarial viewpoint was later taken up by the Rabbinic tradition expressed in the Jerusalem and Babylonian Talmud: Esau and Edom became associated with the city of Rome, where Romans are all deemed Edomites, slayers of Jews and ravagers of Jerusalem. This perspective is alluded to by Johannes in the early part of his autobiography when he characterises the rule of the papacy in Rome as the 'kingdom of Edom' that experienced consternation at the conversion of the Christian Bishop Andreas to the Jewish faith. And later, he refers to the Latin language of the Vulgate as the 'language of the Edomites'. The emotional force in Johannes's mind came to characterise the Papacy, Latin and Christianity as the enemy, a source of error and unbelief: it was a highly personal rebellion and repudiation of his family and his Christian faith and upbringing. Johannes believed he would follow Andreas to embrace Judaism and confound the Edomites. Historical events of long ago were relived and perpetuated in his mind to keep alive this confrontation of Jacob and Esau in the birth of Johannes. He considered Jacob to be the ancestor of the Jews and Esau the ancestor of Rome and, later, of Christianity. The savage destruction of Jerusalem by Roman troops in 70 CE reinforced the catastrophic conflict between Rome and the people of Judea, which followed soon after, between 132 and 135 CE. The result of the rebellion of Simon Bar Kochba in 132 CE was the final razing of Jerusalem to the ground and the destruction of the city of Beitat when the Roman Emperor Hadrian founded a new city on the ruins of Jerusalem. The Jerusalem Talmud proclaimed, 'The voice is the voice of Jacob crying out because of what the hands of Esau did to him at Beitat'. The Rabbinic writings of the Talmud reinforced this belief that Esau was the rejected son who received no covenanted inheritance from his father and God that was his due. Rome and Christianity were also cast out by the Jewish God along with Esau in favour of a relationship with Israel.

Johannes, a Christian Norman, decided to reclaim that biblical relationship for himself, the true one that constituted his birthright, marked by the manner of his coming into the world from his mother's womb. Like Jacob, he moved to claim that blessing from Isaac even though he was the younger son, rejecting his Norman family. Johannes's embrace of Jewishness challenged the rise of Christianity as had been propounded by early medieval commentators. For them, the Christian message had disowned Jews and annulled their ritual law, transferring their inheritance over to the Church that had become the 'true' Israel – a theft that was the cornerstone of patristic Biblical commentary, directed solely towards a Christian view of the world. In this explanation, Judaism was seen as an inheritance that was closed, the historical Israel being merely the 'old Israel' stranded in an unfulfilled past. Johannes now looked to overturn this Christian worldview by casting out his country, education, language and Norman ancestry. His rejection of Christianity was buttressed by an influential book that coloured his opinions.

Sepher Yosippon retells Jewish history

Johannes's progression from Christianity to Judaism is illuminated by a seminal book that appeared in the mid-tenth century in southern Italy, encapsulating these above-mentioned beliefs. The anonymous author, known to later Jewish tradition as Yosippon (Josephus), presents a history of the Jews in the Second Temple period. The title of the work has been taken from the supposed author, erroneously thought to be Josephus. *Sepher Yosippon* propounds a foundation history, recounting in a retelling of the Biblical story, that Esau's grandson Zepho, son of Eliphaz, is the link between Edom and the ancient city of Rome. The anonymous author has Zepho accompany Aeneas to Italy in a fusion with Virgil's famous account, eventually proving the establishment of Rome's Edomite roots through his arrival and settlement:

> In those days Zepho ben Eliphaz, son of Esau, fled from Mizrayim (Egypt). It is he whom Joseph had captured when he went to bury his father, Israel, in Hebron … After Joseph's death, Zepho fled from Egypt and came to Africa to Agnéas (Aeneas) king of Kartagini (Carthage) … Agnéas received him with great honor and appointed him chief of his army.

This rewriting of the history of the Jews in *Sepher Yosippon*, and the part played by Edom in the founding of Rome, through Zepho, grandson of Esau, went through many editions and forms one aspect of Johannes's acquaintance with Jewish history and the links with Edom and Rome.[12] The Norman probably became familiar with this work at a later date, after his conversion and removal to the Levant and after he had mastered Hebrew, but this work no doubt influenced the account of his own life, perhaps even his own use of language. *Sepher Yosippon*, written in classical Hebrew style, proved highly influential and is also a showcase of the rich rabbinical culture of southern Italy, as it mentions many Jewish towns in this region, familiar to Johannes. The Jewish origins of the populations of Taranto and Otranto are recorded. After the Jewish war, we are told, Titus takes 90,000 captives from Judah, leaving 1,500 in Rome and settling '5000 in Taranto and Otranto and other cities in Puglia'. *Yosippon* also mentions the Italian town of Venosa, known to Johannes, suggesting the author had a close knowledge of the town and its Jewish religious and cultural life.[13] The work became one of the most frequently copied titles of the Jewish Middle Ages, for many almost the sole lens with which to view Jewish history. The

---

12 Joshua Holo, 'Gershom B. Judah and the Italian Roots of Early Ashkenazic Jewry', in J. L. Kraemer and M. G. Weschler (eds), *Pesher Naḥum: Texts and Studies in Jewish History and Literature from Antiquity through the Middle Ages Presented to Norman (Naḥum) Golb* (Chicago: Oriental Institute of the University of Chicago, 2012), pp.103–08; Zepho's story in Steven B. Bowman (trans.), *Sepher Yosippon: A Tenth-Century History of Israel* (Detroit: Wayne State University Press, 2023), pp.10–11.
13 David Flusser, 'Josippon, a Medieval Hebrew Version of Josephus', in L. H. Feldman and G. Hata (eds), *Josephus, Judaism and Christianity* (Leiden: Brill, 1987), p.393, on Venosa; Bowman (trans.), *Sepher Yosippon*, p.394 for Taranto and Otranto, and p.88 for Venosa.

significance of this work was the demonstration that Byzantine–Norman Italy had become a most important centre of Jewish learning in Europe.

The route map travelled by Johannes had taken him from his Norman family to an espousal of the Jewish faith that found expression in a powerful anti-Christianity: a reaction to his birth and background that had to be newly understood and refashioned. What lay at the heart of this was a restatement of the Edomite explanation put forward in *Yosippon*. One day, argues Johannes, as it is stated in this work, the Judaic faith will supplant Rome, Christianity and Latin: Zion and Jerusalem would be restored to the Jews. Such hopes were especially poignant in his mind as the crusading armies that had left for the Levant a little earlier regained Jerusalem in triumph in July 1099. This pivotal event now fed into the age-old contest between Israel and Edom: the new crusader capture of Jerusalem could again be compared to the destruction of Jerusalem in 586 BCE, the razing of the Temple in 70 CE and the levelling of the city after the Bar-Kochba revolt. All this would be challenged and undone by an alternative reading of history set out in *Sepher Yosippon*.

A new name

These mournful times now drew Johannes to the Book of Obadiah, the most impassioned anti-Edomite polemic and the shortest text in the Bible, consisting of a single chapter of 21 verses. In these searing lines, the prophet denounces the Edomites for attacking Jerusalem and foresees a terrible vengeance: 'Though thou exalt thyself as the eagle, and though thou set thy nest among the stars, thence will I bring thee down, saith the Lord. / ... / For thy violence against thy brother Jacob shame shall cover thee, and thou shalt be cut off for ever' (*Obadiah* 1:4, 10). The ancient enmity of Jacob and Esau had been rekindled by the victories of the First Crusade, which the prophet Obadiah, seemingly reborn, now denounces, forecasting victory: 'And the house of Jacob shall be a fire, and the house of Joseph a flame, and the house of Esau for stubble, and they shall kindle in them, and devour them; and there shall not be any remaining of the house of Esau' (*Obadiah* 1:18). Now, Johannes, undergoing the prescribed rite of conversion, records with his own handwriting in the colophon previously mentioned the date marking a crucial change of religion and name:

> Obadiah the Norman Proselyte who entered the covenant of the God of Israel in the month Ellul, year 1413 of the (era of) Documents (=1102 A.D.) which is 4862 of the (era of) Creation — he, Obadiah, the Proselyte, has written (this prayer-book) with his own hand.[14]

---

14   Golb (trans.), 'Autograph Memoirs', Document I: Cincinnati, MS Hebrew Union College Genizah Collection no. 8 (prayerbook fragment). Golb places this fragment of the prayer book at the head of the *Autobiography* to begin the story.

This was the short, all-important evidence found by Jacob Mann that showed the date of his conversion and revealed that he was a Norman. This record of his name, appearing for the first time and written by him, and the date and manner he acquired it are found in this autograph statement on the last page of his prayer book (*siddur*) for the Sabbath night. Johannes was gone; he was now Obadiah the destroyer and devourer of Edomites. It was even said in the *Sanhedrin*, a tractate of the Talmud, that Obadiah, this destroyer, had been a convert from Edom, making him a touchstone and an inspiration for those seeking to relinquish Christianity for Judaism. Obadiah, the author of the book bearing his name, was a fifth-century-BCE postexilic prophet that lent his name to Johannes. Now, the newly named Obadiah would shortly depart like Bohemond for the lands of the crusades but carrying different weapons and bearing other aims. Although an apostate, he was still a Norman who sought new lands to conquer but for another faith. The common belief among Jews was that they, the Jews, presently inhabited the exile of Edom and no respite would be offered until the coming of the Messiah. This journey to Jerusalem would become a search for such a messiah, striving to fulfil not only the prophecies of the biblical Obadiah but also those of Johannes, who now bore the same name.

Chapter 4

Letter of Safe Conduct

Johannes was gone. Obadiah, as we must now call him, for that was his new name, imagined biblical precedents for his birth, which for him held the formal clarity and ultimate significance of all timeless things. In his life's journey after conversion to Judaism in 1102 CE, he will be shown to possess that same visionary intensity as when he moved from childhood to maturity. His language continued to be imbued with biblical motifs and images: the very curve and cadence derived from the Old Testament. But now that this new odyssey had begun, his passages of ritualistic description and denunciation from the Books of Joel and Obadiah came to be perceived, in his travels across the Middle East, as texts of messianic Judaism in a largely Islamic world. The great prophets, he believed, thundered against the Edomites, the term used for Christendom. But we must pause before again catching sight of him out there and recount the early travels of the crusaders to the Levant before Obadiah's arrival in the East some five years later.

Antioch and the Holy Lance

The crusaders had reached Syria, on the northern borders of the Holy Land, in the late summer of 1097. Jerusalem was their ultimate goal, but a huge obstacle stood in their way: Antioch, one of the oldest and greatest cities of the Orient protected the route south to Palestine. Before reaching this city, they had already undergone many vicissitudes. The army of 30,000 or more, under various leaders, had been made to swear allegiance in Constantinople to the Emperor Alexios Komnenos, promising to hand over to Byzantium any territory they regained in return for his support. To drive the Seljuk Turks out of Asia Minor was the chief aim of Byzantine policy, and this did not necessarily accord with an army fervently seeking to liberate Jerusalem. But the Byzantines had experienced both a steady onward advance of the Pecheneg steppe nomads and the relentless pressure from the Turks in an inexorable drive for conquest. By 1070, the Seljuk Turks had forced their way into Syria, culminating in the victory at Manzikert in 1071 in eastern Turkey. In addition, taking back Nicaea was crucial to any restoration of imperial control in the East. At this stage, these wars or any contest between Byzantium and the Turks lay far beyond the mental horizon of the Franks. Nevertheless, in July 1097, the crusader army captured Nicaea with the help of Byzantine vessels across lake Askania, which gave onto one of the walls of that city. This was a boon to the Byzantine emperor. Advancing along the main military road across Asia Minor, the crusading army then followed up with a hard-fought victory at Dorylaeum, which established their military reputation with the Turkish Seljuks, currently the dominant power in the region.[1]

The bulk of the army had reached Antioch by the autumn and initiated a fearsome protracted siege from October 1097 to June 1098, a siege that is as famous as it was decisive in the annals of the First Crusade. This huge city, which lay on the River Orontes, some nine miles from the sea, had been a major settlement in the Roman Empire. It was especially holy to Christianity as the place where Peter and Paul had lived and was still one of the five patriarchal seats of the Christian Church. It had remained one of the principal cities of the Byzantine Empire until 1084. The taking of Antioch threw up formidable challenges: it was too big to surround effectively, so the crusaders, lacking siege capabilities, attempted to squeeze the city into submission. As the winter progressed, conditions became very harsh, although the arrival of a Genoese fleet at the nearby port of St Symeon in the spring of 1098 gave some material support. The siege was finally ended when Bohemond secretly persuaded Firuz, a local Christian inside the city, to betray one of the towers to them: on 3 June 1098, the crusaders broke into the city and captured it with Bohemond, who ensured the value of his own triumph by flying his blood-red standard, thereby establishing his claim to the city. But this was not the end, because the citadel towering over Antioch remained in Muslim hands. The situation was made worse by the arrival of a vast relief army led by the local ruler Kerbogha, *atabeg* of Mosul, that surrounded the crusaders inside the city. Now, the besiegers had become the besieged. A lack of food and the loss of most of their horses drove the European invaders to despair. Some of the Franks declared that the expedition was doomed and were ready to abandon the march to Jerusalem, even though they had survived many obstacles along the way. Upon hearing some of these comments, the Byzantine emperor needed little persuading and withdrew his support. This action would be later cited by Bohemond to justify his claim on the city against the demands of Byzantium.[2]

It was at this moment of darkest fortune that a humble peasant from Provence sought an audience with two of the besieged leaders, Bishop Adhémar Le Puy and Count Raymond of Toulouse. He told them he had received frequent visitations from St Andrew accompanied by Christ. One appearance had taken place that very day, 10 June 1098. The informant recounted that he had been told that the Holy Lance of Longinus, the Roman soldier, which had pierced Christ's side at the Crucifixion, now was buried in the Basilica of St Peter in Antioch. He further claimed that the Apostle had declared that it should be recovered to be used as a standard, claiming that he who carries this lance in battle shall never be overcome by the enemy. What

---

[1] Runciman, *History*, vol. 1, pp.175–94; Asbridge, *Crusades*, pp.47–61; Peter Frankopan, *The First Crusade: The Call from the East* (London: Vintage, 2013), pp.64–86.

[2] Tyerman, *God's War*, pp.135–43; Runciman, *History*, vol. 1, pp.213–36. The Firuz incident is depicted on the book cover.

followed seemed to be a true miracle: four days later, the spot pointed out by the humble messenger was dug up, and the lance was discovered protruding from the ground. The inspiration seemed to change everything: two weeks later, through the power of faith – real or imagined – the crusaders, brilliantly led by Bohemond, stormed to an extraordinary victory over a force seven times greater outside the walls of Antioch. The part played by the discovery of a piece of iron in the soil of the basilica became venerated for all time as a miracle: the Holy Lance had guided the Christians to victory.

All this speaks of a time when the supernatural was not considered impossible or very rare: it was a context, as we have seen with Obadiah, in which dreams and visions thrived. Such apparitions came from God, in this case from a relic that had been part of the Crucifixion and the death and resurrection of the Messiah. Monasteries, churches and people of power sought to add to their spiritual authority by possessing such relics of saints, or objects associated with the life of Christ. Relics were usually corporeal remains of men and women venerated as saints or objects deemed sanctified by contact or association with them. Nothing then could beat the power of the Holy Lance, which proved able, in the imagination of the crusaders, to define the journey to Jerusalem and set the seal on the eventual triumph of what came to be known as the First Crusade. It was a time when the power of the miraculous permeated all three religions, Christian, Islamic and Jewish. Soon after, when Obadiah came to this land of the East, accounts of Messiahs and prophetic expectations were rife.[3] Eventually, contemporary Arab historians and chroniclers spoke not of crusades but of wars, or 'the Frankish invasions'. The word designating the Franks was translated in several ways, and we find *'Faranj'*, *'Faranjat'*, *'Ifranj'*, *'Ifranjat'*. The shorter *'Franj'* was also common. This influenced the term for crusaders to become collectively known in Arab eyes as 'Franks'.[4]

After this miraculous victory, there followed months of disagreement over the ownership of the city of Antioch and a protracted struggle for leadership of the march on Jerusalem. By a swift exploitation before and after the city's capture, Bohemond advanced his determination to keep Antioch for himself and step aside from any leadership of the Jerusalem campaign. The intense manoeuvres of Raymond of Toulouse failed to put a stop to this, and, by default, he was inveigled into leading the march south to successfully take the city and liberate the Church of the Holy Sepulchre – the site where the man whose side, 11 centuries earlier, had been pierced by a Roman lance, a holy relic able to inspire the *Franj* to victory outside the walls of Antioch. But Raymond was unable to maintain his position as leader of the victorious army that finally gained the prize of Jerusalem on 15 July 1099, its leadership having passed to Godfrey of Bouillon. The crusaders had positioned their troops around the walls and at first made little progress, as they were unused to besieging such large stone-walled eastern cities, so much larger than most towns in Europe. Besides, they lacked the know-how and materials to build siege structures. By good

---

3   Tyerman, *God's War*, pp.144–47; Runciman, *History*, vol. 1, pp.241–49.
4   Amin Maalouf, *The Crusades through Arab Eyes* (London: Al Saqi, 2006), Foreword.

fortune, when a fleet arrived in Jaffa, they seized the opportunity to dismantle some of its ships and build two towers, which were placed against the walls. Eventually, they succeeded in breaking into the city using one of the towers. Over the next few days, the place was put to the sword in an outburst of religious violence and a release of tension after so many months on the march. In the AlAqsa mosque, the Franks are said to have killed 70,000. A terrible massacre saw many of the Muslim and Jewish defenders slaughtered.

The capture of Jerusalem electrified the Christian world: it was presented as a military achievement with a special providential purpose. By some, the significance was even compared to the Exodus of the Israelites from Egypt to the Promised Land, and the Franks were now seen as the chosen people of God. Jerusalem was now a ladder to heaven for Christianity. But it could not be forgotten that the city was also the centre of Judaism and once King David's capital. It was also the third most holy city of Islam, where the Haram al-Sharif (Dome of the Rock), built in 690–692 CE on the site of the Temple, commemorated where Muhammad had ascended to Heaven and returned after having journeyed from Mecca. Muslims considered that Jerusalem would be the site on which the Resurrection would take place on the Last Day. But, for Jews, the site was also sacred and divine. Obadiah was driven by the loss of Jerusalem to the crusaders to abandon the religion he had been born into and draw nearer to the Holy Land. He looked for a return to Mount Zion where Yahweh's temple in Jerusalem was located and for the reinstatement of Jewish rule. Truly, Jerusalem was the contested place of three faiths, but, for now, Christendom held the city. The person who did more than any other to instigate the march on Jerusalem never heard of it. In Italy, that man was lying sick. On 29 July 1099, a fortnight after the Franks entered the Holy City, but before any news could reach him, Pope Urban II died in Rome, having returned there a few years earlier.[5]

The Latin states of Outremer

Between 1098 and 1109, these so-called Franks, chosen or not, went on to carve out four settlements in the eastern Mediterranean: the County of Edessa, the Principality of Antioch, the Kingdom of Jerusalem and the County of Tripoli. These were new Christian lands overseas (*outremer*) whose identity and government grew apart from Europe in time but remained in some manner outposts of European religion and culture.[6] The expedition that had succeeded in gaining Jerusalem in 1099 and establishing these new states was made up of people from many areas of Europe, including Flanders, Normandy, Languedoc, Lorraine, other parts of Italy, France and, to a lesser extent, Germany. All of these were commonly referred to as Franks

---

5 Karen Armstrong, *A History of Jerusalem: One City, Three Faiths* (London: Ballantine Books, 1997), pp.273–75; Runciman, *History*, vol. 1, pp.286–88, on the massacre and Pope Urban's death. See also Tyerman, *God's War*, pp.157–59, on the massacre.
6 Asbridge, *Crusades*, pp.115–16.

by the Arabs, and, in some Latin accounts of the time, they were also termed 'Latins'. The journey about to be undertaken by Obadiah in the first years of the twelfth century through what is now Syria and Iraq occurred in the period when these four Latin states were beginning their existence along the coast of Syria and Palestine and in northern Mesopotamia. The County of Edessa had been established early in 1098, both east and west of the upper Euphrates, by Baldwin of Boulogne. The Norman Principality of Antioch was founded, also in 1098 as we saw, by Bohemond, the son of Robert Guiscard. The County of Tripoli was initially targeted by Raymond Count of Toulouse, who died in 1105, and the city was finally conquered in 1109 by his son who became Count of Tripoli. The southernmost state was the Kingdom of Jerusalem, founded after its conquest on 15 July 1099, its first ruler being Godfrey of Bouillon, brother of Baldwin, ruler of Edessa.

The Italian city-states were quick to establish that the arrival in Jerusalem of western armies opened up enormous commercial possibilities. Even in the years before the crusaders had reached the Holy City, Genoa, Pisa and Venice already had fleets plying the waters, sailing to Syria and Palestine. Significant material rewards were the driving force, leading to quickened western expansion in the eastern Mediterranean and the exploitation of new markets. The new armies journeying to the Middle East required provisioning of food, goods, arms, men and the pressing need to have lines of communication with Europe. The ports of these new crusader states, such as Haifa, Jaffa, Tripoli and many others, also needed to be speedily secured as points of entry. The port of St Symeon, which supplied Antioch, became an important destination, and, at a critical time during the long siege, a Genoese squadron of 13 vessels had appeared at this port bringing reinforcements in men and armaments. The Italian maritime city-states were able to negotiate highly lucrative concessions and tax privileges for exclusive access to do business in these new ports and cities: Jaffa in 1099 (Pisa); Haifa in 1100 (Venice); Antioch in 1098 (Genoa), for example. But the dangers of sailing across the sea were always an abiding concern.[7]

Maritime travel to the Holy Land

Just how perilous such sea crossings could be is shown in a pilgrimage undertaken by Sæwulf, an Anglo-Saxon merchant, or possibly an abbot, a few months before Obadiah made a similar journey. Sæwulf gave a detailed description, setting sail from Apulia to Jaffa, which was serving as a busy port of entry to Jerusalem, now in Christian hands. Jaffa had played a critical role supporting the Frankish army in the siege of Jerusalem in 1099 and had now become the destination of many pilgrims eager to visit the Holy Sepulchre. But Sæwulf was unable to travel on a direct route to the Holy Land.[8]

---

7 Tyerman, *God's War*, pp.179–80.
8 Sæwulf, 'The Travels of Sæwulf, A.D. 1102 and 1103', in T. Wright (ed.), *Early Travels in Palestine* (London: Henry G. Bohn, 1848), pp.31–50.

Sæwulf recorded that he sailed on the feast of St Mildred (13 July 1102), reaching Jaffa on 12 October 1102, so taking a total of 13 weeks. But the vessel followed a slower route that hugged the coast, both for safety and for business reasons, stopping at several ports for trade. Shipping was customarily concentrated on such coastal routes, a practice known as *cabotage*, to avoid dangerous seas or attacks from pirates. Crossing the high sea, blue-water sailing, was generally halted from November to March in the Mediterranean, when the sea was closed (*mare clausum*). Indeed, conditions even after mid-September and before the end of May were viewed as risky.[9] Sæwulf and his party sailed from Monopoli in southern Italy, but he mentioned other ports such as Bari and Otranto that served equally as points of departure for pilgrims. They met with bad weather a few days out at sea, which threatened to delay any progress, but they proceeded to Hosta, where they journeyed on foot to Negroponte and hired another ship. This was a *dromond*, a type of Byzantine large galley that combined commercial cargo, transport of pilgrims and some naval duties and was able to carry soldiers. The vessel put in at Crete, Samos, Patmos, Rhodes, Myra and Cyprus, with our passenger-pilgrim regularly providing Biblical information of the places visited along the way, like any eager tourist. Here, he also tells us that the vessel was tossed about violently by storms for seven days and nights. They finally docked off the port of Jaffa, their destination. The town of Jaffa lay on the hill overlooking a string of offshore reefs of which Andromeda's Rock was the best known. The danger was that Jaffa, being of shallow depth, had no real harbour and only a limited anchorage between the reefs and the rocks. Farther north, where modern-day Tel Aviv lies, there was no protection from the sea. These disadvantages were so apparent that, as soon as the crusaders went on to conquer Acre in 1104, that port replaced Jaffa as the principal site of disembarkation for pilgrims visiting Jerusalem.[10] Upon arrival, as frequently happened, disaster ensued. Sæwulf was hastily warned to disembark as a violent storm was coming. The next morning, he and other travellers watched in horror from the shore, hearing the roar of the sea and the clashing of the ships. Laden with corn, merchandise and pilgrims, the ships initially managed to hold their anchors, but the volume of the waves threw them up, sending them crashing down upon the rocks, and some ran aground, being crushed to pieces. The violence of the wind prohibited the ships from putting out to sea, and the rocky coast prevented any approach to shore with safety. Out of 30 ships, only seven survived, and more than 1,000 people perished. Many of these would have been pilgrims arriving or returning. These were the perils lurking with sea travel. After Sæwulf's visit to Jerusalem, the return to Europe on 17 May 1103 was more prudent. His ship followed a safer coastal route passing Acre, Tyre and Sidon. Nevertheless, a large Arab fleet bore down on them, and soon his vessel was encircled. Fortunately, the ship was large and able to beat off the attack.

---

9   Michael McCormick, *Origins of the European Economy: Communications and Commerce AD 300–900* (Cambridge: Cambridge University Press, 2001), pp.450–68.
10 John H. Pryor, 'The Voyages of Saewulf', in R. Huygens (ed.), *Peregrinationes Tres* (Turnhout: Brepols, 1994), p.49; Sæwulf, 'Travels', p.36.

It might have been a *dromond*, which had room for 200 soldiers, but could also have been a large sailing ship.[11] Between Cyprus and Romania, they were subjected to repeated assaults by pirates and storms. Sæwulf's account seems to suggest that he was part of a larger group of pilgrims who may have been travelling together in relatively safer conditions. He may have been the tour leader, an abbot possibly, as mentioned earlier.

However, Sæwulf's arrival in Jaffa in 1102 might be seen as straying into the unsafe marginal month of October, although, in the early Middle Ages, ships had begun sailing later into the autumn. Another famous account by Judah Halevi, the Sephardic poet, tells us that he sailed in the summer of 1140 from Almeria in southern Spain, taking a southerly route along the African coast, tracking the shore. He was travelling in a small wooden vessel, a *qarib*, which provided little safety and some discomfort. These were little more than sea-going barges, probably attached to a larger convoy. Passengers were expected to feed themselves, crammed behind sacks of cargo, and provide their own bedding. In all such journeys, as he tells us in his poetry, the vastness of the sea was a frightening contrast to the smallness of the vessel, and the eternal perils of the Mediterranean, both natural and man-made, provoked even greater trepidation: storms and pirates, especially off the coast of Libya. Halevi reached Alexandria on 8 September 1140 just within the customary sailing season, before the winter months, although he was 12 days overdue.[12] This had not been the case with Sæwulf, who had suffered the consequences. All these vicissitudes were the common currency of sea travel.

The departure of Obadiah

Such perils are not irrelevant in attempting to pinpoint a precise date and the manner of Obadiah's departure soon after his conversion. We are fortunate, as we saw earlier, in possessing an almost exact date of this event: in the Hebrew month of Elul in the year 4862. This can be calculated to fall between 17 August and 14 September of the year 1102. The options facing Obadiah would be stark if, as suggested earlier, he was anxious to get away from his homeland once he had abandoned his religion. A monk who had undergone apostasy could be recognised, so he must have opted to maintain his monkish garb or some such dress to make his motive for travel more in keeping with the times: he could pose as a pilgrim like Sæwulf. Even a departure days or hours after this clandestine event could place him dangerously in the winter sailing season, but this was less likely if a vessel was sailing from Bari direct to Antioch with men and supplies, properly armed and in a convoy, and there were many such vessels. It was now a regular occurrence, as maritime traffic had expanded significantly for commercial, passenger and crusader traffic to the

---

11 Pryor, 'Voyages', pp.50–51.
12 Gabriel Levin (trans.), *Yehuda Halevi: Poems from the Diwan* (Manchester: Anvil Press Poetry, 2002), p.23; Goitein, *MS*, vol. 5, p.459.

Holy Land and the Levant in general. Besides, Norman ports in Apulia were closely linked to Antioch, since that city had now become Bohemond's seat of power in the new territories being established in *outremer*. Albert of Aachen recounted that 200 merchant and pilgrim ships, an enormous number, arrived in the Holy Land in 1102.[13] In taking this route, the Norman proselyte intended to reach the Holy Land by arriving at the centre of southern Italian Norman power. Neither was he going to linger in Antioch, as he ran the same chances of detection and recognition he risked in Apulia. We are faced with questions we cannot answer with certainty: the date of his sailing, the time taken, even the exact route. Some accounts have Obadiah in Constantinople for a period, but it is unclear if this took place.

Trips from west to east were usually faster than those against the prevailing winds. One voyage from Venice to Constantinople took perhaps 50 days in the eighth century. A slave ship departing from the Italian port of Taranto in 867 covered the distance from Taranto to Alexandria in 30 days. Sailing times did not get appreciably faster with the onset of the twelfth century, but some sailings were now 24 hours a day if required and if security was deemed adequate.[14] Obadiah could have left Bari sometime in September 1102 or even in August and reached St Symeon, the port for Antioch, in late or early October 1102. Had he waited for the next sailing season, his departure in mid-May 1103 would have him in Antioch 50–60 days later. Given the urgency of his secret abandonment of Christianity, the earlier exit might appear more likely. At this particular time, late or early October 1102, the situation in the Norman-ruled enclave of Antioch was highly unstable, as Bohemond had been taken prisoner in August 1100. His army had been destroyed by Malik Ghazi, the Danishmend emir, on an expedition to the upper Euphrates, and his nephew Tancred made to serve as regent of Antioch from 1101 to 1103. When Bohemond was eventually released in the spring of 1103, with the payment of a ransom, he was reinstated in his authority as ruler of Antioch, and this was marked by a general offensive on the territory around Aleppo ruled by Ridwan the Seljuk Turk. The area between Antioch and Aleppo became a virtual war zone as Bohemond took the nearby town of Basarfut in March 1104. But while an offensive by Bohemond and his allies expanded beyond the borders of Antioch, it was closely followed by a signal defeat of the Franks in a battle near Harran, two months later.[15]

The immediate consequences of these events might seem to augur badly for the safe passage of Obadiah out of Antioch and towards Aleppo, where he was heading.

---

13   Pryor, 'Voyages', p.36, n.7.
14   McCormick, *Origins*, pp.489–93; the passage through Constantinople is mentioned by Alexander Scheiber, 'Der lebenslauf des Johannes-Obadja aus Oppido', in P. Borraro (ed.), *Antiche Civiltà Lucane. Atti del Convegno di Studi di Archeologia, Storia dell'Arte e del Folklore, Oppido Lucano, 5–8 Aprile 1970* (Galatina: Congedo, 1975), pp.227–48; Benjamin Z. Kedar, 'The Voyages of Guiàn-Ovadiah in Syria and Iraq and the Enigma of His Conversion', in A. De Rosa and M. Perani (eds), *Giovanni-Ovadiah da Oppido, proselito, viaggiatore e musicista dell'Età normanna. Atti del convegno internazionale Oppido Lucano 28–30 marzo 2004* (Florence: Casa Editrice Giuntina, 2005), pp.133–47, gives the route followed here.
15   Asbridge, *Crusades*, pp.137–40; Runciman, *History*, vol. 2, pp.32–45.

It is not impossible that, after making landfall, he took another route, avoiding the Frankish-held city. He would certainly not be seeking to linger in Antioch, where he ran the risk of being challenged or recognised as a member of the southern Norman nobility, even if he might be dressed as a Christian in Holy Orders. Any last remaining leg of his passage to the Muslim world needed to take him through Aleppo. This was a highly dangerous undertaking in conditions of perpetual fighting between Muslims and Christians where his new religious identity, if openly displayed, was friendly to neither side. The Norman proselyte had to travel from his disembarkation point at the port of St Symeon, on the Mediterranean coast, approximately nine miles west of Antioch, a route that acted as the city's main link with naval supply forces from Europe and witnessed an intense traffic of trade and pilgrims eager to visit the Holy Land. From Antioch to Aleppo was a further 50 miles to the east, and, although the towns were linked by a Roman road, the terrain was separated by a set of low-lying hills, the *Jabal Talat*, characterised by rocky, arid ground that was difficult to cross. Just to the west of these hills, towards Antioch, were the settlements of Artah and Harim. On a large, fairly flat plain to the east lay al-Atharib and Zardana. The frontier between Antioch and Aleppo, buttressed by these hills, was always changing hands, especially at this period when Obadiah was attempting to negotiate the disputed border zone.[16]

Barukh b. Isaac in Aleppo

The importance of the Jewish population in Aleppo was well attested at this time, not only because of the intense amount of trade that passed through the city but also due to the long-standing presence there of learned Jewish sages and scholars. The city lay between in the region of Al-'Irāq and Al-Shām (Syria) and was a prominent crossroads of commerce. In fact, Aleppo stood at the end of the Silk Road, the vital trunk route from east to west for trade and travel.[17] Expensive silks would arrive mainly from the Orient in endless caravans from regions of Persia and beyond, via Aleppo, to be traded and sold. These caravans crossed cultivated and well-inhabited land – not only desert areas – for greater security. A letter at this time from Joseph b. Sahl Baradani complains that it is two months since the last arrival of caravans from Aleppo and the price of Persian fabric has risen to three or more dinars the parcel. In 1173, Benjamin of Tudela estimated the number of Jews here to be 5,000. This was a relatively high number and could have been lower, but the historic importance of the Jewish community is borne out by the fact that one of its gates, the northern

---

16 Thomas Asbridge, *The Creation of the Principality of Antioch, 1098–1130* (Woodbridge: Boydell Press, 2000), p.50.
17 Guy Le Strange, *Palestine under the Moslems: A Description of Syria and the Holy Land from A.D. 650 to 1500* (London: Alexander P. Watt, 1890), pp.360–67; Al-Muqaddasī and Basil Collins (trans.), *The Best Divisions for Knowledge of the Regions* (Reading: Garnet Publishing, 2001), p.152.

gate, was called *Bāb al-Yahūd* (Gate of the Jews).[18] The thriving Jewish population resided in the north-east area of the city, where a number of synagogues were to be found – one, the Great Synagogue, possibly dating from the fifth century. *Halab*, the old name for the city, was said to come from a story associated with Abraham, who possessed large flocks of sheep that he milked and distributed to the population. The word for milk, '*halab*', might also be linked to the whiteness of the walls of the old town in early times: a time before Abraham had journeyed to the land of Israel. This legend also reinforced the importance of the patriarch's involvement in the foundation of Aleppo, perhaps because of the derivation of this word for milk, '*haleb*' in Hebrew or 'white' in Aramaic.[19] Obadiah had thus chosen with care his first close encounter in the Levant with the world of Judaism: his meeting with Rabbi Barukh b. Isaac was to prove momentous.

The details of Obadiah and Barukh's meeting are set out in a separate letter found in the Geniza and provide another important source for an understanding of Obadiah's journey. The story of its discovery and interpretation, briefly told earlier along with the description of other fragments of the autobiography, is as fascinating as the story of Obadiah himself. The epistle, as we now call it, contains two main sections. The first is a highly wrought lamentation by Barukh, who mourned the destruction of Palestine and Jerusalem. This describes in poetic, almost biblical cadence the slaughter, defilement and captivity of Jews carried out by the Franks in their siege and capture of Jerusalem in 1099. Barukh's account dwells mainly on the sufferings experienced in Jerusalem and the towns taken by the crusaders. Since the arrival of the Franks, such dangers were now ever present for Jewish inhabitants of cities in Palestine. Other cities, farther away from the coast, were now safer, which was why Obadiah had ventured inland to Aleppo, a city that so far had been spared any direct attack. The epistle, written in the hand 'of our master Barukh' as the letter calls him, now concerns us. He was head of the Academy in Aleppo, a renowned commentator and writer on several Talmudic texts that have been identified. As anticipated in the first chapter, Rabbi Barukh referred here to a letter brought to him by Obadiah that certifies his conversion to Judaism in the correct manner. Only at this moment did Obadiah feel able to publicly announce his conversion, after producing the account of the *haverim* (or sages) carried with him from southern Italy for the head of the Jewish *yeshiva* in distant Aleppo. Barukh's epistle then carefully repeats these earlier details of a ceremony held somewhere in Apulia, in his own new letter of recommendation that would validate Obadiah's conversion for a wider circulation in the East. This letter would now override the original document issued in Italy.[20]

---

18 Moshe Gil, *A History of Palestine, 634–1099* (Cambridge: Cambridge University Press, 1992), p.358, on complaining about the price of silk; Adler (trans.), *Itinerary*, p.32, for the population of Aleppo.
19 Le Strange, *Palestine under the Moslems*, pp.362–63, cites this story.
20 Norman Golb, 'Dove avvenne la conversione al giudaismo del proselito Obadiah di Oppido?', in P. Borraro (ed.), *Antiche Civiltà Lucane. Atti del Convegno di Studi di Archeologia, Storia*

In Talmudic Law, full conversion was a legal rebirth, the proselyte being considered to have cut his links with his former family. The ceremony that marks the conversion of a gentile to Judaism is depicted twice in ancient rabbinic literature, first in the Babylonian Talmud, tractate Yevamot 47a–b, and later, with some variations, in the post-Talmudic tractate Gerim 1:1.[21] Talmudic terminology distinguished between the 'righteous proselyte' – *ger tsedek* – who, like Obadiah, took on the full rights and responsibilities of Judaism, observing all the commandments of the Torah as explained by the rabbis, and *ger toshav*, a 'resident alien' who had rejected idolatry but not accepted the full weight of the commandments and had not been circumcised or immersed. The status of a convert was crucially linked to the word '*ger*' (pl *gerim*), a 'stranger' with different shades of meaning. When Abraham had come from Chaldea, before the time of Israel, he characterised himself saying, 'I am a stranger and a sojourner with you' (Genesis 23:4). The ceremony that took place in Italy described in Barukh's letter states that our Norman 'became a proselyte in a law-court of Israel', and the words of the ceremony repeat verbatim well-known phrases set out in the Talmudic tractate Yevamot on conversion, giving the official language and the stages of conversion. This is preceded in Rabbi Barukh's epistle by an important description of Obadiah's family background:

> [This man, the bearer of our letter,] c]a[me t]o ou[r c]i[t]y [w]i[th an] e[p]i[stl]e [fr]o[m s]a[g]e[s]
> who dwell in his lands. They told us that this man is of a great family, that his father
> wa[[s] a great [chief]tain, and that this man is expert in the reading of their boo[k]s. Because of his understanding of what he read [in the b]ooks
> of their error, he [re]turned to the Lord of Israel with all his heart, with all his soul and with all his strength, and became a proselyte in a law-court of Israel.[22]

Barukh's reference to Obadiah as an expert in the reading of 'their books' strongly suggests that the Norman had entered the Church, but the letter from Italy would have been silent on his former status as a monk. The question here is about his conversion, not his former life.

There then follows Barukh's aforementioned letter, giving detailed lines quoted from the tractate Yevamot, which ends with an account of the Norman's circumcision and then the ritual immersion attended by two *haverim*. The all-important passage found in Yevamot 47a–b consists in a description of a ceremony that sets out a series of questions and answers between the convert and the sages (*haverim*).

---

dell'Arte e del Folklore, Oppido Lucano, 5–8 Aprile 1970 (Galatina: Congedo, 1975), pp.217–25; also discussed in Golb, 'Megillat Obadiah Hager', pp.87–92.

21   Shaye J. D. Cohen, 'The Rabbinic Conversion Ceremony', in *The Beginnings of Jewishness: Boundaries, Varieties, Uncertainties* (Berkeley: University of California Press, 2001), p.198.

22   Golb (trans.), 'Autograph Memoirs', Document XVI: Oxford: Bodleian Library, MS. heb. 2873, fol. 1 *recto*, lines 45–49.

The parade of these statements and replies are carefully repeated almost verbatim in lines 49–58 of Barukh's letter, followed by the circumcision and immersion:

> When [he accepted]
> all of the conditions, they circumcised him immediately, and when he was healed
> they ritually bathed him. There were [two]
> sages there, standing on either side of him, and they also informed him of some [lenient and some]
> severe commandments.[23]

The colophon to Barukh's letter stresses its official nature: '… Our master Barukh wrote this letter / that it might be kept by Obadiah the Proselyte (for use) in all communities of Israel to which / he might go'. This appeal to other Jewish communities requires a short explanation.

Obadiah, who had forcibly journeyed away from his native land, had to carry the proper papers, as it were, confirming an officially sanctioned change of religious faith if he was to be entitled to help and support from Jewish communities in the Middle East. The Rabbi of Aleppo now provided him with this safe conduct, a virtual passport in an age when religion defined your identity, particularly in those war-torn times. The lesson from the epistle written by the head of the Academy in Aleppo is that it had the force of law. The Jewish diaspora was closely connected by religious authority, and this in no way appeared to infringe any modern notion of sovereignty. Obadiah had journeyed from southern Italy to the Holy Land without crossing any state frontiers in the modern sense. At the root of this was the concept that law was personal, religious and not territorial. Obadiah was being judged according to the law of his religious community, rather than that of the territory where he happened to be. It was almost possible, outside some local statutes, to assert that states did not possess any law. These were the preserve of the religions. For Jews in Spain or Italy to seek court decisions in Aleppo, Baghdad or Cairo was the natural thing to do.[24]

One important further topic mentioned by Barukh is the background of Obadiah's family and parentage. It would seem that the original account of the conversion ceremony he brought from Italy described Obadiah as coming 'of a great family' and that his father was 'a great chieftain', a translation of the word '*sar*'. We can surmise that the sages in Italy describing the conversion ceremony wished to underline the importance of Obadiah's parentage in the Norman context, as family lineage at times counted for more than nationality or statehood. The translation of the Hebrew word '*sar*' can also mean 'official'. This has been translated variously as 'great lord' and 'chieftain', and some lines from the epistle by Barukh have even had

---

23 Golb (trans.), 'Autograph Memoirs', Document XVI: Oxford: Bodleian Library, MS. heb. 2873, fol. 1 *recto*, lines 58–61.
24 Goitein, *MS*, vol. 1, pp.66–67; Golb (trans.), 'Autograph Memoirs', Document XVII: Oxford. Bodleian Library, MS heb. 2873, fol. 1 *verso*, lines 2–3.

to be reconstructed with considerable difficulty from the partial words that survive, as the citation shows. Earlier, it was established that Johannes of Dreux was indeed the son a minor member of the Norman aristocracy and that the family name could perhaps be linked to the Dreux name of the ruling Hauteville dynasty from Normandy, which might connect him with the family of Bohemond and Tancred. This view has been cast aside by most scholars. One important interpretation gives a sensible opinion: 'the writer of a letter of recommendation would be interested to show his protégé in the best possible light'.[25] Rabbi Barukh repeated the assertion of Obadiah's distinguished family made in the Apulian account given to him, no doubt with some pardonable encouragement by Obadiah, who felt it would strengthen his pedigree and status, even his identity, in the final letter of recommendation, lending him more cachet. In the subsequent years of travel in the Islamic world, as we shall see, Obadiah would be noticed, sometimes with suspicion, for his appearance and distinctive accent in different contexts. When it suited him, he must have volunteered some facts about his background that would appear interesting and impressive. It is also fairly certain that he would not wish to be detained in any way or reside in towns or areas controlled by Franks, as his appearance, even if a Jew, must have looked distinctly Norman.

What might he have looked like? Even setting aside any assumptions of a distant family relationship or blood ties with Bohemond or Tancred, it is not unlikely that Obadiah as a Norman bore some resemblance to the sons of Robert Guiscard: tall, blond and blue-eyed with a pale skin. This is how Guiscard's son Bohemond's Norman appearance was famously pictured by Anna Komnene in *The Alexiad*, the biography of her father, the Byzantine emperor: 'His stature was such that he towered almost a full cubit over the tallest men … The skin all over his body was very pale, except for his face which was pale but with some colour to it too. His hair was light-coloured … His eyes were light-blue'.

A description given in *The Alexiad* of Bohemond's father, Robert Guiscard, the Norman trailblazer, echoes similar physical traits: 'He was a man of immense stature, surpassing even the most powerful of men; he had a ruddy complexion, fair hair, broad shoulders, eyes that all but shot out sparks of fire.'[26] Enough of these features, of the Norman father and son, were probably repeated in Obadiah, although he was not a warrior but a monk and might not have displayed Bohemond's impressive physique also described by the Byzantine princess. The point was, perhaps, that Norman traits of pale skin, size and colouring would have stood out in the context of the Middle East when the Franks arrived. These details had become ingrained in the minds of the people of the Levant as characteristic of Franks or Normans, as Al-Mas'udi wrote in the tenth century:

---

25 Prawer, 'Autobiography', p.114.
26 Bohemond and Guiscard description in Anna Komnene, E. R. A. Sewter (trans.), and Peter Frankopan (rev.), *The Alexiad* (London: Penguin, 2009), Book 13:10, pp.383–84, and Book 1:10, p.31, respectively.

The warm humor is lacking amongst them; their bodies are large, their natures gross ... Their color is so excessively white that it passes from white to blue, their skin is thin and their flesh thick. Their eyes are also blue, matching the character of their coloring, their hair is lank and reddish because of the prevalence of damp mists.[27]

The *Autobiography* of Obadiah later recounts a moment when 'gentiles' (referring to local Muslim inhabitants) sought to slay him upon his arrival in Baghdad and how he quickly looked for the protection of the synagogue. In all likelihood, this reflected the tense conditions in Baghdad between Arabs and Jews, heightened by his suspicious appearance. He looked foreign, perhaps he was viewed as a spy, although this is not mentioned. The inhabitants of Baghdad saw what Anna Komnene and Al-Mas'udi beheld: a tall, pale Norman from the imagined damp mists of northern Europe, even if, as a Jew, he was fully bearded and not clean-shaven like the crusaders. Upon arrival in Baghdad, Rabbi Barukh's final entreaty in the epistle must have saved him, for he would have been guarded and recognised by the Jewish community. The Norman proselyte was taken in and protected, probably housed, fed and clothed. It is legitimate to suggest this, as we have plentiful records from the Cairo Geniza of thousands of Jewish souls in dire straits collecting alms from communal funds around the mid-twelfth century and earlier. Although we do not rule out that Obadiah eventually was able to partly earn his living, the concluding remarks from Rabbi Barukh's epistle signalled that the Jewish community had an obligation to care for him and protect his person. Letters found in the Geniza in Fustāt reveal identical requests to private individuals and the community for alms or charity. This could be a request for a simple gift of cash, food or an article of clothing, or for more substantial assistance.[28] Evidence of poor relief found in Egypt on alms lists suggests that Baghdad cannot have been very different from other Jewish communities of the Mediterranean Islamic world. Obadiah was more than a simple wayfarer: in some eyes, he was a proselyte fleeing to safety in the Islamic world from a distinguished Christian family, but now the danger arose from the war, as he might be mistaken for a crusader. He would have known well the importance of bringing his southern Italian letter to a prominent rabbi in Aleppo to obtain safe conduct.

Before reaching Baghdad, the last stage of the Norman proselyte's journey as he moved eastwards from Aleppo seems to have taken him to Rabbah and Mâkisîn, with a possible stage through Raqqa. Rabbah, on the Euphrates, was home to 2,000 Jews as recorded by Benjamin of Tudela some 60 years later. The Spanish traveller described it as a fine city, large and fortified and surrounded by gardens and

---

27 Carole Hillenbrand, *The Crusades: Islamic Perspectives* (Edinburgh: Edinburgh University Press, 2018), p.270.
28 Mark R. Cohen, *Poverty and Charity in the Jewish Community of Medieval Egypt* (Princeton: Princeton University Press, 2005), pp.125–29; Moshe Yagur, 'The Donor and the Gravedigger: Converts to Judaism in the Cairo Geniza Documents', in Y. Fox and Y. Yisraeli (eds), *Contesting Inter-Religious Conversion in the Medieval World* (New York: Routledge, 2017), pp.115–34.

plantations. Obadiah had arrived at Rabbah after first reaching Mâkisîn, where a bridge of boats spanned the River Khâbûr, which fed into the Euphrates. The *Autobiography* supplies these details:

> Obadiah the Proselyte then went from the city of Maksin [and came unto] Rehoboth which is upon the River Euphrates.[29]

A few lines earlier, Obadiah recounts that, while walking along the road, he saw some troops being pursued and fleeing. A reconstruction of this pursuit in battle apparently seen by Obadiah could perhaps place it at this moment in September–October 1108. The Norman mentions that, as he was walking westwards, some troops rushed by with others in pursuit, but there are many *lacunae* in this part of the surviving fragment. It could refer to a battle that took place between Jāwulī and Tancred's forces, with fighting happening near Tell Bāshir.[30] This intriguing possibility pinpoints the Norman on the verge of his arrival in Baghdad in 1108 – a city that was to become his home for nearly 10 years – some four years or more after his arrival in the Levant.

---

29   Golb (trans.), 'Autograph Memoirs', Document VII: Cambridge: Taylor-Schechter MS 8.271, fol. 2 *verso*, lines 8–9.
30   Golb, 'Megillat Obadiah Hager', pp.83–85; Norman Golb, *Jewish Proselytism – A Phenomenon in the Religious History of Early Medieval Europe* (Cincinnati: University of Cincinnati, 1988), <https://oi.uchicago.edu/sites/default/files/uploads/shared/docs/jewish_proselytism.pdf>, accessed 2024, p.26; D. S. Richards (trans.), *The Chronicle of Ibn al-Athir for the Crusading Period from al-Kamil fi'l-Ta'rikh. Part 1* (Abingdon: Routledge, 2010), p.141; Runciman, *History*, vol. 2, p.114.

Chapter 5

Baghdad: City of Renown

The region of Iraq rose up as the centre of the Arab Empire, after the capital was moved in 762 CE from Damascus to Baghdad in Mesopotamia, the land of the two rivers. Baghdad, founded on an ancient settlement on the banks of the River Tigris, a few miles north of the city of Ctesiphon – the ruined imperial capital of the Parthian and Sassanian Empires – now made it possible to navigate down to the Persian Gulf, overcoming the marshy conditions that affected the Euphrates. Different lines of communication brought routes to and from the East and the Gulf, and from Africa, making use of highly productive irrigated land and intensification of agriculture and taking advantage of a network of canals between the two great rivers, the Tigris and the Euphrates.

The new capital of Islam flourished mightily, becoming a renowned metropolis of culture and commerce. Knowledge, learning, book production and translation of ancient texts soared in the centuries that followed, along with riches and power. Baghdad had been founded as a circular city, four miles in circumference, boasting four equidistant gates with a triple wall, which in concentric circles enclosed the great palace and mosque of the caliph standing in the middle of a wide central area. Before the end of the eighth century, the city spread beyond these modest limits. Suburbs sprung up along the main roads leading out from the four gates, and these neighbourhoods together with East Baghdad or Rusafah, dating from the original foundation, expanded along the east bank of the Tigris. The great Karkh quarter, with its mixture of markets and businesses organised by professions and merchandise, stretched for nearly two leagues on the west side, south of the original Round City, on the road known as the Pilgrim Way that led to Mecca.[1] Over the centuries, these and other districts would grow and contract due to natural hazards such as fire, floods, destruction and ruin from disturbances or riots, for which the metropolis became notorious. According to various sources, in the tenth century, Baghdad initially boasted a population that exceeded 1,000,000 but had probably shrunk to a lower amount. Writing at the end of the tenth century, Al-Muqaddasī, the great geographer of the Arab world, spoke for many when he sounded a sombre

---

1 Guy Le Strange, *Baghdad during the Abbasid Caliphate* (New York: Cosimo Classics, 2011), pp.1–46; Justin Marozzi, *Baghdad: City of Peace, City of Blood* (London: Penguin, 2015), pp.62–91.

note for the city of great renown: '... the authority of the caliphs declined, the city deteriorated, and the population dwindled ... Day by day the city is going from bad to worse'. Despite this gloomy verdict, Baghdad was, he affirmed, the teeming '... metropolis of Islam ... Its people have distinctive characteristics of wittiness, charm, refinement, and correct scholarship'. Baghdad was still, in other words, full of attitude even as it entered this period of descent from its imperial apogee.[2]

Over a century later, as Obadiah came to Baghdad, this verdict had not altered. He was entering perhaps the largest city in the world, still with a population of approximately 800,000, and was joining one of the oldest Jewish communities in existence. The origins of Jewish presence in Babylonia went back to the time of the Babylonian exile in 586 BCE, and the history of this community ran in parallel with the later fortunes of Israel in Palestine. The story told that the city of Jerusalem had fallen to Nebuchadnezzar and that Solomon's Temple had been destroyed. Most elite members of the Judaic population had been sent into exile. Destruction and exile would in time be succeeded by a return of some to Jerusalem, the restoration of the royal line of David and the later rebuilding of the Temple. The core cycle of defeat and triumph, accompanied by exile and restoration, became a central motif, a recurring pattern invoked repeatedly in subsequent Jewish thought. Much of it was forged by the experience of the Babylonian exile. An account of the heritage of the Babylonian Jews from ancient times to the early Middle Ages betrayed these deep roots as well as the uninterrupted continuity of Jewish existence and thought, still vital and enduring up to the moment when Obadiah reached Bagdad but with important transformations.[3]

The enforced exile to Babylon marked a time when the ancient Israelites recorded in the Bible that the people who had arrived mainly from the southern Kingdom of Judah came to be designated as 'Jews'. Since many of these original exiled people were *Yehudi* from Judah, this appellation broadened over time to encompass the cultural transformation brought about by their banishment to Babylon. The term 'Jew' arose in opposition to the more national names 'Israelite' or 'Hebrew', which began to lose their meaning. A disconnect was perceived between a vanished nation and a new kind of dispersion into exile that had sundered any links with a state. The emphasis centred on an identity that was in some manner tribal or ethnic and removed from any geographical reference. Later, the former nation of the Israelites passed into the world of Roman domination, to be known as the province of Judaea. In truth, Israel had no longer existed since its conquest by the Assyrians in 722 BCE. Now, to be in exile was to be a Jew.

When the final victory of the Muslims in 642 CE sealed their presence in Iraq and the East, the Jews of Babylonia and Persia already constituted an enduring element of the population, reaching back into a distant past. Three hundred years after that event, the Muslim geographers still recorded their prominent position especially

---

2   Al-Muqaddasī and Collins (trans.), *Best Divisions*, p.100.
3   Moshe Gil, *Jews in Islamic Countries in the Middle Ages* (Leiden: Brill, 2004), secs 39-46. All references to Gil's work are to sections not pages.

in Babylonia, as it was still called – the land between the Euphrates and the Tigris, home to the ruins of ancient Babylon, where they had originally been exiled. Jews went back to a time well before the arrival of Islam when the Arabs encountered them in Persia and Babylonia. In the late ninth century, Ibn Qutayba said that the vicinity of Sura was mainly inhabited by Jews, and, in 985, Al-Muqaddasī, describing the region of Baghdad, asserted, 'There are many Magians in this region, and *dhimmi*, both Christians and Jews'. This suggests that, in numbers, the numerous Jews came just behind the Zoroastrians, adherents of the original Persian faith, also termed Magians.[4] When Obadiah reached Baghdad around 1108, the arrival of the Hebrews, or children of Israel, had happened over 1,600 years in the past.

The ancient pedigree of Babylonian Jews was exemplified by the title and history applied to the leader of these Jews, whose origin can be traced back to the period immediately preceding the destruction of the First Temple. The word was a Greek translation of the Hebrew '*rosh galut*', 'head of the exile'. To begin, the exilarch, as he was called, exercised power somewhat like a monarch, consorting with the Sassanian emperors and ruling over his Jewish subjects. Tradition and sources in the Bible pointed to the first exilarch being Jehoiachin, the Israelite king of Israel in the line of David, banished to Babylon and perpetuating the line of David. Exilarchs would later be referred to as *al-Da'ūdī* – 'the Davidian'.[5] The special status still enjoyed by the exilarch in the mid-tenth century is exemplified in a description recorded by Nathan the Babylonian, of the virtual ceremony of coronation of the exilarch. What actually took place was a specially convened meeting in the home of a powerful financier of the Jewish community in Baghdad, attended by political and religious leaders, where the 'head of the exile' was elected. Once this was completed, elaborate ceremonies would take place at the synagogue where the exilarch, flanked by the heads of the two religious academies from Sura and Pumbedita, would hear the blowing of the *shofar*, a sound that had only been heard inside the walls of the Temple before its destruction in 70 CE. This was followed by a banquet and other celebrations together with gifts of money, clothing, jewels and precious vessels.[6]

A later description of the exilarch was given by Benjamin of Tudela in his portrayal of the Jewish community of Baghdad, probably around 1168. The outward splendour and circumstance of the relations between exilarch and caliph were memorably described. His account gives a population of 40,000 Jews for the city at this time: a figure that is held to be too high – it is estimated that the number might be less than a quarter of that amount. The 'Exilarch of All Israel', as Benjamin styled him, was Daniel b. Hasdai (d. 1175), who visited the caliph for a formal audience every week – clad in rich silk apparel and a large turban – riding to the palace with a retinue of horsemen. Benjamin tells us that the exilarch had the right to appoint rabbis to

---

4   Al-Muqaddasī and Collins (trans.), *Best Divisions*, p.105.
5   Gil, *Jews in Islamic Countries*, secs 68–70.
6   Gil, *Jews in Islamic Countries*, secs 69–70; Norman A. Stillman, *The Jews of Arab Lands: A History and Source Book* (Philadelphia: Jewish Publication Society of America, 1979), pp.171–75, for Nathan's account.

all the congregations of the Jewish communities in the region as he rendered his formal subordination to the Arab ruler. But all this ceremonial pageantry masked one dominant fact: from 1055, the Abbasid Caliphate in Baghdad was forced to share power with the rising authority of the sultanate of the Seljuk Turks. Tughril Beg the Seljuk had become master of Baghdad, ushering in an age of Seljuk supremacy that lasted over a century. The old ruling dynasty of the Abbasid Caliphate had entered a terminal decline. Many of the above-mentioned problems lie hidden or insinuated behind Benjamin of Tudela's glittering portrait of the exilarch and the caliphate. The Exilarch of All Israel may have been accorded great pomp, but his power was no more than that of a figurehead at the mercy of the demands for money made by the caliphate. At times, the caliph was also a mere figurehead carrying out extravagant court ceremonies but rarely venturing outside his palace complex.[7] Despite these restricted conditions, however, the Jewish community remained influential and continued to serve both the Seljuk sultanate and the Abbasid Caliphate. The Seljuk princes for the most part did not reside in Baghdad but placed a deputy there to enforce their authority. The Abbasid caliphs remained in their magnificent palaces, which were perpetually refurbished. These extravagant building projects required enormous sums of money, and the Jews were one important source.

Baghdad's Jewish population and districts

If Obadiah's arrival in Baghdad (Adinah) took place in 1108–1109 or thereabouts, the surviving fragments of his *Autobiography* give a detailed account of the persecution of Jews for their clothing during the reign of Caliph al-Muqtadī (1074–1094), a few years before his arrival:

> the king of Adinah, whose name was al-Muqtadi, empowered his second-in-command, whose name was
> Abishuga (=Ibn Shuja), to take discriminatory action against the Hebrews dwelling in the city of Adinah. He sought many times
> to cause them to perish, but the God of Israel thwarted his intent, this time also
> hiding them from his wrath. (Abishuga) put gleaming signs upon them, on the head of each and every Jew: one on the head
> and the other on (the) throat, and about a silver-*mithqal* of lead hanging from the throat of each and every Jew, upon which was inscribed
> (the word) *Dhimmi* — for the Jews were taxed. He moreover had a girdle placed around the loins of each
> and every Jew. Abishuga further had placed upon the Jewish women two signs: the shoes belonging to each and every woman had to be
> one red and the other black, while upon the throat of each and every woman

---

7   Adler (trans.), *Itinerary*, pp.39–42.

or upon her shoe was placed a small brass bell to make a noise
so that one might clearly distinguish between the women of the Hebrews and the
women of the gentiles.[8]

A stylistic detail preserved in the translation made by Golb, the phrase 'of each and every Jew' patterning the narrative, suggests that Obadiah at times seeks to emulate a frequent feature of Hebrew writers in the language of *Tanakh*: the tendency to employ repetition as a descriptive formula. A more profound examination of the medieval Hebrew language in the *Autobiography* would assuredly reveal a greater understanding of the nuances in the Norman's thoughts and motives, as initiated by Golb's work.[9]

Turning to the content, the fact that all these events affecting the dress restrictions of Jews are recounted suggests that such incidents of persecution were still flaring up after Obadiah's arrival. These years saw frequent rioting and demand for money made upon Jews, described in the Norman's account, together with harsh punitive impositions on what to wear. The discriminatory dress edicts demanded of the Jews in 1091 are uniquely set out by Obadiah and were common and long-standing currency. Jews and Christians were required to wear yellow badges and a heavy lead coin around the neck bearing the word '*dhimmi*' as well as a special belt. Jewish women had to wear one red and one black shoe and a copper bell around the neck that would tinkle. The point is that the imposition of these punitive dress codes rumbled on, being constantly removed and reinstated. All this arose not only out of tension with the Jewish community and the authorities but also due to extremist Muslim sects, mainly the Hanbalis, who sparked riots against the Jews. These were followers of Ahmad ibn Hanbal, a revered founder of a Traditionalist school of Islamic law. The power of 'urban gangs', known as *al'-ayyārūn*, grew in Baghdad and became a serious and near permanent disruption. All this worsened the living conditions in Baghdad, exacerbating political tensions.[10]

The above should not obscure the fact that these dress restrictions were designed to be immensely aggravating, even unbearable: a ruse to pressure more sums of money from the Jews. In 1121, for example, these were renewed, but later an agreement was reached whereby the Jews were to pay 20,000 dinars to the sultan and 4,000 for the caliph for their removal. The discrepancy in the amounts shows where the proportionate power to exact monies lay. Obadiah's account also mentions harsh

---

8   Golb (trans.), 'Autograph Memoirs', Document VIII: Budapest: Kaufmann Genizah Collection, MS 134, fol. 2 *recto*, lines 7–19, and Document IX: Budapest: Kaufmann Genizah Collection, MS 134, fol. 2 *verso*, line 1.
9   John Barton, *A History of the Bible* (London: Penguin, 2020), pp.42–45; Golb, 'Megillat Obadiah Hager', pp.77–107; Rendsburg, *How the Bible is Written*; Robert Alter, 'The Characteristics of Ancient Hebrew Poetry', in R. Alter and F. Kermode (eds), *The Literary Guide to the Bible* (London: Fontana Press, 1989), pp.611–24.
10 Richards (trans.), *Chronicle of Ibn al-Athir*, pp.32, 82.

taxation of the Jews in Baghdad on a sliding scale from the wealthy to the poorer Jews. The exilarch had to appear before the rulers in that same year to guarantee the entire amount due then raise these sums from his people.[11] This was the true tale behind any lavish weekly ceremonial visit to the caliph by the exilarch.

These details of discrimination against Jews regarding clothing are legion in the dictates and orders of the time. It has removed attention from what Jews actually wore: there are no specific references in any sources to 'Jewish' attire, other than numerous instances of vestments for special occasions, religious functions and descriptions of women's clothes for marriage, for example, which were elaborate and luxurious. One reference out of many survives in a recorded set of details from a mid-twelfth-century Fustāt wedding, found in the Geniza archives: a dazzling trousseau including robes of silk with gold thread, a pomegranate-coloured festive robe, panelled robes, luxurious pieces of cloth and much more. In all, 40 percent of the wealth a bride brought to her marriage was invested in silks, cloths and clothes. The value of these was listed in this particular wedding document at 373 dinars, but there were many other costly items, giving a grand total of 2,100 dinars. Such lists provided security for the bride in case of divorce or widowhood, setting out the assets so that the woman would be no worse off financially than when she entered marriage.[12] But any attempt to differentiate Jews from Arabs in their everyday life was not clear: most probably because, from day to day, ordinary people largely dressed alike. At the end of the tenth century, Al-Muqaddasī remarked that 'the people here like to dress well, and wear the *taylasān* (mantle or cloak). They wear sandals, dress up their turbans so they are tall, and clothe themselves in fine calico'. These details were given for the region around Iraq but were largely repeated for an account of apparel in Al-Sham (Syria):

> The Syrians dress well, both the scholar and the simple wearing the loose outer *ridā'* (cloak). They do not go shod in summertime, except in the use of the single-soled sandal ... The people here wear their raincloaks thrown open; and they do not scallop their *taylasāns* ... It is only the villagers and scribes who wear the *durrā'a* [loose garment with sleeves, often made of wool or brocade]. The clothing of the rustics in the country district around Jerusalem and Nābulus is the single *kisā'* [long shirt-like enveloping garment], and without drawers.[13]

It is evident that ordinary inhabitants of Baghdad, Arab or Jew, would sport a form of cloak and other shirt-like loose garment and sandals, which might be omitted in the hot summer months. The head was covered by a turban, which might be tied or wound about in differing ways to signify a particular status.

---

11 Gil, *Jews in Islamic Countries*, sec.245.
12 Cambridge University Library (CUL): T-S J1.29: Trousseau list; Goitein, *MS*, vol. 4, pp.185–88.
13 Al-Muqaddasī and Collins (trans.), *Best Divisions*, pp.108, 154.

All these conspicuous aspects of discrimination against non-Muslims mentioned earlier were from the outset proclaimed as an attempt to mark Jews as being different from Muslims. Over the centuries, numberless edicts in the Muslim world stated that Jews were forced to wear badges, special colours and whistles, to cut their sleeves differently, to not wear turbans and so forth. As shown above, Obadiah describes these impositions in eleventh-century Baghdad, but they were not unusual. Some of these sanctions are mentioned in the Pact of Umar in the seventh century and repeated in the decree of the Caliph Al-Mutawakkil in 850, where Christians and Jews are commanded to wear honey-coloured *taylasāns* and the *zunnār* belt. This belt became commonly associated with non-Muslims but may go back to pre-Islamic times. In addition, Jews had to wear badges of the same honey colour as the cloaks.[14] These orders were directed at both Jews and Christians, but their uniformity or strictness varied greatly across the Arab world and changed in time. Essentially, members of these two religions were placed in a higher category of infidels as non-Muslims, but non-Muslims who are recognised in the writings of Muhammad as recipients of the divinely revealed scripture in the Koran. Obadiah was thus a *dhimmī* belonging to the community of *ahl-al-dhimma* termed 'people of the book', and he would have faced the same conditions had he remained a Christian. The essential trade-off was that *dhimmīs* had to pay a poll tax and sometimes a land tax, accepting a series of discriminatory regulations in return for the ruling authorities lending them protection and freedom to practise their religion. It was a bargain not always honoured by the Muslim authorities.[15]

None of these factors restricting dress and status impeded the growth in size and prosperity of the Jewish community in Baghdad where Obadiah now resided, but it is difficult to pinpoint with exactitude their areas of residence. Many of the poorer members might have lived in a known Jewish quarter, but merchants and tradesmen lived elsewhere, probably in Al-Karkh, the large commercial district on the west side of the Tigris. At times, the bridge connecting Karkh with the eastern zone was called Kantarah al-Yahûd (Bridge of the Jews), connecting to 'the Jews' fief', as it was sometimes termed.[16] At the end of the tenth century, Al-Muqaddasī stated that 'Most of the assayers, the dyers, cambists and tanners in this region are Jews'.[17] Benjamin of Tudela's account depicts a wealthy Jewish presence in the city: the great synagogue had columns of marble of various colours overlaid with silver and gold, and on the columns were sentences from the Psalms in golden letters. At the time of Benjamin's visit, as his *Itinerary* tells us, there were 28 synagogues on either side of the Tigris. The enormous personal wealth of the exilarch, not to mention the thriving Jewish financiers and merchants of the city, underpinned the needs of the caliph and the state. Benjamin of Tudela's account adds that the exilarch owned hospices, gardens

---

14   Stillman, *Jews of Arab Lands*, pp.167–68, for Al-Mutawakkil decree.
15   Mark R. Cohen, *Under Crescent and Cross: The Jews in the Middle Ages* (Princeton: Princeton University Press, 1994), pp.52–57.
16   Le Strange, *Baghdad*, pp.149–50.
17   Al-Muqaddasī and Collins (trans.), *Best Divisions*, p.153.

and orchards in Baghdad, as well as many holdings of inherited land. This wealth protected the Jews, who bought off violence and persecution whenever possible. The caliph required large sums, for he 'has a palace in Baghdad three miles in extent, wherein is a great park with all variety of trees, fruit-bearing and otherwise, and all manner of animals'. Benjamin of Tudela gave a circumference of 20 miles for the walls of the city.[18]

Just before Obadiah's arrival, dating from the reign of Caliph al-Muqtadī (1074–1094), many new quarters were laid out to the north and east of the caliphs' palaces, which came to form the new town of East Baghdad. This had been partly necessary because of a serious flood in 1074. In time, assisted by a flow of migration from Karkh, this area grew strongly, and soon East Baghdad became recognised as the main part of the city by Caliph al-Mustazhir (1094–1118), the ruler when Obadiah was in residence. The neighbourhoods of Baghdad were constantly changing, due to floods, riots and other disasters. There was a damaging fire in July 1108 (the year Obadiah supposedly arrived). This happened in Ibn Jarada, a run-down area in the Jewish neighbourhood in the eastern sector of the city. All the Jews in Baghdad happened to be away on the western side because of the Sabbath. When they returned home, property worth 300,000 dinars had been destroyed. That same neighbourhood had already suffered a conflagration in recent times, the residents returning to rebuild it, and now it had gone up in flames again. Another fire in 1116–1117, broke out along the Tigris grassland, burning townhouses and synagogues. Riots are mentioned in 1051 when the Sunni objected to an inscription for a gateway in Karkh, leading to the murder of a Sunni leader by the Shi'i and resulting in the destruction of a Shi'i mosque. Later, in 1177, Jews were involved in a violent affray when they objected to the noise of the call to prayer next to their synagogue. This caused a surge of protest by the Muslims before Friday prayers: a mob attacked shops belonging to Jews and destroyed a synagogue. Baghdad was a rich but violent city.[19]

Baghdad: the synagogue and the Academy

Fragments of the *Autobiography* mark Obadiah's arrival in the great metropolis, calling it '… the city of Adinah which is Baghdad, / [capital of the Ishma]elites'. He goes on to mention, as always giving his account in the third person, '… The gentiles (=Muslims) sought to slay him'. 'Gentiles' in this context means Muslims, and we surmise, but cannot be sure, that he was taken for some kind of enemy or Frank, following the recent battle mentioned earlier that had taken place near Mosul in late 1108 between the forces of Jāwulī Saqao and Tancred. Obadiah's appearance and accent were no doubt heavily 'foreign'. All this seems to have led to some 'tribulations' mentioned in passages of this account, although the surviving text is damaged. But after this incident that is lacking in detail, 'Obadiah the Proselyte', as

---

18   Adler (trans.), *Itinerary*, pp.35, 42.
19   Gil, *Jews in Islamic Countries*, secs 244–45, for fires and violence with the Hanbalis.

he now calls himself, may have '… stood before the doorway of the sy[nagogue]'. In the narrative of the *Autobiography*, when Obadiah recounts his arrival in Baghdad just after these tribulations and the attack he mentions, this doorway scene becomes clearer, as he then tells us that he was taken in and lodged in the synagogue or the *yeshiva*:

> the academy. The servant installed Obadiah the Proselyte in the house
> wherein the Jews would pray, and they brought him provisions.
> It happened thereafter that Isaac, the head of the academy, directed that
> Obadiah the Proselyte be with the orphan youths, in order to teach him
> the Torah
> of Moses and the words of the prophets in the script
> of the Lord and the language of the Hebrews.[20]

From this passage, it can be deduced that Obadiah was sent back to school to learn Hebrew with the young orphan children in the synagogue. It seems clear that, although he was deeply familiar with the Bible in Latin and something of a Christian scholar, he was not yet fully conversant with the Hebrew language and script, even if he had encountered tenets of the Jewish faith and could have known some vocabulary. Children, as well as adults, were known to study in the synagogue, especially at night on the Sabbath and on holidays. The general area of the synagogue was also considered a desirable place to live, especially if Obadiah was a refugee, an orphan like the boys with whom he now studied.

A great part of Jewish community life depended on synagogues, also serving as hospices for travellers in need and for foreigners seeking shelter and receiving charitable assistance. Even if we are ignorant of which synagogue in Baghdad is mentioned, it must have been a more prominent one, one perhaps sanctioned by the leader of the Baghdad Academy. In most cases, a large arched space in the interior of a synagogue had at its centre the *bima* reading table. At the far end stood the Ark, the *aron hakodesh*, and worshippers gathered around the perimeter or sat on cushions and rugs. Women were separated and watched the prayers and proceedings through a screen from a gallery, a practice that might have originated because of Islamic custom. Bronze oil lamps lit the darkened spaces as the scrolls of the Torah, now removed from the Ark, were carried around the synagogue. In some synagogues, the entire building could be viewed as a compound fulfilling many functions. The records for a synagogue, found in the Geniza, describe in some instances a large sprawling complex: an adjoining house (*mulāziq*), others adjacent to its vestibule (*dihlīz*) or to its *sukka* (the hut for the Feast of the Tabernacles). Also mentioned are the living quarters for a man (*sukn*) and the apartment (*ṭabaqa*) of another, making up one of the buildings in the immediate vicinity of the compound. Within this veritable collection of annexes and buildings, Obadiah must have studied and

---

20 Golb (trans.), 'Autograph Memoirs', Document VIII: Budapest: Kaufmann Genizah Collection, MS 134, fol. 2 *recto*, lines 1–6.

resided for some amount of time, now learning, now protected, fed and becoming very much embedded in a new life and identity.[21]

When, years later, the Norman proselyte set out these happenings in his memoirs, he recalls that the decision to initiate him in his educational programme was taken by one Isaac, head of the *yeshiva* or academy in Baghdad. The mention of academies and *yeshivot* needs to be made clear. The two main academies originally located in Sura and Pumbedita had now relocated to Baghdad. The term '*yeshiva*' is synonymous with 'academy' in Hebrew, so the two major academies headed by *geonim* were the highest authority and should not be confused with the more local academies where the Babylonian Talmud was also studied. This Isaac, mentioned in the above extract from the *Autobiography*, has been linked to Isaac b. Moses, also known as Isaac b. Sukkari from Spain, who was ordained *gaon* at this time.[22] There is a suggestion here that Obadiah had been fast-tracked, perhaps due in part to the glowing write-up he was accorded by the rabbi in Aleppo, telling of his education and family background, which must have been quickly shown to the Baghdad authorities. The 'authority' he mentions in his *Autobiography* was perhaps the leader of one of the two academies, now resident in Baghdad. Another possibility is that he is referring to the rabbi of the synagogue, a more likely interpretation. The two Baghdad academies that had originally been located at Sura and Pumbedita had by now moved to the capital, to maintain influence and access to the networks of power. At times, this reflected a fierce rivalry between them and with the exilarch. Sura, originally located south of Baghdad, was frequently referred to as Mata Meḥasia, an earlier centre. Pumbedita or El-Anbar on the River Euphrates (today Fallujah) had been important as a major Jewish centre since the Second Temple, located at one time in nearby Nehardea.[23] The influence of the two Babylonian *yeshivot*, or academies, with their collection of religious scholars was enormous and had created and promoted the emergence of the *Talmud Bavli* (Babylonian Talmud), which, over many years, had brought together the wisdom, teachings and commentaries of these scholars between 400 CE and 600 CE, the high point of rabbinical Judaism.

A *yeshiva* or academy was dedicated to the study of these Hebrew texts: their leaders were known as *geonim* (sing. *gaon*). Although elected by the Jewish community before receiving approval from the caliph or his representative, a *gaon* possessed enormous intellectual and religious clout, perhaps far more than an exilarch. The high point of their influence over the entire diaspora of the Muslim world may be considered to have lasted from the mid-sixth century to the mid-eleventh century.

---

21   Simon Schama, *The Story of the Jews: Finding the Words 1000 BCE–1492 CE* (London: The Bodley Head, 2013), pp.253–54; Jacob Lassner (ed.), *A Mediterranean Society: An Abridgement in One Volume* (London: University of California Press, 1999), pp.150–54; Menahem Ben-Sasson, 'The Medieval Period: The Tenth to Fourteenth Centuries', in P. Lambert (ed.), *Fortifications and the Synagogue: The Fortress of Babylon and the Ben Ezra Synagogue, Cairo* (Montreal: Canadian Centre for Architecture, 1994), pp.213–14.
22   Gil, *Jews in Islamic Countries*, sec.261.
23   Robert Brody, *The Geonim of Babylonia and the Shaping of Medieval Jewish Culture* (New Haven, CT: Yale University Press, 1998), pp.35–42.

When the Norman proselyte arrived in Baghdad, their renown had passed its zenith: the Geonic period was waning internationally. Nevertheless, their authority remained significant and enduring in the lands of Persia and Babylonia, particularly so in this world of political intrigue and rivalries dominating the metropolis of Baghdad. A hierarchy had developed within these academies, and leadership was personified by its head scholar, or *Rosh Yeshivat Ge'on Ya'aqov*, meaning 'the head of the Academy which is the pride of Jacob'. Both academies also had a vice principal (*Av Bet Din*), and, below these figures, 70 outstanding scholars reflected the prestige of these centres of learning. Their reputation was enhanced by the tradition that they and their forbears had perfected the study of the Talmud over the centuries and now constituted the sole authoritative channel of dissemination of the oral and written codification of Rabbinic Jewish Law. When the academy was in session, the *gaon* presided, facing seven rows of 10 scholars, each member occupying a designated place in a strictly observed seating plan. Outside these chosen members, a crowd numbering approximately 400 part-time students had no fixed place or obligatory programme of study. The senior elite core of 70 scholars were usually assigned sections from two tractates (chapters of the Talmud) to study and comment on at each session. Each row of 10 was headed by a *resh* or *rosh kallah* (head of a row): the corresponding title was *alluf* (chief). Wealthy or prestigious members of the Jewish community, bankers or merchants from all parts of the diaspora, could even be accorded this honorary title and membership of the academy, no doubt as a reward for their donations and influence.[24]

The magnetic pull of these academies could not be shunned, and Obadiah might have felt drawn to their meetings, but it is unlikely that he was initially well enough prepared to be part of this, not only because of his poor acquaintance with Hebrew but also because of his unfamiliarity with Babylonian Aramaic, which had once been the lingua franca of the pre-Islamic Middle East and had recorded a large part of the oral and written message of the Talmud from ancient times. After the Arab conquest of the region in the mid-seventh century, Hebrew and Aramaic were now joined by Arabic as the principal languages of government within the expanding Muslim world. Nevertheless, Obadiah's passing mention of one Isaac as 'head of the academy' is an intriguing detail: such a mentor could have been decisive in any career advancement when his activities became more settled and established. In the meantime, his progress in those studies in the synagogue proved more important. He must have earned his living from other skills he already possessed or developed over the coming years, in Baghdad and other centres. This will become clearer when we look at his messianic experiences that had determined his pilgrimage to this part of the world.

---

24   Brody, *Geonim*, pp.43–53.

Chapter 6

Awaiting the Messiah

The Norman proselyte was indeed drawing closer to messianic experiences that had awakened his thought and visionary imagination when he was still Johannes in southern Italy. Now, he had journeyed as far as Baghdad, ensconced on a course to master the Hebrew language, and immersed himself in an intensive study Judaism under the tutorship of the sages of the *yeshivot*. This much we are told in his *Autobiography*, but this narrative conceals a deeper engagement. The fall of Jerusalem on 15 July 1099 to the knights of the First Crusade had left the world of Christendom awestruck and seemed to promise the road to heaven. But, for Obadiah, it had opened up a different path pointing to another conquest: the road to Zion and a reconquest of Jerusalem aiming to take the city back for Judaism. Journeying east was for him an undertaking that told of another more personal Norman crusade, comprising other challenges and battles needing to be fought. It was a project that now consumed all his energies during his hours of reading and study. His own personal exile and the abandonment of his family and country of birth accorded closely with his newly acquired faith, a faith marked by this peculiar feature that distinguished it sharply from other religions: the question of exile as a central motif. The story of Judaism also recounts how, in the beginning, Abraham, considered by Jews to be both patriarch and ancestor, had broken with his family and ancestral religion when he journeyed to Palestine, leaving behind Ur in Chaldea. It was later foretold that, one day, Abraham's descendants would also experience exile and humiliation in Egypt before being freed from slavery and promised a return to a land of their own. Exile therefore figured prominently as a constant leitmotiv in the Jewish self-view, underlined by their uprooting from Jerusalem and their enforced removal to Babylon. This was Obadiah's mindset as he grappled with Jewish studies in the synagogue in Baghdad.

Such an experience was powerfully counterbalanced by an expectation that, in his own time, their God would send a messiah to redeem the Jews, restoring them to Jerusalem. The arrival of such a figure was continually announced in the chronicle of Judaism. The redemption was to be an earthly one, and, when He manifested himself, the Messiah, the 'Anointed One', would once again sit on David's throne. But such a time was never indicated exactly. The need and yearning to announce the tidings of his coming was all-consuming in those frequent ages of oppression and suffering, such as in twelfth-century Baghdad. Excited groups of believers speculated endlessly on the nature of this 'End Time' or 'Last Days', as it was also known, when all who return to the law of God will assemble in the Holy Land, an event sometimes referred to as an 'in-gathering'. These expectations loudly prophesied by Ezekiel and Isaiah are repeated in the Dead Sea Scrolls, running on in early and medieval Rabbinic literature. All these texts speculated on the confusion of the great final battle to come against hostile powers and the eventual renewal of Jerusalem – a gathering of the dispersed and a kingdom of glory in the Holy Land. Such an End Time was felt in varying degrees to be rapidly approaching, and one of the most frequently repeated visions was a description of the signs that would signal this moment. There would be prophets who announced the Messiah, and signs in the heavens, while others warned of a time of troubles before the resolution. Obadiah had already prepared for the onset of such times when, before his departure from Italy, he had forecast such a great and terrible day in his reading of the Book of Joel, when there would be portents in the sky and on the earth. One way or another, as we shall see, this paradigm was mentioned and dwelt upon by all three Abrahamic faiths. The Norman proselyte, in his immersion in Biblical studies, had now become consumed with the prospect of the Messiah and this gathering in Jerusalem. Upon resuming his travels and leaving Baghdad, Obadiah would soon confront such a person, one who claimed to be this divinely anointed one – all of which would take place after enduring some harrowing times in Aleppo, which we will describe.

For now, exile highlighted the gaping disparity between the tenets of his new religion and the vanished state of Israel, where four formative periods of Jewish history could be discerned: under Abraham the first patriarch, later under Moses (after leaving Egypt, when the covenant was forged on Mount Sinai), thirdly during the Babylonian exile and followed lastly by the destruction of the Second Temple, when Judaism in its final form was concluded as a religion of exile and dispersal. The first two periods fashioned the religion of Yahweh for the Israelites; the second two developed this further into Judaism for the Jews of the diaspora. Now, in twelfth-century Baghdad, Jews continued to live in exile in the age of Edom, so central to Obadiah's vision, at a time when Christianity, the inheritors of Rome, controlled the former land of Israel and occupied Jerusalem. This was the insight and experience that had driven the Norman to convert and embark for the Holy Land. Here, in Baghdad, he was to encounter a teeming world of prophets and sects beneath the seemingly ordered society of the Arab Caliphate, a multitude of sermons and prophecies that reinforced and encouraged this idea of a saviour and prefigured his own account.

A messianic moment in Baghdad

Several folios found in the Cairo Geniza depict an episode of an allegedly messianic proclamation in Baghdad that, despite its fragmentary preservation, tells a fascinating story taking place close to the time of our Norman proselyte's presence in the city. The leading voice we hear is that of a pious woman known as 'the daughter of

Joseph the son of the physician'. The woman, deemed to have led an ascetic life, is said to have appeared in public preaching that she had seen the prophet Elijah in a dream and had been told by him that the redemption of Israel was at hand. The fragments of this document date this event to 25 Elul 1120 (21 August), a moment when Obadiah could have been in Baghdad but may have already departed for Aleppo and Damascus.[1] The story of this woman's proclamation has become confused with a dispute between the Jewish community and the Seljuk Sultan over some allegedly illegal taxes he imposed on them, a dispute that sheds some revealing light on what could take place in respect of these harsh financial demands, which were a constant threat. The caliph became involved in this affair because the woman had stated that the arrival of the Messiah would lead to the establishment of a Jewish kingdom, thereby calling into question the validity of any other independent state such as the Abbasid government. This lent a strong political dimension to the affair. The outcome was that the caliph ordered the imprisonment of all prominent Jews in the imperial mint after he had consulted the *Qadi* al-Dāmghānī – the chief legal authority – to determine if he was entitled to sanction this detention. The caliph was told in no uncertain terms by the judge that he could not enforce this act upon the Jews, but the ruler demurred, giving orders that the pious woman should be burned and the sentence carried out on the Jews. That same night, the document says, Elijah appeared to the caliph in a dream, and the caliph was greatly overawed. Although the story is patchy because of the report's fragmentary survival, it goes on to say that the Jews were released because of the *Qadi*'s opinion and because of Elijah's night-time appearance before the caliph. In reality, this story hints at an earlier dispute, already mentioned, about edicts against the Jews, their continuing restrictive dress codes and how they managed to survive, even though they stopped paying a tax. So the messianic tale may partly be a confrontation about tax. Subsequently, after the appearance of Elijah in the dream, an order was issued by the caliph to release the Jews from the poll tax. Even so, it appears that these Jews were careful to raise money from every household to placate Muslims with bribes so that the caliph would waive the tax on this occasion and remove the dress restrictions. So the affair of the dress codes and the payment of sums to the sultan and the caliph already alluded to earlier here gets another mention. But, in an account by Ibn al-Athir, a main source for the tax episode, he made no reference to the Jewish messianic affair, so prominently set out in the aforementioned Geniza fragment.[2] This was not unusual, as Arab records tend to pass over without interest details of any Jewish affairs, and such messianic troubles could just as commonly occur inside Islam. This is evidenced in the same passage, where the chronicler Ibn al-Athir also gave another story, setting out an account of a man of the family of 'Alī who appeared in Mecca preaching repentance and winning a following, looking to have himself proclaimed caliph. Although

---

1 S. D. Goitein, 'A Report on Messianic Troubles in Baghdad in 1120–21', *JQR*, 43:1 (1952), p.58. The document Bodleian Library (BoL): MS. Heb. f. 56, no. 2821, sets out a full translation the text.
2 Richards (trans.), *Chronicle of Ibn al-Athir*, pp.233–34; Goitein, 'Report', p.65, for the story of Ali.

these episodes appear to centre on messianic redemption, the real goals, as we saw, were often political. Appearances of Elijah as the Great Messenger, the announcer of the advent of a greater figure, were frequent in these stories. A messiah was often preceded by such a herald or messenger.

The presence of messengers and prophets occurred not only in Baghdad but also repeatedly in earlier Jewish messianic movements, springing up in outlier regions of the Middle East from the seventh century onwards, voicing opposition, it would appear, to the rabbinic mainstream. These messengers were precursors of a phenomenon that Obadiah was later to witness and describe at length.

Early Jewish sects

The transition from Persian to Arab rule in the seventh to eighth centuries brought into question the beleaguered condition of existing Jewish settlers in the sparsely populated provinces to the east and north of the recently created territories of Islam, on the borders between Iraq and Persia. The remoteness of these frontier settlements, distant from the new metropolitan centre of power in Baghdad, presented a land that was drawn to independent action, removed in both religious and secular matters from any Jewish authority emanating from the exilarch and the Geonic academies in the cities. There was little expectation among Jews that the collapse of Byzantine and Persian power in the outlying regions followed by the rapid ascent of an Arab Empire would be the harbinger of any long-awaited miraculous redemption of Zion and the restoration of Israel to the Holy Land. In addition, a complicated host of influences from the underlying Persian religion of Zoroastrianism, and from the newer offshoot of Islamic Shiism, must necessarily be noted. The Shi'i variant to mainstream Islam grew up partly as an important driver of resistance to Sunni rule by the Abbasids. These factors also played a part in the emergence of another variant to mainstream Judaism that needs to be taken into account: the Karaite movement. Early Jewish groupings fed off this multitudinous parade of other sources producing, at a very early date, principles common to a large number of so-called schismatic movements. All these movements seem to draw water from the same well. To understand the history of such Jewish sects, it is therefore relevant to bring into relief both the Shi'i background of Islam and the importance of the Karaite movement in Judaism. There is, perhaps, a tendency to define Karaism solely as a deviant group or sect that broke away from an already mainstream rabbinic Judaism.[3]

In 937 CE, Abû Jûsuf Ja'qûb Al-Qirqisānī, so-called because he may have hailed from ancient Circesium or Karkemish in Upper Mesopotamia, on the left bank of the Euphrates, was one notable scholar who collected crucial details of messianic

---

3   Leon Nemoy, *Karaite Anthology: Excerpts from the Early Literature* (New Haven, CT: Yale University Press, 1963), pp.xii–xvii; Marina Rustow, 'The Qaraites as Sect: The Tyranny of a Construct', in S. Stern (ed.), *Sects and Sectarianism in Jewish History* (Leiden: Brill, 2011), pp.149–86, treats the question of Karaism as a sect.

movements in an important text. His *Book of Lights and Watchtowers* (*Kitāb al-anwār-wa'l-marāqib*) furnishes descriptions and a chronicle of such early Jewish and other sects. In the introduction to his book, Qirqisānī also singled out certain Karaite communities in Persia, which, he said, were hostile to criticism and to the secular sciences in general, considering them harmful to belief and to religious sentiment. Qirqisānī's opinion was to develop into a long-running point of disagreement that emphasised the opposition between Karaism and mainstream Rabbinical Judaism. Like many religious chroniclers of this time, Qirqisānī was a polymath who travelled widely, studying botany, zoology, geography and even metallurgical processes. He must have collected information from his travels and conducted first-hand interviews, and his commentaries on Jewish sects and prophets constitute an original source where few survive.[4]

The provenance of these prophetic names is uncertain: at times, other sources provide somewhat different details and nomenclature. Abū Īsā al-Isfahānī appears to be one of the earliest in a series of figures endowed with prophetic, even messianic, pretensions. In one account, he asserted that the coming of a messiah was to be preceded by five messengers, of whom he himself was the last. Other sources, such as Ibn Hazm, say his name was Muhammad b. Īsā: 'Father of Jesus' the prophet of Islam ('Īsā' is 'Jesus' in Arabic). This is a common detail, namely a connection with other Abrahamic religions even if the figure is from a Jewish group. Of course, Jesus is also included among the recognised prophets of Islam, but Qirqisānī also referred to al-Isfahānī – an early messianic or prophetic person – by the name 'Obadiah' (Hebrew name for 'Abdallah'). This conflation of the name of Obadiah in connection with al-Isfahānī had led E. N. Adler to speculate wrongly in 1919 that the fragment of the life of the Norman proselyte he had found was a reference to al-Isfahānī. Was there however a suggestion that al-Isfahānī was a Muslim? He was certainly a religious figure who preached and believed in Muhammad's prophetic mission as well as in the role of Jesus. He claimed adherence to the sequence of prophets that were divinely sent, which included prophets worshipped by the different faiths, though nothing in this regard can be claimed with certainty.[5] He was, as his name suggests, from Isfahān in Persia, and it is not irrelevant that a large Jewish community was known to reside there. A source describing the early conquest of this town by the Arabs in 642 CE tells of Jews dancing and singing as they awaited the king of the Jews, who was to arrive the next day and with whose help they would defeat the Arabs. To this legend, we can add the story of the Muslims who believed that a false Messiah would rise up against them at the end of days, springing up from the Jews of

---

4   Nemoy, *Karaite Anthology*, pp.43–45; Bruno Chiesa and Wilfrid Lockwood, *Ya'qub al-Qirqisānī on Jewish Sects and Christianity: A Translation of "Kitāb al-anwār". Book 1, with Two Introductory Essays* (Frankfurt: Peter Lang, 1984), pp.14–31.

5   Chiesa and Lockwood, *Ya'qub al-Qirqisānī*, pp.144–45, on text of Qirqisānī's account of al-Isfahānī; Fred Astren, 'Non-Rabbinic and Non-Karaite Religious Movements', in P. I. Lieberman (ed.), *The Cambridge History of Judaism: Jews in the Medieval Islamic World* (Cambridge: Cambridge University Press, 2021), vol. 5, pp.612–15, on Isfahānī and multiple religious identity.

Isfahān.⁶ The episode of al-Isfahānī was also repeated by Maimonides – perhaps the greatest Jewish philosopher and legal scholar of the medieval period – in his later Epistle to Yemen, a central account narrating different messianic events:

> One of these is the exodus of a multitude of Jews, numbering hundreds of thousands from the East beyond Isfahan, led by an individual who pretended to be the Messiah. They were accoutred with military equipment and drawn swords, and slew all those that encountered them. According to the information I received, they reached the vicinity of Baghdad. This happened at the beginning of the reign of the Omayyads.⁷

The embellished account given by Maimonides, consistent with other accounts of false messiahs, also suggests that al-Isfahānī was descended from David – usually an obligatory trait for a messiah. Additionally, said Maimonides, his followers were said to come from the land 'beyond the river', meaning the River Oxus and the land of Khurāsān, at the borders of the Arab Caliphate. The time of al-Isfahānī was placed by Maimonides at the outset of the Umayyad dynasty, that is, soon after 661 CE. Other accounts put his activities in 684–705 CE or even later, at the time of the Abbasids and al-Manṣūr (754–775). Qirqisānī certainly recounted that al-Isfahānī claimed to be a prophet, leading a revolt against the government, a detail of an insurrection that is repeated by Obadiah the Proselyte in a later narrative. Qirqisānī also stated that al-Isfahānī's following became an army of many thousands, an observation taken over by Maimonides. Other sources specifically tell of a battle supposedly waged against the army of Caliph al-Manṣūr. One account has him leading his soldiers against the caliph at Ravy in Persia, where all were killed; another recounts that he drew a line in the ground around his men and said that they would not be harmed inside this circle. In Qirqisānī's account, some of his followers say that he was unharmed, taking refuge in a cave on the mountain, and that nothing more is known of him.⁸ This is another recurring detail in the many descriptions of a messiah: he is not dead but will return. He is awaited.

After al-Isfahānī, either in hiding or in concealment, the movement was led by a disciple named Yūdghān ('Judah' in Arabic), who is described as a prophet or even the Messiah. Qirqisānī stated that he claimed to be a prophet but that his followers called him the divine Redeemer. In such stories, either the prophet who announced the expected arrival or the coming of the actual Messiah was a constant source of overlap. Yūdghān's followers called him (in Aramaic) *rayā*, the shepherd. Yūdghān, we are told, commanded his followers not to eat meat or drink wine, bringing him closer to some ascetic habits of the Karaites, as we see in a later meeting with a

---

6   Gil, *Jews in Islamic Countries*, secs148–50, for al-Isfahānī.
7   Maimonides, 'The Epistle to Yemen', in A. Halkin (trans.), *Crisis and Leadership: Epistles of Maimonides* (New York: Jewish Publication Society of America, 1985), p.127.
8   Gil, *Jews in Islamic Countries*, sec.150.

messiah reported by Obadiah.⁹ Another so-called messiah of the eighth century is Sāwīrā, also known as Serenus or Severus, mentioned in Spanish and eastern sources. In many parts of their diaspora, the Jews came to believe that the Messiah would bring about their flight to the Holy Land – another favoured topic in these stories, which Obadiah himself mentions in his report of a later messianic movement he witnessed. The flight was literally that, a flight through the air, an experience described by Obadiah first-hand.

This yearning for Zion, a return to Jerusalem, the 'in-gathering' as we termed it, was repeatedly expressed in later centuries, most powerfully by the poet Judah Halevi – a near contemporary of Obadiah – who asked, in his *Ode to Jerusalem*, for the wings of an eagle to carry him there. His poetry expresses better than all others this ardour for the homeland. Halevi declared that he cannot live a complete religious life in Islamic lands while Palestine is under Christian control. The Holy City, reached by flight, is at the heart of all messianic longing. Halevi captured this in his *Ode*:

> … I wish that I could wander
> where the Lord appeared to visionaries, prophets;
> wish that I had wings
> to fly to you—so far!—
> and place the pieces of my broken heart
> among your jagged mountains,
> throw my face down to your ground,
> fondle your gravel and caress your soil.¹⁰

The irony of exile from Zion, its conquest by Christianity and the domination of Islam are all powerfully expressed by another of Halevi's verses:

> While Zion is in Christian hands
> and I am trapped in Arab lands?¹¹

Such sentiments, so well uttered by the poet, conveyed the passionate feeling in these prophecies and the intense following these longings stirred up in the expectant mass of Judaic adherents. None of this could be long denied, and, increasingly, this sentiment took hold of Obadiah's mind.

---

9   Chiesa and Lockwood, *Ya'qub al-Qirqisānī*, pp.145–46; Gil, *Jews in Islamic Countries*, secs.151, 157.
10 Raymond P. Scheindlin, *The Song of the Distant Dove: Judah Halevi's Pilgrimage* (Oxford: Oxford University Press, 2008), p.173.
11 Scheindlin, *Song*, p.169.

A revolt in the mountains

Obadiah's own later account uniquely records a messianic movement that shows similar features and must have spanned a good few years, possibly several decades, even preceding his arrival in the Levant:

> in the days of the chief named al-Afdal. In those days there arose
> "children of the violent" amongst the nation of Israel, who lifted up their souls to establish
> a vision and stumbled in their words. In the mountains of Assyria, in the land of Hakkeriya.[12]

The date of this insurgency, which, as he notes, had violent features, has to be placed later than 1094, when al-Afdal was appointed the vizier of Egypt, and his mention provides a time reference for Obadiah's readers. The Norman proselyte is no doubt recording this militant movement much later, probably in the mid-1120s or later still, when the *Autobiography* was recollected and written up after his final arrival in Egypt, certainly after 1121. But Obadiah probably learned about it from oral sources during his stay in Baghdad, after 1108 – possibly earlier. Again, like the previous schismatic manifestations discussed, this was a movement located in the borders, namely the mountainous region of Upper Mesopotamia described as *Hakkeriya* in the *Autobiography*. The town called Hakkāriyya was in a rural area where the Kurdish Hakkāri were found, spreading south and east of Lake Van in today's Armenia and Azerbaijan.

However, other sources pinpoint the nearby town of Amadiya as the location.[13] The messianic unrest described by the Norman appears to have continued into the 1140s, perhaps even later, which suggests that Obadiah must only be referring to the earlier stages of this movement. The historical memoir of this revolt as told by the Norman proselyte names three figures: a certain Jew named Solomon b. Ruji, his son, whose name was Menahem, and a man called Ephraim b. R. Azariah, described as a 'glib man' in the account, also known as b. Fadlun. Some form of messianic pronouncement took place in this mountainous area, and, as Obadiah claims, Solomon b. Ruji was put forward as the anointed messiah. Letters were sent to that effect far and wide by b. Fadlun announcing that Jews everywhere would soon be transported in the air to Jerusalem, as the *Autobiography* asserts:

---

12 Golb (trans.), 'Autograph Memoirs', Document X: Cambridge: Taylor-Schechter, MS 10K 21 fol. 1 *recto*, lines 1–3.
13 Guy Le Strange, *The Lands of the Eastern Caliphate* (Cambridge: Cambridge University Press, 1905).

88 THE SCROLL OF OBADIAH

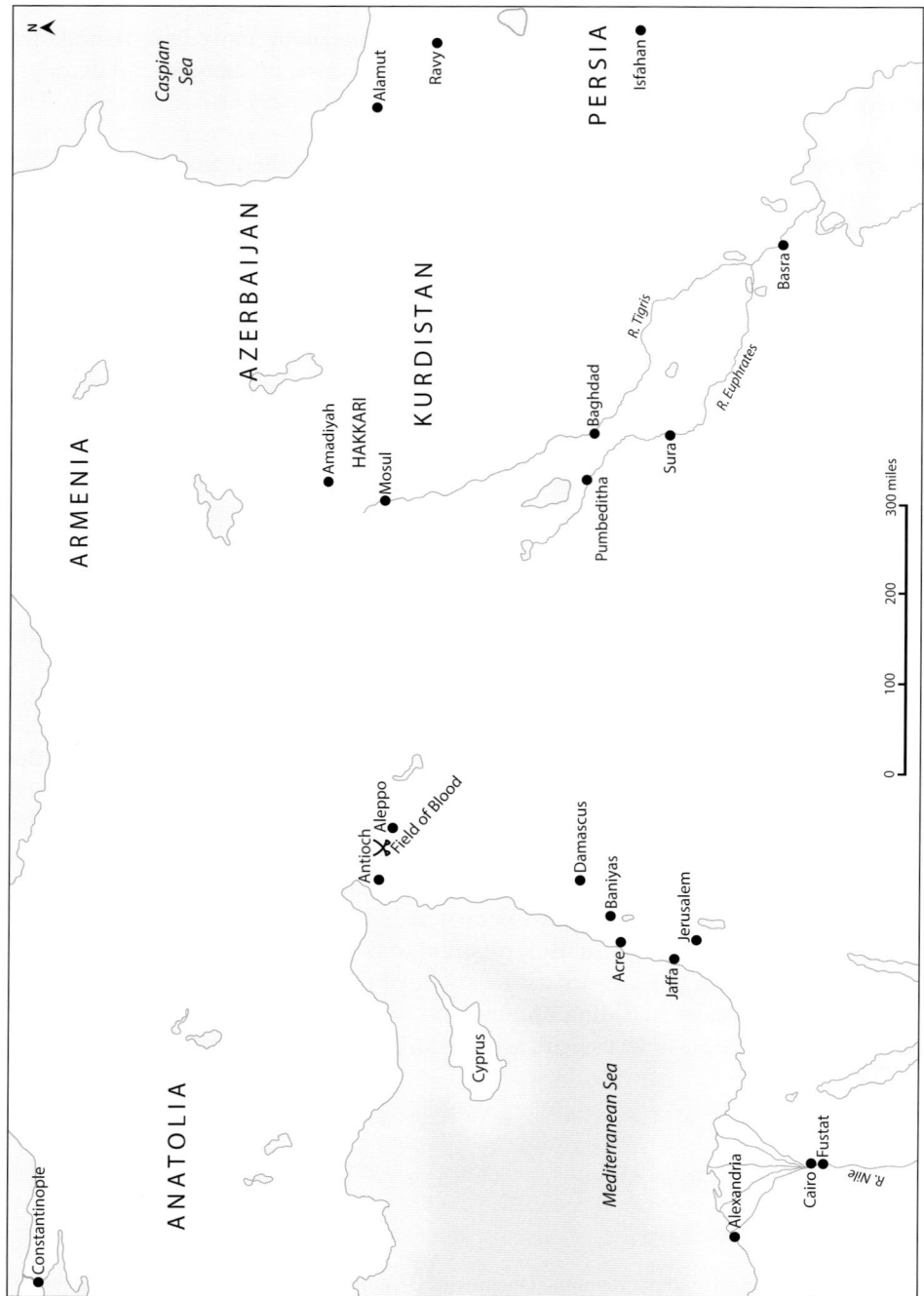

Map 2 The Levant and the world of Islam, 750–1150 CE.

> All of them said that the time had come when the Lord would gather
> his nation Israel from all lands unto Jerusalem
> the holy city, and that Solomon b. [R]uji was the king
> Messiah.[14]

The remainder of Obadiah's tale is chiefly taken up with the ridicule thrown at the Jews for falling victims to the claims of flying with wings to the Holy City. Obadiah closes this episode with a brief mention of another pretender, one bin Shaddad from Ba'aquba, near Baghdad, who 'told lies in abundance' and was seized by the caliph and thrown in prison. We have no more details of this last sect or of its leader, as the manuscript of the *Autobiography* is damaged at this point.

The bare bones of this messianic movement in the mountains, captured by Obadiah, is also repeated in two other important later accounts telling the same story of the Jewish revolt but with significant added details. In his *Itinerary*, Benjamin of Tudela connected these Jews and their militant stance with the powerful Nīzārī Ismaili band of far greater importance, to be found in the mountainous district of Alborz under the leadership of Ḥasan-i Sabbaḥ – famous in later times for their policy of targeted killings. Since their seizure of the fortress of Alamut, (known as 'the eagle's nest') in 1090, their leader Ḥasan had laid the virtual foundation of a Nīzārī state in Persia and Syria comprising a network of impregnable mountain fortresses. Ḥasan had been converted to the Ismaili doctrine, of which the Fatimid caliphs were the patrons, in opposition to the Sunni Caliphate, and he espoused an esoteric form of Ismaili lore. Arab chronicles sometimes refer to his movement as the Bāṭinīya.[15] The attacks and killings successfully carried out by such Nīzārī forces are frequently cited in Arab chronicles of the period. These assassinations later gave rise to the gripping legend of drug-induced killers in which Ḥasan, dubbed 'the old man of the mountains', presided over the preparation of these acts of asymmetric warfare, mainly in a famous description by Marco Polo that has resonated down the centuries in European histories. The term 'assassin', which has passed into western vocabulary, is a corruption of '*Hashishiyyin*', another term for the sect, supposedly alluding to the taking of hashish or Indian hemp to induce visions that prepared the assassins for their mission.[16]

But this aura of insurgency and violence associated with a mountain site of warriors was also crucially brought up by Benjamin of Tudela in his account, which forms part of Obadiah's description of the messianic Jews residing in the heights

---

14 Golb (trans.), 'Autograph Memoirs', Document X: Cambridge: Taylor-Schechter, MS 10K 21 fol. 1 *recto*, lines 13–16.
15 Adler (trans.), *Itinerary*, pp.53–54; Le Strange, *Lands*, p.221; Richards (trans.), *Chronicle of Ibn al-Athir*, pp.40–44.
16 Teresa Waugh (trans.), *The Travels of Marco Polo: A Modern Translation* (London: Sidgwick and Jackson, 1984), pp.38–39; Farhad Daftary, *A History of Shi'i Islam* (London: I. B. Tauris, 2013), pp.12–15; Bernard Lewis, 'The Ismā'īlites and the Assassins', in M. W. Baldwin (ed.), *A History of the Crusades: The First Hundred Years* (Madison: University of Wisconsin Press, 1969), vol. 1, pp.108–09.

of the border lands of Persia. Such a blending of Ismaili, Jewish and Persian backgrounds, already cited, reinforces the development of similar prophetic figures appearing and disappearing in Shi'i doctrine, such as the *Mahdī*, 'the divinely guided one', a personage who, after a period of concealment, will manifest himself and initiate a new era of righteousness and divine law.

All the sectarians previously examined, who arose in earlier centuries, were awaiting prophets: they invariably supported the claims of one *Mahdī*-like figure or another. This term, which has various messianic interpretations, has been applied to a number of individuals by Shi'i and Sunni Muslims. Belief in the coming of the *Mahdī* became a fundamental tenet of the faith of Shi'i Islam. Until such a figure appeared, mankind would require guidance or a need to rely on the teachings of imams. It is of some significance that the Shi'i appear connected to the insurgent Jews: in his version of the story, Benjamin of Tudela had 'four communities of Israel who go forth with the Nīzārī in war time'. The term 'Nīzārī' is another name given to the extreme Shi'i sect of the Ismaili, under the leadership of Ḥasan in the mountain redoubt of Alamut. This detail dovetails with Obadiah's description of them in his memoirs as 'children of the violent'. Descending from the heights, we are told, these Jewish warriors plunder and pillage and return to their hideouts in the mountains. These fighters are therefore adherents of a Jewish messianic movement who had certainly been in existence for about two generations since the last years of the eleventh century, before the arrival of the Franks and the crusaders. The insurgency is also located or based in the city of Amadia or Amadiya, 'where there are about 25,000 Israelites' according to Benjamin of Tudela, on the fringes of the land of Media.[17] Here, the story introduces an element of revolt against the king of Persia, led by a figure whose name has passed into modern times as something of a misnomer: David Alroy. The name 'Alroy', when clarified, is seen to be a corruption of 'Al-Ruji' so that David Al-Ruji was the son of Solomon al-Ruji. The error of the family name and the confusion of the first name created the figure of David Alroy, repeated in later medieval texts and resurfacing in the nineteenth century in a fantastical novel by Benjamin Disraeli titled *The Wondrous Tale of Alroy*. Alroy's persona even survived in street names in modern Jerusalem and Tel Aviv in the centuries that followed, having gained a foothold in the popular imagination as a notable messianic pretender.

This David Alroy has to be the figure of Menahem, the son of Solomon mentioned by Obadiah in his first account, and his full name would be Menahem ibn-abi-Da'ud Suleiman ibn al-Ruji, misremembered as Da'ud Alroy (David).[18] Menahem, son of Solomon Ruji, described by Benjamin of Tudela as David Alroy, proclaims that he has been sent to lead the Jews to capture Jerusalem and free them 'from the yoke of

---

17 Daftary, *Shi'i Islam*, pp.202–03, definition of *mahdī*; Adler (trans.), *Itinerary*, p.54.
18 Norman Golb, 'The Messianic Pretender Solomon Ibn al-Ruji and His Son Menachem (The So-Called "David Alroy")', *Oriental Institute, University of Chicago* (2009), p.3, <https://isac.uchicago.edu/sites/default/files/uploads/shared/docs/false_messiah-1.pdf>, accessed 2024; Gil, *Jews in Islamic Countries*, secs 248, 271, on al-Maghribī, David Alroy and sources.

the Gentiles': the Christian crusaders. Benjamin's account, notable for linking the Jewish insurgents with the Shi'i Assassins, ends with a confrontation with the king of Persia, who consigns Alroy to prison. Menachem, in this version, miraculously escapes through sorcery and other tricks, crossing the water on his mantle and then returns to Amadia. The Persian king threatens to slay all Jews in his territories unless Menachem desists from carrying out his plan. Finally, the exilarch and the head of the Baghdad Academy put an end to Menachem's designs by successfully bribing his father-in-law, who is said to have gone to his house and slain the would-be messiah whilst asleep in his bed.[19]

Many elements of this account concerning Menachem are perhaps given a more balanced treatment by a second source that also complements Obadiah's story. A certain Samuel ibn Abbās al-Maghribī converted to Islam after abandoning Judaism and may have done so because of the failure of Menachem's movement, of which he was a member. Maghribī included this story in his highly polemical treatise *Silencing of the Jews*.[20] It is also possible that Maghribī was known to Benjamin of Tudela and that he provided him with an oral source for his account in *The Itinerary*. Here, Maghribī, in his own account, described Menachem and the Jewish agitation for no other purpose than to poke fun at the credulous Jews, but there are some details that need mentioning. He placed the story of Menachem at a time when he was an educated young man, both clever and handsome. In this account, Menachem obtains possession of the fortress of the town of Amadia from its commander, from where he writes to the Jews and appeals for all to come with weapons concealed in their clothing, creating a large force from Azerbaijan and its borders. Eventually, the commander kills Menachem, and this force is dispersed, but many Jews of Baghdad about this time believed his proclamations through the deceitful letters forged by a number of Jewish swindlers and waited to fly to Jerusalem by night whilst assembled on the rooftops dressed in green clothing. Other pseudo-messianic incidents describe green veils and turbans worn by such prophetic figures to signify their mission. Sometimes, these were termed 'paradise garments'.[21]

The story told by Samuel al-Maghribī, which repeats details of Obadiah's account, rings true in some respects, especially when he mentioned the persisting memory of the messianic movement: 'the Jews of Amadia hold Alroy even today in higher esteem than many of their prophets. Many consider him to be the expected Messiah himself, and I have seen many Persian Jews in Khoi, Salmas, Tabriz, and Maragha who invoke his name in the most holy of oaths'.[22] The editor of this work situated Samuel Maghribī and his life between 1126 and 1175, making him contemporaneous to Benjamin of Tudela. He converted to Islam in Maragha in 1163 when he wrote his account as a resident of this region, where Menachem also lived. He seems

---

19 Adler (trans.), *Itinerary*, pp.54–56.
20 Moshe D. Perlmann (ed. and trans.), *Silencing the Jews* (New York: American Academy for Jewish Research, 1964), a translation of al-Maghribī.
21 Golb, 'Messianic Pretender', pp.4–5; Israel Friedlander, 'Jewish-Arabic Studies, I. Shiitic Elements in Jewish Sectarianism', *JQR*, 2:4 (1912), p.505, n.122.
22 Perlmann (ed. and trans.), *Silencing*, p.73; Golb, 'Messianic Pretender', p.5.

to refer to the persistence of Menachem's memory from past events, describing how he subsequently became the object of a cult following. A most significant detail provided in this account calls Menachem a *qā'im*, meaning the prophet or announcer of the Messiah. The Nīzārīs also spoke of the *qiyāma*, the long-awaited Last Day. The figure announcing this was called the *qā'im al-qiyāma*. This appellation accords more accurately with Obadiah's own account, where Solomon al-Ruji was the Messiah and Menachem, his son, was the messenger or announcer of the father. Of course, in subsequent years, the followers inevitably also accorded the son the title of Messiah, such an upgrading being a common topic in tales of messianic experiences, but nowhere in the existing statements examined is this ascribed to Menachem by himself. Menachem can therefore be seen as his father's *qā'im*, an extremely revealing term, also used by the Shi'i sectarians to denote a precursor or representative of the greater one: the saintly pretender or redeemer such as the *Mahdī*. The details of Obadiah's earlier account would therefore make sense.[23]

In short, in his account, the Norman proselyte would be referring in his memoirs to a Jewish messianic movement spanning from the end of the eleventh century and persisting into the first decades of the twelfth century, a movement originating in the Hakkāri region of Kurdistan, centred, as we are told, in the region of Amadiya and spreading into wider areas of the eastern Caliphate. The father, Solomon al-Ruji, was the Messiah while the son, Menahem, was his father's messenger (*qā'im*) seeking to raise an army of mountain Jews to capture Jerusalem from the crusaders. Passages seemingly quoted or paraphrased by Samuel Maghribī from Menachem's actual words exhort the followers to stand before the leader or spokesman (*qā'im*) to show their opposition to the rulers. It appears to be the case that Obadiah would only have registered the early years of this movement, going back to the last decade of the eleventh century, a time when the father was still alive and the son was by his side. Both Obadiah's story and these later accounts of the revolt take us into the politics and wars of the caliphate and bring in the mounting confrontation between the Sunni and Ismaili Nīzārī or *Batini*, centred around the upcoming struggle for Aleppo in the second decade of the twelfth century to which Obadiah, according to his *Autobiography*, appears to have been a direct witness.

---

23   Perlmann (ed. and trans.), *Silencing*, p.72, cites *qā'im*; Golb, 'Messianic Pretender', p.6; Daftary, *Shi'i Islam*, pp.134–35, on *qā'im al-qiyāma*.

Chapter 7

Siege of Aleppo

Obadiah's account certainly situates him in Aleppo roundabout the year 1117 in the midst of tumultuous events that arose out of a crisis springing from factional fighting between three parties: the nominally Seljuk-supporting rulers of the city, the forces of the Nīzārī-led Assassins attempting to gain control of Aleppo and finally the mounting threat to the city of the Frankish crusaders led by Roger Prince of Antioch, who had inherited the command of that principality following the death of Tancred in 1112.[1] This is a moment when the Norman proselyte's *Autobiography* provides a rare eyewitness testimony, both political and military. As always, however, it has to be remembered that these details are recalled some years after the events and only some were directly experienced by him.

In 1115, the power and prestige of Roger of Antioch – the inheritor of the principality of Antioch from Tancred – was at its height, and he appeared to cement the Frankish position of control around Aleppo. The crisis had been brought to a head in December 1113 by the death of Ridwan, ruler of Aleppo, which had followed the stabbing of Mawdūd, an important Turkish leader, carried out by the so-called sectarian Assassins. Some elements of the Aleppo population vehemently loathed the Batini Assassins, who had been staunchly supported by Ridwan. Following the end of Ridwan's life, many of the Assassins were arrested, notably their leader Abū Tāhir, also called 'the Goldsmith', who was executed along with a large number of his supporters. This 'Goldsmith', a Persian envoy sent by their leader Ḥassan from his mountain fastness in Alamut as part of a concerted drive to expand westwards and set up centres of Batini power in Syria, had greatly influenced affairs in Aleppo through his authority over Ridwan. The Goldsmith was in reality another Persian *dā'i*, a term signifying a preacher or messenger propagating in Aleppo the belief of the Nīzārī cause, an act of policy known as *da'wa*. Now, the power vacuum caused by Ridwan's departure was filled by the rise of Lulu Al-Yahya, also known as 'Lulu the Eunuch', who ruled over Aleppo as regent for Ridwan's younger son.[2] Meanwhile, Roger and the Franks were continuing to tighten their virtual encirclement and siege

---

1 Maalouf, *Crusades*, pp.82–92; H. A. R. Gibb (trans.), *The Damascus Chronicle of the Crusades: Extracted and Translated from the Chronicle of Ibn Al-Qalānisī* (Mineola, NY: Dover Publications, 2002), pp.144–47; Richards (trans.), *Chronicle of Ibn al-Athir*, p.164.
2 Maalouf, *Crusades*, p.92; Gibb (trans.), *Damascus Chronicle*, pp.144–50.

of Aleppo, occupying all the fortresses around the city, a position made worse by the murder of Lulu in May 1117. At this critical juncture following Lulu's demise, an appeal by the citizens of Aleppo was sent to Ghazi bin Urtuq (also known as Ilghazi) to come forward to take control of Aleppo. This Ghazi or Ilghazi was the leader of the Turkish Artukid dynasty serving under the Seljuk Sultan. Ilghazi embarked on an immediate offensive against the Frankish forces of Roger of Antioch.

It was at about this time that Obadiah was in Aleppo, as we shall see, witnessing the climax of all these deaths and killings that were now played out in a critical battle between Ilghazi and Roger of Antioch outside the city. The march of events that were seemingly bringing the city of Aleppo steadily under Roger's Christian control would have signalled a significant advance of the crusader states led by the Kingdom of Jerusalem. The struggle now reached a turning point, and, on the morning of 28 June 1119, 15 miles or so from Aleppo, the Christian army with many Syrian and Armenian mercenaries was surrounded. Then, the wind turned, driving a violent cloud of dust into the Frankish faces. Roger fell fighting with many of his knights, either killed or taken prisoner at what became known as the Battle of the Field of Blood (*Ager Sanguinis*). One account describes a prostrate mass of dead horsemen and foot soldiers alike, with Roger stretched out among them, his head cleaved down to the nose. The horses, in one description, resembled hedgehogs riddled with arrows. At sundown, Ilghazi made his triumphant entry into Aleppo with many Frankish prisoners behind him in chains.[3]

This bloody encounter between Muslim and Frankish forces merits a more detailed account to bring out Obadiah's involvement. The main source is to be found in Walter the Chancellor's *Antiochene Wars*. Walter was the chancellor of Antioch from 1114 to around 1122 and mentioned that he was captured in this conflict, later being ransomed. He asserted that the Latin side numbered 700 knights in the battle, as well as a significant number of mercenaries. Matthew of Edessa specifically had some 600 Frankish cavalry, 500 Armenian mounted fighters, 400 infantry and an assorted number of 10,000 on the Christian side. He also gave a total of 80,000 for Ilghazi's host, but this may have been an exaggeration. What is definite is that his forces were much larger than that of the crusaders. All told, the Frankish army may have totalled 20,000 horse and foot.

The Franks were encamped at the eastern edge of the plain of Sarmeda, close to the small fort of Tel-Aqibrin, some 15 odd miles west of Aleppo. The broken territory was surrounded by mountains to which there was only access by three sites, and the Franks believed no one could move against them because of the difficult access of the terrain they controlled. In fact, on the morning of 28 June, scouts brought word that the crusader camp was surrounded. Roger, still full of confidence, was now inclined to move forwards, as he saw that he must break this encirclement, for he had already made a fateful decision. He had decided not to wait for the arrival of

---

3   Nicholas Morton, *The Field of Blood: The Battle for Aleppo and the Remaking of the Medieval Middle East* (New York: Basic Books, 2018), pp.83–112; Maalouf, *Crusades*, pp.93–94; Gibb (trans.), *Damascus Chronicle*, pp.160–61; Runciman, *History*, vol. 2, pp.149–51.

support and reinforcements from Baldwin of Jerusalem, which he had summoned northwards for aid. After kissing with fervour the standard of the Holy Cross, containing a fragment of the True Cross – a relic of supreme importance obtained after the conquest of Jerusalem in 1099 – he gave orders for battle lines to be drawn up. At the first sound of the bugle, all were to put on arms and armour; on the sound of the second bugle, battle lines were drawn up, both knights and foot soldiers assembled. Finally, on the sound of the third clarion call, individual battle lines or divisions advanced paying homage at the sign of the True Cross. One division took the lead from the right, advancing to strike the enemy, followed by five companies in sequence. Walter, our main source, narrated that these attacks failed to follow through with enough force and suffered grievous losses inflicted by Muslims with spears, lances and a hail of arrows. One cohort of mercenaries on the left, a force of Turcopole cavalry charging with the main crusader contingent, failed to hold their line and, when it started to break up, disrupted Roger's main forces, partially contributing to the loss of the battle for the crusaders. As mentioned earlier, this was aggravated by a whirlwind blowing north and throwing up a large cloud of dust that appears to have got into the eyes of the warriors, rendering them unable to fight. It was at this moment that Roger was struck by an enemy sword through the middle of his nose right into his brain. He perished at the foot of the jewelled cross that was his standard.

The outcome of the Battle of the Field of Blood highlighted important features in the military context to be found in the Levant. For over a century, Turkic tribes had been moving steadily into the Islamic world, and this had expanded into a tide of conquest. The Turks, pushing into the Christian Byzantine Empire, had defeated their army in Anatolia at the Battle of Manzikert, in August 1071. Now, the army of Ilghazi showed yet again that these forces were successfully implanting themselves farther south in the Islamic world. In some respects, the Battle of the Field of Blood was not a standard war of east and west but rather the latest stage of a struggle pitting these nomadic fighters from Central Asia against the armies of a more settled agricultural society from the Frankish world. The Frankish crusaders had to adapt and learn to fight highly skilled horsemen and archers who rode smaller, extremely agile steeds and did not wear the heavy armour of the crusader knights. In the battle, the Franks suffered enormous losses from the bow of the Turkish archers, and few of them escaped. Hundreds of captives were bound and beaten with rods. This description of Latin captives given by Walter is gruesome, and, even if exaggerated, it might suggest that he was witness to some of these events. A number of the leading knights were ransomed, and Walter must have been amongst those. It cannot be ruled out that Obadiah was also present at some of these occasions.

Many of these figures and incidents are alluded to in Obadiah's narrative, and it does seem incontrovertible that he was present in Aleppo sometime from 1117 onwards enduring the terrible conditions of a final Frankish siege before the battle that put even greater pressure on the city. From his account, the situation certainly did not favour the Jewish inhabitants. This was a very different Aleppo from the one he had experienced around 1104 when he met with Rabbi Baruch to obtain the important letter of validation and safe conduct about his conversion. Now, some 13 years later, after a decade or so in Baghdad, his sojourn in Aleppo recorded grave hardships for himself and his fellow Jews, who must have suffered from the attacks of both Muslims and Christians.

Obadiah's own account in his memoirs, cited below, dwells on the harsh plight of many Jews in Aleppo – men, women and children, seeking protection during the siege of Roger of Antioch and the Frankish forces. Although they were helped and supported by others of the sizeable Jewish community, many of them, probably refugees, died from hunger, and others became weak and impoverished. He suggests they did receive help from the local population and even acknowledges that he himself was helped by them 'in some small measure', for which he blessed them. The central event for him, as he recalls, was clearly the saving of Aleppo from the harsh treatment of crusaders by the victory of Ilghazi, the Turkish leader, described by him as 'a great man', and this is perhaps not surprising. The Battle of the Field of Blood between the Muslim army and the Franks, apart from recalling the massacre in Jerusalem in 1099, is remembered by Obadiah as an anticipation of the great wars of redemption to come that would result in the defeat of Edom, the Christian host. Even if this victory at Aleppo had been won by soldiers of the Arab faith led by a Turk, it was a virtual deliverance, since in his mind Christianity constituted the greater enemy. The experience in Aleppo is, for the Norman proselyte, a precursor of the battles that will take place in the looming Last Days with the expectation of the coming of the Messiah. Obadiah rounds off his account alluding to this sentiment, characterising Ilghazi as a chosen figure:

> For the city of Aleppo had remained in dire straits because of
> Sir Rogier king of Antokhia (=Antioch) and because of the Togarmites
> [..........] the Ishm]ae[l]ites, while so[me] of them would [..........]
> [............to] the commands of the king of Aleppo. Jews
> [in abundance in A]leppo died, while those who remained were weak and impoverished.
>
> So the Lord raised up a saviour for the inhabitants of Aleppo —
> Ghazi bin Urtuq of the chiefs of the Togarmites.
> For it happened when the wickedness of the Franks was great in the sight of the Lord.[4]

---

4   Golb (trans.), 'Autograph Memoirs', Document XII: Cambridge: Taylor-Schechter, MS Loan 31, *recto*, lines 18–19, and Document XIII: Cambridge: Taylor-Schechter, MS Loan 31, *verso*, lines 8–10, 17–19. Account of the battle in Thomas S. Asbridge and Susan B. Edgington (trans), *Walter the Chancellor's The Antiochene Wars* (Aldershot: Ashgate, 1999), pp.125–29, 136–38 (for torture of prisoners in Aleppo), 188–89 (number of 10,000 in battle); Gibb (trans.), *Damascus Chronicle*, p.200, total of 20,000; Morton, *Field of Blood*, pp.102–06, for Turkish nomadic and Frankish military tactics.

Obadiah's closeness to Hebrew and Arabic is brought out, for example, in the name he gives to the Franks. In the original Hebrew text of the *Autobiography*, they are called *Afrangiyyim*, a Hebraised form of the Arabic '*Franj*' or '*Ifranj*'. On the other hand, he calls the Turks by the biblical name '*Togarmin*'. His cultural context often places him in an Islamic space rather than a Christian one, but he calls Roger by his name used in the Italian vernacular pronunciation and gives him his European title of a knight. Indeed, some of the Arabic sources refer to him as 'Sirodjal' or 'Sirdjal'. Here, as in other parts of the *Autobiography*, Obadiah demonstrates that he sometimes oscillates between four different languages for names and places: Arabic, Latin, a southern Italian version influenced by Old French and Biblical Hebrew.[5]

Subsequently, after the battle, we are told that Obadiah journeyed to Raqqah (named as Kalneh in his account), 150 miles east of Aleppo, on the left bank of the Euphrates. He describes this as a return, as he had been there before, over 10 years earlier, on his way to Baghdad, but there are no details provided on the length of his visit, other than the comment that he stayed there 'some days'. The move to Raqqah must have occurred in 1119. It is likely that this stopover may have been occasioned by the disturbed conditions in the region after the recent clash between Christian and Turkish armies, as the town had a large Jewish community and at this point had not been directly affected by the wars with the crusaders. Unfortunately, most of the details concerning his move to Raqqah and an onward trip to Damascus are unknown, because of missing pages from the surviving fragments of the *Autobiography*. A direct route from there to Damascus might take Obadiah along a convoy route crossing the Syrian desert between Damascus and Palmyra, through Tadmor – an important trading post with a large presence of Jews that the Norman proselyte always looked to for help. His account suggests he now spent a few months in Damascus, as always supported by the charity of the Jewish community: Obadiah refers to 'a collector' who obtained weekly contributions from the Hebrews for his upkeep. This would be a gabay, a synagogue assistant or beadle who administered charitable funds. Again, the Norman proselyte recalls with rejoicing and gratitude the generosity shown to him.[6] The suggestion of continuing support offered to Obadiah denotes some peculiar status he may have enjoyed, which now becomes clearer on the next stage of his journey.

End-game in Bāniyās

Obadiah appears to have been well received and looked after in Damascus with contributions from the community, and this is continued in the next reported location, which is Dan or Bāniyās: 'Then Obadiah the Proselyte arose from Damascus

---

5 Kedar, 'Voyages', p.141.
6 Golb (trans.), 'Autograph Memoirs', Document VII: Cambridge: Taylor-Schechter MS 8.271, fol. 2 *verso*; Golb, 'Megillat Obadiah Hager', p.89.

and went / to [Dan] (=Banias) which is in the land of Israel', says the Norman.⁷ This town was traditionally seen as the border of northern Israel and was a centre of refuge for both Jews and Muslims fleeing from the earlier Byzantine incursions in the tenth century.⁸ Later, the town is described as comfortable and prosperous, 'the granary of Damascus'. Obadiah seems to have proceeded there from Damascus accompanied by a number of followers, which suggests that he was attracting disciples. The attacks of the Franks on Aleppo in 1117–1119 and earlier on in Damascus in 1112 had caused great panic and hardship on the Jewish population, which was poor and unprotected, and Jews were looking for some form of comfort from the travails they had been suffering earlier in both cities. Later, Bāniyās became the target of the Assassins, now chased out of Aleppo but pursuing the same tactics of expansion. They succeeded for a time in gaining the foothold of a frontier fortress there, ceded to them by Toghtekin, the ruler of Damascus. On the border between the Kingdom of Jerusalem and Damascus, the town of Bāniyās was repeatedly attacked as a gateway to the territory of Jerusalem and the coastline stronghold of Tyre.⁹

These events, however, still lay in the near future. But, in August–September 1121, upon his arrival in Bāniyās, Obadiah had a fateful encounter with a presumed leader of a group of Karaites. It gave rise to another outburst of messianic pretensions on the part of this Karaite figure. He was a *Kohen*, that is, of a priestly lineage, by the name of Solomon and was now confronted by the Norman proselyte. Obadiah's arrival in the town appears to have been greeted warmly by a 'few poor men', as he recounts, who came forward, suggesting that he was the bearer of a special message and had a reputation that preceded him by word of mouth. Now ensued Obadiah's meeting with Solomon the Karaite, an Aaronite priest, who also had a retinue listening to him. He can now be called Solomon ha-Kohen, to give him his proper title, and the narrative licenses us to imagine that some form of public encounter took place between these two men, surrounded by a group of listeners made up of their respective followers, as Obadiah recalls in his *Autobiography*:

> He said to Obadiah the Proselyte and to the Je[ws]
> who were in Dan that in two and a half more months
> the Lord would gather in his people Israel from all the lands
> unto [Jeru]salem the holy city. Obadiah the Proselyte said
> to Solomon: "W[hence k]now you this thing, my lord?"
> Solomon then said: "Because I am the man whom the Israelites
> are seeking."¹⁰

---

7   Golb (trans.), 'Autograph Memoirs', Document XIV: New York: Jewish Theological Seminary of America, MS Adler 4208=3098, fol. 7 *recto*, lines 7–8.
8   Gil, *History of Palestine*, sec. 214; Al-Muqaddasī and Collins (trans.), *Best Divisions*, pp.136–37, on Bāniyās.
9   Farhad Daftary, *The Ismāīlīs: Their History and Doctrines* (Cambridge: Cambridge University Press, 2007), p.348; Lewis, 'Ismā'īlites', pp.116–17.
10 Golb (trans.), 'Autograph Memoirs', Document XIV: New York: Jewish Theological Seminary of America, MS Adler 4208=3098, fol. 7 *recto*, lines 12–18.

The exchange continues with Obadiah stating categorically that, because Solomon, a Levite, is descended from the seed of Aaron, he cannot be that messiah who must spring from the line of David, or even be the figure of Elijah, the announcer of the Messiah. Most importantly, Obadiah also now recalls, three lines further down, that the day of this exchange in Bāniyās with Solomon was 'nineteen years from the day on which I entered into the covenant of / the Lord God of Israel'. The exact mention of this day by Obadiah is only one of two dates that can be securely attributed in the account of his life: August–September 1102 for his conversion and August–September 1121 for this meeting with the Karaite messianic pretender in Bāniyās. On this later date, also in the month of Elul (August–September), the Karaite went on to assert that, in two-and-a-half months' time, the Lord would gather in 'his people of Israel' from all the lands to Jerusalem, the Holy City. This all-important 'in-gathering' mentioned earlier is repeatedly invoked as a significant moment marking the return of Jerusalem to the Jewish faith: the invocation of Zion in all its panoply of glory. Such a moment will herald the future emancipation of the Jews, a changed life for Israel and the gathering of all people in Palestine from all parts of the globe. This, as we saw, would take place by miraculous flight when the revived Hebrew state would be proclaimed by the King Messiah at the head of a Hebrew army – an army that will slay the Edomites (the Christians) and take possession of the city of God. Some accounts of this event describe a frightful battle between fierce armies struggling for world supremacy in a war lasting seven years. All of this had been endlessly proclaimed and preached by previous false-messiah figures described earlier and again in the conversation between Solomon ha-Kohen and Obadiah. The foretelling of such multitudes being brought to Jerusalem for the 'in-gathering' is to be found scattered in the many writings of the prophets, of which the prophet Zechariah is an oft-cited example:

> Thus saith the Lord; I am returned unto Zion, and will dwell in the midst of Jerusalem: and Jerusalem shall be called a city of truth; and the mountain of the Lord of hosts the holy mountain.
> …
> Thus saith the Lord of hosts; Behold, I will save my people from the east country, and from the west country; And I will bring them, and they shall dwell in the midst of Jerusalem: and they shall be my people, and I will be their God, in truth and in righteousness. (Zechariah 8:3, 7–8)

In the biblical Book of Zechariah, this forms part of what has sometimes been called the *Decalogue of Promises to Zion* heralding the new era. The historical context for this grand vision of Zion and Jerusalem may have simply originated at the time in an incantation by the prophet exhorting Jews to finish the rebuilding of Jerusalem and the Second Temple. It may have been composed some 20 years after 539 BCE, which marked the return of Jews from exile in Babylon. We know from the psalms mentioning Jerusalem that the Temple was associated with Mount Zion. The return of the Jews to the Temple and to Mount Zion is at the heart of what drove Obadiah to await the Messiah's return. The Jews, he believed, would flock back to Jerusalem to participate in the moment. However that may be, these passages and many others were constantly cited in succeeding centuries to announce the coming of the Messiah. But, before entering more deeply into this matter, we must return to the dialogue between the Karaite and the Norman proselyte, which went on to take an unexpected turn.

Obadiah was now urged by Solomon ha-Kohen not to go to Jerusalem for two-and-a-half months until he and all the dispersed Israelites shall have gathered there in the manner described. The reply given by Obadiah suggests that he would be journeying to Jerusalem at a time of his own choosing after reaching Egypt: "'I shall go to Egypt and shall return / with our brethren the children of Israel who are in Egypt to / Jerusalem.'"[11] This remark drew no comment from Solomon: '... Solomon was silent', says the account – with a heavy dose of meaning. This part of the *Autobiography* breaks off here after telling us that Solomon and Obadiah journeyed on separately to Tyre. We hear no more of what became of either the Norman proselyte or the Karaite after their exchange.

The sense of this passage in Obadiah's account has remained enigmatic, not to say puzzling. But it seems most likely that Obadiah was contradicting Solomon and saying that he, Obadiah, was going to Jerusalem at another time accompanied by his own followers and that this riposte was meant to silence Solomon. Even if Obadiah had earlier scorned other messianic pretenders such as Al-Ruji father and son, there was a more personal dimension in his response to the Karaite. Was Obadiah, as some have wondered, harbouring his own messianic pretensions?[12] A journey to Jerusalem by a Jew had to be charged with a messianic meaning, as Jerusalem was not only in Frankish hands but also the only city in which the crusaders barred the Jews. Jerusalem was out of bounds. This meant that the aim of going there actually signified its liberation from Christian rule. If Jerusalem was his final destination, then clearly Obadiah saw himself as having embarked on a journey of redemption, as he explicitly states. According to his account, the band of followers accompanying him from Damascus to Bāniyās was meant to be swelled by more followers when he got to Egypt. This would also explain why he was looked after and held in some esteem in Aleppo and Damascus and, when in Bāniyās, surrounded by his disciples, why he had brusquely countered Solomon ha-Kohen, brushing aside his messianic pretensions. It begins to look as if Obadiah had departed from Baghdad around 1118, or earlier, with some specific mission in mind.

Whatever Obadiah held to be his identity, it was unlikely that he was putting himself forward as the Messiah. More likely, as we have suggested, he had come to inhabit that world of numerous sectarians who so often came forward supporting the claim of announcing one divine appearance or another. Obadiah would evidently see himself as a messenger or apostle of the Messiah. Earlier, we noted how

---

11 Golb (trans.), 'Autograph Memoirs', Document XV: New York: Jewish Theological Seminary of America: MS Adler 4208 = 3098, fol. 7, *verso*, lines 16–18.
12 Prawer, 'Autobiography', p.128.

Isfāhanī, an early messianic pretender, could sometimes also be characterised as a *rasūl* or messenger of the Expected One. In Islam, Muhammad was the Messenger of God – *rasūl Allah*. At times, such messiahs could have more than one messenger. This characterisation, which became widespread in the Islamic world, overlapped or perhaps influenced other Jewish sectarians. This was in addition to the messianic idea and to the variety of forerunners, in one of which, the prophet Elijah, appears frequently as the announcer of the Jewish or even the Christian Deliverer. Such a figure was also conveyed by the persona, already mentioned, of the *Dā'i*, denoting a variety of roles, from the religious propagandist to that of public communicator. All these particular features are already gathered in the earlier descriptions of Isfāhanī and Yūdghān. The term '*Dā'i*', associated with '*da'wa*', a much-used word that proclaimed a programme or mission carried out by a *Dā'i*, played a huge role in the preaching or dissemination of Ismaili faith amongst the Shi'i. In the heightened and intense world of Jewish and Islamic sects, the propagandist or his followers sometimes manifested that he too was a messiah, as we saw earlier when Yūdghān was elevated to a messianic status, like his predecessor Abū 'Isa Isfāhanī.

Here, the shared world of Islam and Judaism overlaps in Obadiah's self-definition: he was akin to a *Dā'i* (propagandist) proclaiming a *da'wa* (policy) or fulfilling the role of a *rasūl* (messenger).[13] These terms are also enhanced by the earlier description given by Samuel Maghribī in his naming of Menahem al-Ruji, son of Solomon al-Ruji, as his father's *qā'im*, another term associated particularly with a Shi'i description of a precursor or representative of an imam who proclaimed a saintly pretender or redeemer. But the term '*qā'im*' was evidently also in use among Jews. Obadiah was no doubt personifying such a role and saw himself on a mission to preach, proclaim or disseminate the coming of the Messiah without having a divine standing of his own. In all likelihood, the Norman was presenting himself as some kind of announcer or messenger spreading the news of the coming of a Greater One. This vision, which would have taken hold of him in Baghdad after his intense readings of the Prophets, drove him to set out on this phase of his travels to Aleppo and Damascus with an important stop in Bāniyās – a stop that caused him to reveal something of this prophet-like vocation.

Obadiah had hitherto espoused a mainstream position of Rabbinic beliefs, as codified in the Talmud, and these adhered to the authority of the official administrators and interpreters, the heads of the *yeshivot*, and the *gaon* of the Academy under whom he had perhaps studied in Baghdad for a decade or more. It seems that he did not put himself forward as a disciple of Solomon ha-Kohen, the priestly leader of the Karaite group – a movement that had arisen first in the Persian world, co-mingled with sectarians such as some local Jewish schismatic movements. The Karaite ideology stood unflinchingly for a rejection of the Talmud and an opposition to the leadership of the *gaon* and the exilarch. Chiefly, they promulgated an insistence on the freedom of each individual to interpret the Bible – the oral law – as

---

13   Israel Friedlander, 'Jewish-Arabic Studies, I. Shiitic Elements in Jewish Sectarianism', *JQR*, 3 (1912), pp.258–63.

the sole manifestation of the Law. Karaism also put forward an aggressive messianic nationalism, chafing with impatience at the endless delay in the redemption and restoration of Israel. Finally, Karaism exhibited a strong sense of unworldly asceticism. As we saw, some of the characteristics of early Karaism seem to have Shi'i parallels, but it is unclear which sect was the origin or the chief influence of the other. Since the birthplace of Karaism was to be found in the north-eastern frontier of the Arab Empire, whose culture was essentially Persian, there were doubtless connections with the local Jewish groups, as was studied earlier. The answer to these questions remains somewhat obscure: did Karaism develop out of such schismatic sects that had preceded it, or was this a new departure influenced by the Muslim environment but with motives that were intrinsic to Jewish society?

One story that has resonated and served to heighten the tension between Karaism and the mainstream Rabbanites is the life of Anan b. David. Anan, it was said, was a rabbinic high-flyer who was passed over by his brother for the position he coveted and so failed to obtain the post of exilarch in Babylon. The humiliating loss of such power and prestige, so the story goes, drove Anan to set up his own dissident sect, and, whilst his opposition to the Rabbinic establishment is not clear, his own doctrines – set out in the *Sepher ha Mitzvot* (Book of Precepts) sometime between the tenth and twelfth century – only add to the enigma concerning the origins of Karaism and the centrality of any one individual or school of thought. He is first mentioned around 850 CE, but his so-called defection and subsequent teaching might have happened in the previous century. It is only the later Karaite tradition that accorded Anan the status of a founder of Karaism. Anan, who challenged Geonic authority, can probably be set among the leaders of the numerous movements of eastern Persia, even if he later appears to be linked to Baghdad. His probable legendary story, or some of its details, would have served to reinforce the origin of Karaism as an offshoot or protest to mainstream Judaism, when the two groups parted company.

Intriguingly, when the Norman proselyte met Solomon ha-Kohen, this Solomon told him that the sign of his elected status as the Messiah was that he did not eat bread or drink water. Commonly, Karaites declared that it was forbidden to eat meat or drink wine. This declaration, we are told, had also been repeated earlier by Isfahānī and his successor Yūdghān and serves to underline that Karaism could have developed from the previous sects previously described. Solomon's asceticism regarding bread and water was passed over by Obadiah in his remarks to him, but the general restriction of meat and wine has an explanation: this austerity arose because the destruction of the Temple had led to the prohibition of any slaughter of animals or sacrifices. Jews were now in exile, and such practices could only resume in Palestinian territory when Jerusalem reverted once more to Israel and the Temple was restored.[14] Such restrictions only reinforced the need to hasten any messi-

---

14 Friedlander, 'Shiitic Elements', 3, pp.293–95; Yoram Erder, 'The Doctrine of Abū 'Īsa al-Iṣfahānī and Its Sources', *Jerusalem Studies in Arabic and Islam*, 20 (1996), pp.178–79; Gil, *History of Palestine*, pp.777–79; Nemoy, *Karaite Anthology*, p.xviii; Martin Goodman, *A*

anic deliverance, if necessary by force of arms. Some of these premises lay behind Solomon ha-Kohen's remarks to Obadiah.

Departing Bāniyās, Obadiah travelled to Tyre, the fortified harbour city, in the autumn of 1121. A few years later, in 1124, that city would fall into the hands of the Franks, followed by Bāniyās in 1129.[15] But, for now, this route to Tyre provided safe passage along the coast in Muslim-held lands, avoiding crusader-held territory in Palestine. After the encounter with Solomon the Aaronite priest, a messianic expectation of a Zionist redemption in Jerusalem loomed on the horizon. This challenged Obadiah to proceed to the Holy City, even if it was not clear when it would take place. The full topic of redemption and a final battle is a subject that requires addressing. The Norman proselyte's beliefs must now be set in a wider context.

The coming of the hour

The story recounting the End Time or the Last Day, repeatedly told in the books of the Prophets, describes the signs and visions that would precede this moment. A time of troubles before the resolution was set out in graphic terms by Joel, as we saw mentioned earlier in Obadiah's memoir: a great and terrible day and the gathering of the remnant that would follow on Mount Zion and in Jerusalem, after the sun had been turned to darkness and the moon into blood. This much had already been prophesied years earlier by the Norman when he cited his reading of Joel on the eve of the First Crusade, but, now in Bāniyās, he had sensed its imminence. The general invocation of the building of the Holy City was widespread in salutations and correspondence, as is illustrated in a business letter to three senior Karaite Tustari brothers in Egypt in 1026: 'God knows of the strength of my longing for you—may he always support you. I ask Him to bring us together when His Holy City will be built'.[16] The argument about the number of years and the triumph of Israel was endlessly debated. Every pretended messiah or self-appointed prophet announced a date. In 840, in Córdoba, the earlier Frankish apostate Bodo had calculated the Messiah's arrival in 867–868.[17] Saadia b. Joseph, *Gaon* of Sura (892–942), in his influential study of Judaism that appeared in 933, *The Book of Beliefs and Opinions*, spoke of a date. Here, in a section on the Last Times, he maintained that this time was foretold in the Book of Daniel to occur at the end of the fourth Roman Empire

---

History of Judaism (London: Penguin, 2019), pp.301–08, on Anan and Karaites; Rustow, 'Qaraites', p.151; Moshe Gil, 'The Origins of the Karaites', in M. Polliack (ed.), *Karaite Judaism: A Guide to Its History and Literary Sources* (Leiden: Brill, 2003), pp.73–118, on the origin of Karaites.
15 Gibb (trans.), *Damascus Chronicle*, pp.170, 194.
16 Goitein, *MS*, vol. 5, p.392.
17 José Madoz (ed.), *El Epistolario de Álvaro de Córdoba. Edición Crítica* (Madrid: Consejo Superior de Investigaciones Cientificas, 1947), p.234; Frank Riess, *The Journey of Deacon Bodo from the Rhine to the Guadalquivir: Apostasy and Conversion to Judaism in Early Medieval Europe* (London: Routledge, 2019), p.82.

when, Saadia added, the Muslim state would also collapse with it. The appointed hour for this inevitable end, variously construed by commentators of Saadia's book to happen in 965 or 968, showed his interpretation of the End Time, prophesied in Daniel, to be enigmatic, even unintelligible to the ignorant, but not so to the wise.[18] Saadia was certainly held to be one of the wise. He harboured some opinion as to when the Messiah was to be expected, and, whilst refraining from expressing it openly, he sought to proclaim that the hour was not far off: some 30 years after the completion of his work on Judaism. Like all these dates, Saadia's prophecy came and went, and, two centuries later, in the time of Obadiah, yet another figure and Hour awaited, according to his exchange in Bāniyās.

This uncertain and ambiguous coming of the Messiah is also reflected in the work of Maimonides. Whilst agreeing that the Hour will come upon the allotted end of Edom (Rome), he was reluctant to be drawn on the year. In the Epistle to Yemen, written in 1172, Maimonides castigated Jacob ben Nathaniel al-Fayyumi, who had written to him on behalf of the Jews of Yemen seeking confirmation for such an event, or even the identity of a messiah: 'First of all, it devolves upon you to know that no human being will ever be able to determine it precisely', asserted Maimonides. Even so, a few pages on in this work, he unexpectedly revealed an ancient tradition handed down from his father regarding the future restoration of prophecy in Israel, which was meant to inaugurate the messianic era and which he set in 1216.[19] The sages of Judaism were mindful that, although their belief in the Hour to come was undoubted, the actual date remained unknown and should not to be exactly sought. If this is illustrated in the examples told by Saadia and Maimonides, it is even clearer in the patriarchal story of Jacob, who, in his old age, gathered his sons before him when he wished to describe, in his final words, the time of the *ketz* (end of days). This was the blessing of Jacob given to his sons (Genesis 49:1–27) that, as the *Talmud* later recounts, he was unable to carry out because the spirit of God (the *shekhinah*) had departed from him, rendering him unable to prophesy. Jacob declared in this account that this had come to pass because one of his descendants was unfit. Such opinions were also held by Saadia, for example, because he declared that the Jews had to repent if the expected era of redemption was to happen. Otherwise, the spirit of the nation would have to be crushed and forced to seek God. Israel will come to God either through love and conviction or through force and affliction.[20] Jacob therefore seemed to have the last word in his understanding of why he could not name the Hour. Such wise minds cautioned that intensive involvement in awaiting a messianic apocalypse and probing ceaselessly for the timing of the End lacked any uplifting of spiritual value and added nothing to our future, which in any case is unknown. No one could or should calculate the End, some seemed to say.

---

18   Samuel Rosenblatt (trans.), *Saadia Gaon: The Book of Beliefs and Opinions* (New Haven, CT: Yale University Press, 1955), pp.295–301.
19   Maimonides, 'Epistle', pp.114, 122.
20   Rosenblatt (trans.), *Book of Beliefs*, p.301.

Even if this approach counselled rejection, men like Obadiah and the Karaite at Bāniyās passionately espoused an extreme position: a messianic tradition that envisaged the formation of a new world brought about by a mighty world war. This event also seemed to them to be close at hand and drove the Norman proselyte into the territories of Palestine towards the Holy City of Jerusalem. The story as set out by Saadia had two outcomes: in the first of these, if the inevitable end approaches and Israel has not yet made repentance, the woes of the pre-messianic state will be fought out between the messiah b. Joseph and the local lord Armilius over the possession of Palestine. He will appear in Galilee, said Saadia, and proceed at the head of a small army of Hebrews to take Jerusalem, presently in possession of Rome under Armilius. But although Messiah b. Joseph, a lesser messiah, will rout Armilius, his victory will be short-lived, for Armilius will drive the Jews back into the desert and slay this messiah. The second outcome, if Israel has fully repented, makes the first outcome unnecessary: then the King Messiah ben David will appear suddenly, proceeding to Jerusalem at the head of a Hebrew army, slaying the Roman chief and thereby taking control of the Holy City. Even so, this is not the end: the King Messiah will wage a long and bloody war against the fierce army of Gog, lasting seven years.

This last story of a battle, the redemption of Israel and the hour of Zion, coalesced in Obadiah's mind, taking hold of his vision and imagination. The source of this prophecy, found in Chapters 37–39 of the Book of Ezekiel, a pivotal work in the history of prophecy, became the great declaration concerning the millennial agenda of Israel's restoration and redemption. Ezekiel's oracle recounts how, in the 'latter days', God unleashes a formidable enemy from the north to bring down and conquer Israel and, after a period of 170 years, Israel emerges triumphant. This enormous span of time is in stark contrast to Saadia's seven years. Israel's victory is associated with the vision of the 'valley of the dry bones', also described by Ezekiel. Here, the fallen, or the dead generally, are resurrected as living beings and fighters, who usher in the final victory. The formidable enemy is called Gog from the land of Magog, whose identity has been endlessly debated, variously taking in King Gyges of Lydia, Alexander the Great and a personification of evil derived from the Sumerian word for darkness. This Gog from the land of Magog passed into the Christian apocalypse, fleshed out in the final work on the New Testament canon, the Revelation of John, where 'Gog and Magog', summoned by Satan, are gathered for battle.[21]

Similar expectations of the Last Days were equally well known to medieval Muslims. Speculations of these Last Days and the role of the *Mahdī* were frequently intertwined with prophecies about Islam's triumph over Christianity and the fate of Jerusalem. In his *The Beginning of the End*, the Arab chronicler Ibn al-Kathir set out a comparable panorama in similar detail. One portent of the approaching end would be announced by a dark sun rising in the west, followed by the barbarous hordes of Gog and Magog, called in Arabic Yājūj and Mājūj. Other Islamic accounts state that, before their disappearance, they would drink Lake Tiberias dry. Such a terrible happening would be followed by the appearance of the one-eyed Antichrist

---

21 Rosenblatt (trans.), *Book of Beliefs*, pp.301–06.

Dajjal, riding through Palestine on an ass, followed by a retinue of 70,000 Jews. The Muslims of the twelfth century also longed to repossess Jerusalem, and the city became the focus for a campaign culminating in its reconquest by Saladin in 1187. Muslims believed that the Prophet Muhammad had made the Night Journey on the winged steed into the Heavens from Jerusalem and that the city would be the site on which the Resurrection would take place on the Last Day. On the Day of Judgement, when the Trumpet of the Resurrection sounded, all creatures would be brought to life again and assemble in the valley of Gehenna, just outside the eastern wall of Jerusalem.[22] These Arab versions of victory often included many repetitions of the Judaic details that set out the triumph over Rome, now led by the *Mahdī*. In the period just prior to the coming of the First Crusade, Muslim and Jewish expectations dwelt on the imminence of the year 500 AH (corresponding to 1106–1107 CE).[23] No doubt these dates were in the background that drove messianic expectations described and witnessed by Obadiah, stirred also by his readings of Ezekiel during his time in Baghdad. All told, such visons of the End Time, held by Obadiah, depicted a similar world espoused by Islamic figures of Shi'i sectarian movements. Later, in August 1164, the fourth ruler of Alamut, Hasan II, proclaimed the *qiyāma*, or Resurrection, which heralded the awaited Last Day when all would be judged and consigned forever to Paradise or Hell. This manifestation would be unveiled in the person of the imam or *Mahdī*. Obadiah could therefore be seen to be familiar with, or echo, Ismaili and Muslim accounts of the appearance of a messiah, as everybody fed off the same corpus of stories and sources. Evidence from documents found in the Geniza indicates that some Jewish sages read books of Shi'i Islam.[24]

Obadiah's anticipation of this great life-and-death struggle for world supremacy is paralleled in Saadia's account by the gathering of the people in Palestine from all parts of the world: now, the Temple will be rebuilt in accordance with Ezekiel's detailed description of the restoration of Zion. Seemingly transported in an ecstatic trance to Jerusalem from his exile in Babylon, Ezekiel gives a vision of the new Jerusalem and the rebuilt temple complex. (Ezekiel 40). As Saadia proclaimed, 'Then the light of God's presence will appear shining upon the Temple with such brilliance that all the lights will become faint or dim in comparison'.[25] However, we find no further evidence of Obadiah the Proselyte heading to Jerusalem as he proceeded from his meeting in Bāniyās. With these thoughts of the End Times in his mind, he was now following a path, it would seem, via Tyre, to Egypt.

---

22   Hillenbrand, *Crusades*, pp.141, 149; Robert Irwin, 'Islam and the Crusades, 1096–1699', in J. Riley-Smith (ed.), *The Oxford Illustrated History of the Crusades* (Oxford: Oxford University Press, 1995), p.223.
23   Irwin, 'Islam and the Crusades', pp.217–18; Goitein, *MS*, vol. 5, p.404.
24   Goitein, *MS*, vol. 5, p.399; Farhad Daftary, *The Assassin Legends: Myths of the Isma'ilis* (London: I. B. Tauris, 2011), pp.40–41, for Hassan II and proclamation of the Resurrection.
25   Rosenblatt (trans.), *Book of Beliefs*, p.310.

Chapter 8

The Gift of the Nile

The city that Obadiah reached around the year 1121 was at this time the imposing capital of a most ancient land and civilisation that had witnessed many empires, long preceding the Arabs and their arrival. This latest manifestation of a principal urban centre in Egypt, however, reflected a pattern that had been adopted after other early Arab conquests. The Caliph Umar ibn al-Khattāb (634–644) had decreed that Muslims should not disperse through the conquered lands, settling as proprietors or farmers, but establish Muslim cities known as *amṣār* (sing. *miṣr*), signifying garrison settlements of soldiers. This Arabic term '*miṣr*' was eventually also applied generally to signify the land of Egypt. Muslims were thereby meant to draw revenues and supplies from the conquered population and become a minority tax-consuming class, a standing army retaining their distinctiveness, religion and culture. Not long before, Kufa and Basra had been established in the Middle East in this manner: now, in Egypt, this was also to be the story. The aim of creating a separate caste of conquerors, paid from the local revenues of the conquered, did not survive for long, but it was what initially occurred on the banks of the Nile. The back story of the founding of Fustāt is as follows: in 642 CE, General Amr ibn al-'As had laid siege to the Byzantine fortress of Babylon, overlooking the Nile.[1] A pre-Roman fortress had already been constructed on this site centuries earlier by Nebuchadnezzar, after his conquest of Egypt, and named after his own Mesopotamian city of Babylon.[2] The capture in 642 CE of both the fortress and its surrounding area then provided the space for the foundation of the future great settlement of Fustāt. The name, al-Fustāt, is said to derive from the Greek word '*fossaton*', meaning a moat – since a moat connected with the location of the fortress. More recent archaeology points to a canal that entered the fortress camp here from the Nile running back to the Red Sea: an anticipation of the Suez Canal. This was probably linked to the waterway constructed by the Roman Emperor Trajan, the *Amnis Trajanus*, around the year 112 CE, connecting Babylon via Bubastis to the Red Sea.

---

1   Hugh Kennedy, *The Great Arab Conquests: How the Spread of Islam Changed the World We Live In* (Philadelphia: De Capo Press, 2007), pp.160–65.

2   Peter Sheehan, 'The Roman Fortifications', in P. Lambert (ed.), *Fortifications and the Synagogue: The Fortress of Babylon and the Ben Ezra Synagogue, Cairo* (Montreal: Canadian Centre for Architecture, 1994), p.58.

Another story, told in the early chronicles, is somewhat more colourful. According to this account, the name 'Fustāt' came about after a dove laid an egg on the tent of the Muslim general, who, upon his return from battle, declared that the nest was a sign from God. The first city, it was claimed, arose around this tent and the dove, and the name was thus etymologically linked to the word for tent in Arabic.[3] Fustāt may indeed have started as a garrison city of soldiers and their families, but it was to grow in later centuries into an enormous conurbation. The rise of this city eclipsed Alexandria, founded by the Greeks at the mouth of the Nile: it was a return to the ancient geography of the Pharaohs, where nearby Memphis had once been the capital.

Panorama of the city

These modest and haphazard beginnings were to have a spectacular future. The small encampment below the Nile delta that began in 642 as a governorate of the Umayyad Caliphate gradually shifted north by dynastic expansion to the new walled city of al-Qāhira (the 'Victorious'), to become Cairo, a city established in 969 by the Fatimids as an imperial enclave. The Fatimid period (910–1171) was the golden age of the Isma'ili movement. This regime, having ruled over Morocco, Algeria and Tunisia, had become the master of Egypt and ushered in a new caliphate, announcing the Fatimid rise to power that presided over the consolidation of Egypt into a new entity. There followed over time a large influx of emigrants from the Maghreb countries, including a sizeable number of Jews, many of them wealthy merchants. Fustāt certainly continued as a thriving centre of population and commerce until 1168 or thereabouts, when some areas were burned down on the orders of Vizier Shawār to impede a threatened crusader invasion. Nonetheless, at the time of Obadiah's arrival in the 1120s, Fustāt was still at its apogee. Although the growing success of al-Qāhira meant that the new foundation increasingly became a government centre and the residence of the ruling political elite, an appreciable amount of goods, manufacture and commerce still remained in the hands of merchants and traders in Fustāt. Al-Muqaddasī, the chronicler from Jerusalem, gave a famous description of the city towards the end of the tenth century when he termed it '… a metropolis in every sense of the word …' – to him, it seemed a wonder, possessing enormous political as well as commercial power. He declared that it had superseded Baghdad and was '… the glory of Islam, and is the marketplace of all mankind'. The size of the population more closely matched that of Baghdad, where Obadiah had resided for a decade or more before emigrating to this new metropolis. Ibn Hawkal, in an earlier view, described open streets, splendid gardens and elegant urban outskirts. It was, he said, a city one-third the size of Baghdad that extended some three to four miles along the river: one aspect that particularly struck him were the apartment blocks between four and seven floors high, some with roof gardens irrigated by water wheels

---

3   Amitav Ghosh, *In an Antique Land* (London: Penguin, 2012), pp.36–37.

with water drawn from the Nile. Al-Muqaddasī compared these tall edifices to lighthouses, seemingly giving off a bright radiance from their central areas. Finally, he also marvelled at the quantity of ships on the river, ceaselessly coming and going with trade, perhaps guided safely by the lights of these tall buildings. He added that Cairo had grown to join Fustāt, forming a vast metropolis in size and prosperity.[4] Other descriptions mention the extreme heat and lack of rainfall only alleviated by the flooding of the Nile during the month of Elul (August–September) providing water and a thick carpet of silt and topsoil for abundant crops, together with a rich supply of fish for the markets. A large octagonal marble column marked the height reached by the annual flood up to a measure of 16 cubits, a level that could proclaim a year of plenty with well-stocked warehouses: food supplies reflected the delicate ecological balance of the Nile. The extent covered by the annual flooding of waters was said to irrigate the land to a distance of 15 days' journey. Like a stock market index, the annual fortunes of Fustāt rose and fell, recorded by the height attained on the column. The so-called 'Nilometer', rebuilt in 861, stood on the edge of Rawda (al-Jazīra), the island in the heart of the city. Benjamin of Tudela gave some of these details when visiting Fustāt in the late 1160s.[5]

A century before Benjamin's arrival, the Nilometer had plummeted to dire levels of 13 and 14 cubits: this was the harbinger of disastrous drought and famine that started in 1065. Such times of disruption, poverty and violence seemed to presage the fragmentation of the Fatimid Empire. Although Fustāt continued to prosper somewhat, it had increasingly lost out to neighbouring Cairo. The great days of Fustāt were finally brought to an end with the threatened invasion of Egypt by Amalric, king of Jerusalem, who, in November 1168, was stopped from entering Cairo by a huge fire ignited in Fustāt to halt his attack. The enormous fire, started by 20,000 barrels of naphtha and 10,000 lighted torches, is said to have lasted 54 days.[6] Whatever the true extent of this conflagration, the great days of the Fatimid ascendancy had passed. Even if the old city was rebuilt in part, some of its areas were still said to be in ruins, according to Benjamin of Tudela.[7] This was the aspect presented by old Fustāt half a century after Obadiah's arrival.

Jewish communities in Fustāt

The Jewish population of Fustāt, though diverse, generally comprised two main communities: Rabbanites (divided into Palestinian and Babylonian) and Karaites. These two main groups seem to have intermarried and lived together without incident despite bitter theological disputes that had frequently taken place earlier,

---

4   Al-Muqaddasī and Collins (trans.), *Best Divisions*, pp.166–67; J. H. Kramers and G. Wiet (trans), *Ibn Hawkal. Configuration de la Terre (Kitab Surat al-Ard)* (Paris: Editions G. P. Maisonneuve & Larose, 1964), vol. 1, pp.144–45.
5   Adler (trans.), *Itinerary*, p.72.
6   Maalouf, *Crusades*, pp.168–69.
7   Adler (trans.), *Itinerary*, p.73.

especially in Palestine. A decree issued by the Fatimid caliph of Cairo arose out of a long-standing quarrel that, in 1024, had initially proclaimed a deed of protection for the Karaites, one that was initially disregarded by the Rabbanite chiefs. Now, the caliph stated that neither of the two denominations should interfere with the affairs of the other. A closer examination of the Geniza sources shows that any estrangement or complete break was not evident between the two communities and that Rabbanites and Karaites maintained contact in their writings and daily lives.

A tradition situated around 882 says that the Jews of Fustāt acquired a church from the Coptic patriarch Michael III and converted it into a synagogue, which was subsequently named in honour of the scribe Ezra and from then on became the main synagogue of the Jerusalem/Palestinian community. An alternative view held that the synagogue of the Palestinians represented the original pre-Islamic Jewish place of worship. Here, in this Ben Ezra synagogue, the fragments of Obadiah's account that form the source of this story would be discovered centuries later.[8]

But matters, as we have suggested, were not always tranquil between Rabbanite and Karaite: Rabbanites had attempted to excommunicate the Karaites in 1029 as 'eaters of meat with milk' – one example of many such earlier incidents. Something of this antagonism had surfaced in the curious exchange between Obadiah and the Karaite pretender in 1121, when Solomon ha-Kohen had told the Norman proselyte of the peculiar diet that gave him messianic credentials. Now, in more peaceful times, Karaites resided mostly in the Al-Mamsusa quarter of Fustāt on the eastern side of Qasr al-Sham, also a Jewish area where a majority of the two large communities lived. At the time of Obadiah's residence, friendly relations seemed to prevail between leading families belonging to the two denominations.[9] With the Fatimid arrival in 969, the Jews of Egypt gained a sizeable measure of social and economic prosperity. The Fatimids, being a Shi'i Ismaili sect, preferred to deal with Jews and Christians rather than depend on members of the Sunni majority. The wealthy merchants, many of whom were Karaites, also achieved prominence under the Fatimids in Egypt. Two of the most important members of the Tustari family, originally hailing from Khūzistān, who had migrated to the Maghrib, were appointed after a generation as heads over the entire Jewish community and were known by the title raīs al-yahūd. During the Fatimid period, Egypt was developing into one of the most prosperous commercial centres in the Mediterranean, provoking a surge in emigration from Babylonia and adjacent regions and the consequent growth of the Babylonian community in Fustāt, including other arrivals from Christian lands of Byzantium and Europe. Many also came from the Maghrib, like the Tustari, who had followed the Fatimids into Egypt. These migrations, combined with the rise of

---

8   Charles Le Quesne, 'The Synagogue', in P. Lambert (ed.), *Fortifications and the Synagogue: The Fortress of Babylon and the Ben Ezra Synagogue, Cairo* (Montreal: Canadian Centre for Architecture, 1994), p.80; Le Quesne, 'Descriptions', p.245, for Coptic view; Goitein, *MS*, vol. 2, p.148, sets out both sides.

9   Marina Rustow, *Heresy and the Politics of Community: The Jews of the Fatimid Caliphate* (Ithaca, NY: Cornell University Press, 2008), pp.347–49; S. D. Goitein, 'A Caliph's Decree in Favour of the Rabbinite Jews of Palestine', *JJS*, 5:3 (1954), pp.118–25.

the Fatimids, undermined the security and dominance of Iraq as a centre of international trade. It would appear that the persistent urban unrest in Baghdad contributed to the decline of the Jewish population in Iraq and a migration westward.

Another important family was represented by Joseph Ibn 'Awkal (970–1040), whose commercial organisation became very powerful over four generations.[10] He was a notable example of the recipient of the honorary title *alluf/resh kalla*. As a young man, he had served in the Academy at Pumbedita studying under Sherira *Gaon* and had later officiated as a representative of the Geonic centres in Fustāt. It reflects the prominent position and honours given to such business figures, obtained as a reward for their donations and charity work. As head of the family firm based in Fustāt, Joseph not only presided over the gem-trading exchange but also handled many different commodities including spices, aromatics, medicines and precious metals. The family probably came originally from Babylonia but settled in Egypt like so many merchants and traders in the move westward. Their imports were mostly from their extensive Indian Ocean trade: Fustāt became the hub for commerce between the Indian Ocean and the Mediterranean, but the company also traded with Tunisia and Sicily. All this was accentuated in the opening years of the eleventh century, after the Fatimid rise to power had witnessed the consolidation of Egypt, Tunisia and Sicily under one government, bringing about a shift in economic power to Fustāt. These developments mirrored a sustained economic boom, accompanied by a substantial population rise all over Europe and the Mediterranean, which is reflected in the stories of these merchant families.[11]

Streets, bazaars and squares also bore the names of different trades. This suggests that people who engaged in different occupations tended to live or work together, although this is not certain. There were nonetheless streets named after activities: Alchemist, Cobbler or Leather-Bottle Maker, for example. One street was called the 'Street of the Jews'. Other descriptions also added that the streets were narrow and winding with many that were cul-de-sacs. There were markets that were also divided according to the crafts or goods they dealt in, such as the market for fishmongers, the market for the wool merchants and the market for the Jews.

The heart of the Jewish presence in the old city, where Obadiah must have resided, consisted in the two closely connected synagogues on the southern corner of the old fortress of Babylon. One street, known as the Street of the Two Synagogues, also called the Street of the Poor, or Dead End Street, bisected the courtyards of the Babylonian and Palestinian synagogues. The political and institutional influence of the community was promoted through the Great Synagogue of al-Fustāt

---

10 Elinoar Bareket, *Fustāt on the Nile: The Jewish Elite in Medieval Egypt* (Leiden: Brill, 1999), pp.5–13.
11 S. D. Goitein, *Letters of Medieval Jewish Traders* (Princeton: Princeton University Press, 1973), pp.26–34; Chris Wickham, *The Inheritance of Rome: A History of Europe from 400 to 1000* (London: Penguin, 2009), pp.365–68; Wickham, *Medieval*, pp.121–40; Phillip I. Lieberman, 'Demography and Migrations', in P. I. Lieberman (ed.), *The Cambridge History of Judaism: Jews in the Medieval Islamic World* (Cambridge: Cambridge University Press, 2021), vol. 5, pp.383–86, for westward migration.

– the Palestinian synagogue, *Kanīsat al-Shāmiyīn*, also known as the Ben Ezra synagogue of our story. The prosperity of the community can be seen reflected in the documents and the dated copies of books from the tenth and eleventh centuries, while later fragments reflect the economic and spiritual decline of the immediate neighbourhood from times of greater wealth. At the outset of the tenth century, the synagogue was surrounded by homes of prosperous Jews. Later, by the second half of eleventh century, established members of the Jewish community moved north, away from this densely populated area to the more spacious and up-market neighbourhoods of Cairo. Those who remained were not only the poorer inhabitants but also those religious leaders of al-Fustāt who were still linked to the synagogue of Palestine. Even if the neighbourhood was sinking into lower economic levels, new immigrants continued arriving throughout the course of the twelfth century. Some were artisans, such as glassmakers and perfumers, who set up workshops that created unhealthy conditions for residents. This exacerbated the drift to rentals for poorer tenants. Even so, a house adjacent to the fortress wall and outside it – the official house of the *Nagid* – had a private passage leading to the courtyard of the Palestinian synagogue. This was the home of the head of the Jewish community. His residence in Fustāt and not in Cairo signals the abiding importance of the Fustāt synagogue to the Jewish community.[12]

None of this can help to incontrovertibly pinpoint Obadiah to any exact part of the Jewish neighbourhood of this teeming and crowded old city, and we are led to extrapolate details of his work and life from suggestive nuggets of information about him gathered from Geniza fragments and other texts that have come to light. These other findings compensate for the loss, after 1121, of passages from the *Autobiography* as a source: they furnish tantalising facts about his life, work and past experiences in Egypt that might have extended for at least two decades or more into the early or late 1140s. The inferences drawn from these examples, certain up to a point, serve to illuminate his life and work in his later years, stopping short from straying into any excessive or imagined depiction regarding the Norman proselyte. Even so, one has to be prepared to be sidetracked and follow paths that throw up 'hidden perspectives and retrospectives' departing from the straight and narrow and pursue a more digressive approach.[13]

Obadiah and his marriage

A seventeenth-century text of Crimean origin picks up a surprising reference to Obadiah. The unexpected mention of the Norman proselyte in a document over a century after his life attests to his enduring name. The contents refer to a commentary by one Rabbi Shemaria b. Elijah Jacob Ikriti (1275–1355), a Rabbanite scholar

---

12 Bareket, *Fustāt on the Nile*, pp.27–30; Ben-Sasson, 'Medieval Period', pp.204–10.
13 Richard Holmes, *Sidetracks: Explorations of a Romantic Biographer* (London: Vintage, 2001), p.ix, 'hidden perspectives and retrospectives in autobiography'.

who was also accepted by the Karaites. Ikriti was later attached to the court of Naples, devoting his time to Biblical studies and commentary, and must have been familiar with the life of Obadiah because of his known connection with Norman Italy and the persistence of his memory. Rabbi Shemaria cited a response given by an unidentified *gaon* to a question posed by one Rabbi Obadiah, clearly mentioned, to a verse of Proverbs 19:14: 'Houses and riches are the inheritance of fathers: and a prudent wife is from the Lord'. The response also refers to Deuteronomy 20:7, 'And what man is there that hath betrothed a wife, and hath not taken her? Let him go and return unto his house, lest he die in the battle, and another man take her'. Why was this matter raised? The questioner from this surviving document appears undoubtedly to have been Obadiah, but it is not clear who the respondent to his enquiry was. Nor is it stated if this took place in Baghdad or Egypt, although the context would point to the latter. From the tone of the query, Obadiah appears to have been recently married, or else concerned or fearful about the deferment of his impending marriage, perhaps because he still was expecting to depart to fight in the wars of the Last Days. Jewish law allowed for deferment for up to one year.[14]

We could also surmise that this new or intended wife was financially well endowed and that Obadiah had 'married up' above his station, to an intelligent, richer wife with significant assets. Perhaps his Norman background of noble ancestry in Italy counted for something, as well as his learning. That this is not irrelevant is brought out by the conditions set by a bride in one instance: in 1047, in Fustāt, Fa'aiza, the daughter of Solomon, stated in her marriage contract (*ketubah*) that the bridegroom, Tuvia, son of Eli, must declare, amongst other things, that he 'will not leave Fustāt, Egypt, to travel abroad, unless she specifically agrees'. This pre-nuptial style agreement was common and could cover many subjects, such as the right of the woman to demand a divorce or protect her inheritance rights.[15] The concern that was uppermost in the mind of the bride and her family was that the woman should be provided with security in case of divorce or widowhood and be no worse off financially than when she entered marriage. Such sensitive questions, or some of them, might have been in Obadiah's mind as he asked the question of the *gaon*. The inference of his marital status is strongly reinforced by another fragment found in the Bodleian Library, which may have been part of a set of liturgical poems – a subject that we cover in more detail later. The colophon of this text records the fact that one Elijah, named as the son of Obadiah, was its copyist. The examination of the script shows that the shape of the handwriting is similar to that of Obadiah's. The script can be compared with other examples known to be that of the Norman proselyte, particularly the writing in the statement that gives the oft-mentioned date of his conversion in the end pages of a prayer book (*siddur*) and where he adds, in his own words, that this is recorded in

---

14   P. E. Miller, 'Rabbi Shemaria's Commentary on Proverbs 19:14', *JQR*, 73:2 (1982), pp.146–51; Mauro Perani, 'Una menzione di Obadiah il Proselito da Oppido Lucano in un commento a Proverbi 19,14 di Shemariah ben Elijah ben Jacob Ikriti', *Sefer Yuhasin: Rivista per la storia degli Ebrei nell'Italia Meridionale*, 7 (1991), pp.3–15.

15   Cambridge University Library (CUL): T-S 20.160: Legal Document; Reif, *Jewish Archive*, Illustration 43, pp.184–85, of this marriage contract.

his own handwriting.[16] Other examples of accounts from scribes found in the Geniza show that such people seem to have transmitted their art of writing to their descendants even more frequently than was the rule in other trades. Their writing skill and style was their most valuable asset, a precious gift to be inherited by their children. The details of a person's handwriting were like a DNA trace revealing an identity, or, as in this case, even a family connection. Many Jews held prominent positions at the Fatimid court as scribes (*Sofer*), which were passed on from one generation to another.

A notable example of this custom was Yefet b. David, one of the best-known scribes of eleventh-century Fustāt, whose father was the court scribe and whose grandfather Shekhania referred to himself as *safra* ('scribe' in Aramaic). The family had emigrated from Palestine and continued their work in Egypt, proudly memorialising their heritage. Obadiah had followed the same pattern of westward migration to Egypt, establishing himself in a new profession, perhaps as a scribe, and setting up a trade that would be taken up by his son. The details of such families repeat the same movement from parts of the Levant to the growing attraction of Fustāt, free from crusader control. During the eleventh century, a large contingent of Jews had already been settled there for generations and had been joined by further migrants. It is particularly noteworthy that, in the colophon of books, it is not uncommon to find the copyist mentioning his forefathers for several generations, many of whom originated elsewhere. The movement of proselytes fleeing their European places of birth and arriving in the Islamic world may have been considerable. It is estimated that Obadiah formed part of a total of 15,000 such men and women between 1000 and 1200 CE. This estimate could be greater.[17]

Similar writing styles of father and son are traceable, especially if the son was taught by the father, as appears to be the case in the example mentioned above, which we now turn to and which links Obadiah the father and Elijah the son. The original Hebrew has no punctuation. The tone of prayer and encouragement suggest a liturgical poem:

> Whatever was done in the name of the young servant
> The smallest (youngest) of pupils
> Elijah of Rabbi Obadiah the proselyte
> Be strong and we shall be strengthened
> And the writer of this shall be my Holy Seed
> Amen forever and may it be so
> I am a boy and lacking learning
> Teach me perhaps

---

16 Golb (trans.), 'Autograph Memoirs', Document I: Cincinnati, MS Hebrew Union College Genizah Collection no. 8 (prayerbook fragment); Bodleian Library (BoL): MS. Heb. f. 99, p. 36a (Elijah); A. Scheiber, 'Der normannische Proselyt Obadja, der Aufzeichner der erstern hebräischen Melodie', *Studia Musicologica Academiae Scientiarum Hungaricae*, 8:1/4 (1966), pp.178–80, for Elijah text and Figure 4 illustration.

17 Bareket, *Fustāt on the Nile*, pp.160–76, Yefet b. David; Goitein, *MS*, vol. 2, p.240, for family writing styles; Golb, *Jewish Proselytism*, p.36, for proselyte numbers.

That Obadiah is referred to as a rabbi suggests that, after a few years of marriage and the fathering of a family, he gained some status and regard as a scribe – or even as a cantor, as will be examined shortly. The term 'rabbi' in Geniza documents could sometimes also designate a scholar whose opinions or work had acquired some authority. This son, named as Elijah, perhaps no more than a youngster, seeks instruction from his father. It is not improbable that there were other children, but, in all these assertions, we are constrained when it comes to pinpointing time and place. Certainly, none of this can be placed at any period prior to 1121 CE covered by the *Autobiography*. These details can reasonably be assigned to his life in Egypt. The contents of this fragment point to the strong possibility that Obadiah took up or continued some manner of work related to that of a cantor or a scribe.

Cantor and scribe

The records of the Geniza show that the office of cantor, or *hazzan*, was important in the community and could comprise other tasks. The prominence of music, melody and chanting in the service encouraged the rise of the professional cantor, and, during the eleventh and twelfth centuries, they became noteworthy in the Egyptian capital. A query addressed to Maimonides at this time proves that several cantors appeared at the same time during a Sabbath service.[18] The skills required were many, and more established cantors were also expected to compose appropriate poetical additions to the service, so they sometimes added their own melodies. In one account given by Nathan the Babylonian, the role of the cantor in Baghdad is described in some detail as leading the prayers and chanting the psalms, even delivering a sermon on the appointment of the exilarch. A highpoint of this service was the reading of the Torah, where the cantor took the Torah scroll from the Ark.[19]

The ornamental Ark, or *hēkhāl*, that housed the scrolls was at the back end of the synagogue, and facing this, in the centre of the synagogue's open space, was a raised platform known as the *bima*. Here, parts of the Torah were read, and prayers were recited by the cantor. In the Ben Ezra synagogue, which Obadiah must have attended, certain Sabbath ceremonies were conducted that were unique to the worshippers of the Palestinian rite, such as the ceremony known as *Sefer ha-Shir* (Book of Song), in which the Torah scrolls were promenaded. At the commencement of this ceremony, when the Ten Commandments were read, the singer stood on the *bima* facing the *hēkhāl* with the Torah scroll in his arms. Here, he recited the Commandments together with the people while standing upon the *bima*. Upon completion, the cantor descended the stone steps from the platform and returned the scrolls to the ark. Such might have been the actions of the cantor in the Ben Ezra synagogue of Fustāt.[20]

---

18 Goitein, *MS*, vol. 2, pp.219–20.
19 Stillman, *Jews of Arab Lands*, pp.272–74.
20 Ben-Sasson, 'Medieval Period', p.213.

In Fustāt, one could find cantors from all over the world, including Christian Europe, Muslim Spain and Persia. Foreign cantors appear regularly in the list of receivers of fees from the community. This description of cantors suggests that they were required to be linguists, with knowledge of other languages, further underlining a probable overseas provenance, and the nature of their office meant that their work could diversify into writing and scribal work. Many such documents that have come to light in the Geniza, written and co-signed by cantors from the eleventh to the thirteenth centuries, testify to this multitasking, where cantors turned their hand to other activities.

Some of these details just set out could certainly form a profile of Obadiah, originating from Italy whilst living in Egypt and attending the Ben Ezra synagogue, and this licenses us to propose that he engaged in areas covered by such work. The trade of a scribe would have led Obadiah to draw on his skills and develop activities he had begun in the synagogue in Baghdad in order to earn fees and better his professional standing. The *dayyānīm*, as cantors were also known, had regular functions at weddings and funerals and were paid for this work. Some cantors were community officials with direct links to the synagogue and lived in the synagogue compound, reminding us that Obadiah had done so when he started his Judaic education as an adult in Baghdad and was studying the Hebrew language.

Details of such remuneration are not known precisely, but many documents give differing accounts with amounts paid. Some cantors earned significant sums, and others barely scratched a living. One example can stand for many: the cantor and scribe Hillel b. Eli evidences these ups and downs. He was in service from 1066 to 1108, with some of his letters describing a well-regarded position and others complaining of neglect and fearful of the tax collector. According to records found in the Geniza, this Hillel b. Eli was the father-in-law of Halfōn ha-Levi, one the most productive scribes, with documents that can be dated from 1100 to 1138.[21]

More information can be gleaned about scribes and copyists, as a good script constituted a precious and remunerative skill. Some were government clerks known as a *katib*, a term for a civil servant. Generally, these were proficient in Arabic script for official documents. What we know about Obadiah does not preclude him from this, but the evidence we do have has him writing in a distinctive Hebrew calligraphy that has made it possible to pinpoint other examples of his writing, even, as we have just seen, when the style has passed to his son Elijah.

In this particular case, Obadiah could have worked as a copyist for private correspondence or as a copyist of books either for himself or for third parties. Here, as previously mentioned, the term for someone carrying out this activity was a *sōfer*, but there was also a *nāsikh*, a more specialised expert who copied out biblical texts. These two terms, especially the latter, were connected to an intimate knowledge of religious and liturgical law. This had a value in the community, and copyists were paid for their services. Whether Obadiah copied for himself or was paid to do so by others, a fragment of a copy made by him of the Prophetic lessons (*Haftaroth*)

---

21   Goitein, *MS*, vol. 2, pp.220–24.

has been found, and this has encouraged Alexander Scheiber, who discovered the fragment, to suggest that, in his last years, Obadiah turned into an indefatigable scribe and writer of Hebrew texts, copying the most essential religious books for his library. Such an imagined context has not been confirmed by any further findings, but it may well be so.[22] The discovered fragment of *Sefer Haftaroth* refers to a series of extracts that were publicly read or chanted in the synagogue as part of the service, following the Torah reading, on each Sabbath and other festivals. This also buttresses the argument that Obadiah must have copied it for the synagogue service as part of his professional work as a cantor for which he would have been paid.

What languages did Obadiah speak or read? Evidence reinforces what is already known: that the *Autobiography* survives in an elegant and classical Hebrew, the language used for biblical texts, prayers and liturgical poetry as well as for other religious purposes in the Jewish community. Obadiah probably knew and spoke Arabic and possessed some reading knowledge of Aramaic, and he certainly preserved his Latin from the early days. More generally, perhaps around half the documents found in the Cairo Geniza are written in Judaeo-Arabic – Arabic written in Hebrew characters. Aramaic had a largely scholarly purpose, used chiefly in Jewish religious law and commentary on the Talmud. But Obadiah had learnt and perfected his Hebrew during the years of study in Baghdad.[23] The Jews who have left us the records of their daily life in the Geniza mostly wrote as they spoke, in the Arab vernacular of their region, interspersed with Jewish words. In short, from the multitude of evidence drawn from these findings, we know that the Norman proselyte remained close to these worlds of writing, copying and cantillation in various forms, probably establishing his position in the Jewish community and earning a living from this work. As we shall see, his most original language came to be seen as a bridge between the music and the notation he learned in Italy and he now remembered in Fustāt, more than 20 years later.

22 Goitein, *MS*, vol. 2, pp.228–31; Bareket, *Fustāt on the Nile*, pp.63–64; Scheiber, 'Der normannische Proselyt Obadja', p.178: ENA. 3579 *Sefer Haftaroth* fragment.
23 Goitein, *MS*, vol. 1, pp.14–15; Reif, *Jewish Archive*, pp.210–24.

Chapter 9

The Sound of Music

Augustine's *Confessions*, an autobiographical work of great influence in the early Christian world and beyond that saw the light in the first year of the fifth century, speaks of the attractions of the sung Psalter as a sensual gratification: 'I have no wish to exclude from my ears, and from the ears of the Church as well, all the melody of these lovely chants to which the Psalms of David are habitually sung'.[1] Augustine, however, seemed to adopt a moral stance, concerned that the attractiveness of the music and the melodies might detract from his understanding of the true meaning of the words of the Psalms. He worried that he was at times more moved by the singing than by the religious import of what was sung. Seven hundred years later, the enduring sounds of these musical forms remained a sensual gratification that had equally filled Obadiah's ears and mind in those earlier times spent in a Benedictine monastery.

We should remind ourselves of the routine governed by the Rule of Benedict. In the daily life of the monastery, a prescribed order of events began at two o'clock in the morning when the brothers arose to celebrate Matins. During the course of the day, they attended eight services. These generally began with an invitationary (a call to worship) and a hymn, followed by three to six psalms or canticles, three to four readings from the Gospel, a responsory and, on Sundays and feast days, a mass. The central part of these services was the chanting of psalms, and Benedict's rule devoted no less than nine chapters to the order and manner in which these were to be sung throughout the year. These instructions were very precise, with the result that the book of 150 psalms was chanted in its entirety every week, beginning afresh on Sunday at Matins. We cannot ignore the centrality of this day and night experienced by Obadiah. The music and words of the psalms arising from this perpetual cycle of repetition, together with the chants and responses, became hardwired for all time into the memory of Johannes of Oppido – now Obadiah the scribe and cantor – and were to resurface years later in his work in a most striking manner. But, before we hasten to describe such coming together of Jewish and Christian musical forms in the mind of the Norman proselyte, we must briefly set out the historical development of the forms of singing in Jewish liturgy prevailing in the eleventh century.

---

1   R. S. Pine-Coffin (trans.), *Saint Augustine Confessions* (London: Penguin, 1961), Book 10, Chapter 33, p.231.

The hymn form in Jewish liturgy did not continue unchanged from ancient Judaism: it was said by some to have been restored back into the Jewish service – possibly due in part to the success of early Christian church music – because the lack of singing after the demise of the Second Temple in 70 CE had been keenly felt by Jewish attendees of the synagogue, now mindful of the new prominence of early Christianity in the following centuries.[2] Even if the process is debated and not entirely clear, it seems evident that fresh forms of music and poetry were reinserted at some later date into the synagogue service. The word 'psalm' is a translation via the Greek of the Hebrew '*miznor*', denoting a song performed to musical accompaniment. The Hebrew word for the entire collection of psalms is '*Tehillim*' (Praises), a noun derived from a verb frequently used by psalmists, '*hallel*' (to praise), and retained in the word '*hallelujah*' (praise the Lord). Certainly, there had been praise, music, chanting and responses associated with the daily singing of the psalms in the Temple, but, after its destruction, this music almost disappeared altogether with the Levites, the trained singers who had cultivated it. With regard to the origins of the music, it is even possible that singing and chanting of the psalms might have started outside the original Jerusalem Temple, only later making an appearance therein. It seems that it was not till the Second Temple period that hymns and song took on a central role. In 180 BCE, Ben Sira described King David, who 'established harp-singers before the altar, also to make sweet melodies with their singing sounds'. In his *Antiquities of the Jews*, Josephus echoed this, repeating that David promulgated the custom of hymns sung by the Levites. A notable example is in Psalms 120–134, each of which bears the superscription 'a song of ascents', signifying a ceremony held during the days of *Sukkot* (Feast of Booths). The main aspect of the festival involved the waving in the Temple of agricultural produce kept in a booth rather than at home. This festival in the early autumn marked the completion of the agricultural year and was probably the best attended of the pilgrim feasts, perhaps because, with the gathering of the harvest, it was easier for farmers to leave their fields. This 'song of ascents' alluded to the 15 steps of the Temple that went down from the court of Israel to the court of the women, as described in the tractate Sukkah 5:4: 'And the Levites accompanied them with harps, lyres, cymbals and musical instruments without number – on the fifteen steps that go down from the court of Israel to the court of the women, corresponding to the fifteen Songs of Ascent in [the Book of] Psalms, on which the Levites would stand and recite in song.'[3] All this changed after the Temple's destruction.

---

2   Eric Werner, *The Sacred Bridge: The Interdependence of Liturgy and Music in Synagogue and Church during the First Millennium* (New York: Columbia University Press, 1959), pp.234–37.

3   Gary A. Rendsburg, 'The Psalms as Hymns in the Temple of Jerusalem', in J. H. Charlesworth (ed.), *Jesus and Temple: Textual and Archaeological Explorations* (Minneapolis: Fortress Press, 2014), pp.106–12, here noting Ben Sira, Josephus and the 15 Songs of Ascent; festival of Sukkot, Goodman, *History of Judaism*, pp.48–50; John A. Smith, *Music in Ancient Judaism and Early Christianity* (Burlington: Ashgate, 2011), pp.77–82; Alter, 'Characteristics', pp.611–24, for etymology of psalm and praise.

Initially, after this removal of music from Jewish worship, synagogue services were centred on intimate prayer that replaced the pomp of the Temple's lost music after the year 70 CE. Additionally, in the diaspora, synagogue services found themselves restricted by Christian authorities as to the practice of praying. In the case of the Babylonian Jews, ruled by Persia prior to the arrival of the Muslims, public Jewish prayer was prohibited, so, around the fifth century CE, the Jews in Palestine began inserting poems that they added to passages from their official prayers.[4] Melodies, known as *piyyutim*, were then composed for these poems, which were sung in the synagogues. When the Persians rebuked them for contravening the ban on public prayer, the Jews replied they were not praying but merely making music. This story, true or not, but frequently told, was also recorded by Samuel Maghribī, that same Jewish scholar spoken of earlier, who – after converting to Islam – had told of the messianic movement witnessed by Obadiah in the twelfth century and recorded in his *Autobiography*. Maghribī, in his book *Silencing of the Jews*, had called these musical forms *al-hizana* (songs), the Arabised word for the Hebrew '*hazamut*', a cantorial chant. Today, there is no firm consensus among scholars as to the reasons that led to the rise of *piyyūt*, and the medieval view that the singing was invented as a subterfuge to elude religious persecution is not generally held, although Maghribī, who proffered this account, was a near contemporary of Obadiah.[5]

Whatever the reason, after the arrival of the Arabs and Islam in 636–650 CE, Jewish liturgy, now free of Persian restrictions according to Maghribī's story, never returned to the simple prayers bereft of music. The synagogue ceremony became the object of a priestly resurgence with such melodious compositions harking back to the vanished ceremony of the Temple. At the outset, there was strenuous resistance to this musical initiative, whipped up by the rabbis and sages as being of non-scriptural origin and therefore viewed as a degradation of the integrity of the service: a blasphemy in some cases. The insertion of these poems and music was initially even questioned by Maimonides. But, in time, the poetical segments known as *piyyūt* (pl *piyyutim*) added wonderful music and melody to the liturgy, winning the affection of Jewish worshippers and restored an imagined link, however distant, with the lost glories of the Temple. The word given to these liturgical poems was said to be derived from the Greek term '*poiēt(ēs)*' and now went on to become a mainstay of accepted religious worship.[6]

Fustāt, in the early twelfth century – Obadiah's time – was alive with cantors writing such liturgical offerings with both music and texts: wherever their origin, it seemed that congregations were demanding ever-new examples of musical content to enchant them at the synagogue. It seems probable from the evidence that Obadiah was one of those participating in this trend. Often, the *ḥazzān* was composer of

---

4   Goodman, *History of Judaism*, p.248.
5   Perlmann (ed. and trans.), *Silencing*, p.62; Goitein, *MS*, vol. 2, pp.159–61; 'subterfuge' challenged and new consensus in Ezra Fleischer, 'Piyyūt', in S. Safrai (ed.), *The Literature of the Sages: Second Part* (Philadelphia: Fortress Press, 2006), p.365.
6   Werner, *Sacred Bridge*, pp.237–44; Lassner (ed.), *Mediterranean Society*, pp.154–56, 216, on Maimonides and music.

both the *piyyūt* and the melody to which it had been set, or perhaps he was creating an adaptation from an existing model. Most times, the driving force was a quest for novelty and originality to evoke pleasure in the listener. Much of these considerations can now be ascribed to various examples of music produced by Obadiah that, centuries later, have been deemed to be highly original in the history of Jewish music.

A landmark in the notation of music

An item from the Cairo Geniza was initially observed to contain a previously unknown *piyyūt* inscribed in Hebrew characters and set to music with medieval neumatic notation on a four-line stave. Its adopted title was identified later according to the opening words '*mi 'al har Horev*' (Who stood upon Mount Horeb).[7] This poem with the notation remained a puzzle to music specialists from its finding and publication in 1921 until the 1960s, when two Jewish scholars independently recognised it to be written by none other than Obadiah the Norman Proselyte.[8] The fact that there was a melody discernible in a possible Italian or Gregorian style adapted to Hebrew poetry and notated in the twelfth century has accorded the Norman proselyte a singular place in afterlife, a 'watershed moment' in the development of Jewish musical history.[9]

In Europe, musical notations in the form of dots written in the open space above a text would remain for most of the tenth century the principal practical way of representing musical sound in writing. The word for these signs is derived from the word '*nota*', which came to be known as neumes. Such neumatic notation preceded the development of modern musical notation and involved the use of these notational 'dots' and other signs that provided for fixed singing or chanting of Christian liturgies or plainsong. One of the first incipient neume systems in the West is said to date from the late ninth century, found at the abbey of Sankt Gallen in Switzerland and promulgated in part by a monk named Notker, but such systems were also emerging in France and in Italy, where it would doubtless have been taught to Obadiah, in some form, in his Benedictine monastery. At first, scribes simply placed acute and grave accents above the text to show rises and falls in pitch. In time, these accents developed into neumes, signs indicating relative pitch by their high

---

7   Golb (trans.), 'Autograph Memoirs', Document XVIII: The Music of Obadiah, Song 1 (musical version and translation), pp.20–21, 24.
8   Norman Golb, 'Obadiah the Proselyte: Scribe of a Unique Twelfth-Century Manuscript Containing Lombardic Neumes', *Journal of Religion*, 45:2 (1965), pp.153–56; Alexander Scheiber, 'Obadiah the Norman Proselyte Notator of the First Known Hebrew Melody', *Tarbiẕ*, 34 (1965), pp.366–71.
9   Israel Adler, 'The Music Notations by Ovadiah the Norman Proselyte and Their Significance for the Study of Jewish Music', A. De Rosa and M. Perani (eds), *Giovanni-Ovadiah da Oppido, proselito, viaggiatore e musicista dell'Età normanna. Atti del convegno internazionale Oppido Lucano 28–30 marzo 2004* (Florence: Casa Editrice Giuntina, 2005), pp.207–17.

and low position. But, to begin with, the neumes only sketched the general contour of melodies without measuring the size of intervals.[10] Around 1000 CE, a line was introduced to indicate the tone. From there, it was but a short step to the musical staff. Obadiah's use of ruled lines in the examples found demonstrates, as we show later in the illustration, that he was conversant with an early form of the stave or staff notation, a set of lines above which such notes were written. The graphic mode was to create a system of lines with meaningful spaces between them, rendering it possible eventually to notate plainsong. The Norman may have been exposed to the work or, more likely, to the influence of the Benedictine monk and theorist Guido of Arezzo, active in the first years of the eleventh century, who developed this system of lines and spaces representing pitches defined by letters (clefs) and a technique of sight-singing initially based on the first syllables in each phrase of a hymn *ut, re, mi, fa, sol, la* – the crucial stepping-stone to today's musical notation – known as solmisation or solfeggio (today referred to as *do, re, mi, fa, sol, la, si, do*). The first three syllables, *do, re, mi*, became the title of the popular modern song sung in *The Sound of Music*, which tells the listening children how, with these syllables, 'you could sing most anything'. The earliest neumes had been simply signs placed above the text of a chant to indicate the ascent and descent of a melodic line. With this new notation system, singers could visualise the chant they were learning: together with the lines and clef signs indicating the exact pitch and size of the intervals, this provided an early musical score they were able to see and sing. Letters on the left-hand side of the page were a primitive clef that signalled the musical pitch right across the page along that line.[11]

Although all this has only been laid bare after the other circumstances of his life, the discovery has handed Obadiah a significant and much-debated prominence. The unearthing of a notated eastern, or perhaps European, chant by a twelfth-century Norman proselyte living in Egypt still remains the earliest such example in Jewish music. The liturgical poem mentioned earlier, *mi 'al har Horev*, celebrates the figure of Moses and his revelation on Mount Sinai and is probably linked to the feast of *Śimḥat Torah* that ends the annual cycle of the reading of the Pentateuch. Another musical fragment of some importance in Obadiah's work came to light at about the same time – spotted during the unending searches of fragments from the Geniza Collection at Cambridge.[12] *Barukh haggever* (blessed is the man who trusts in the Lord), followed by three verses from the Old Testament, is almost certainly a musical formula composed for the synagogue. The music also appears to have characteristics of Gregorian chant, recorded on clear musical stave lines ruled on one side of the

---

10   Susan Rankin, *Writing Sounds in Carolingian Europe: The Invention of Musical Notation* (Cambridge: Cambridge University Press, 2018), pp.157–62, 358–61 (for Sankt Gallen); Christopher Page, *The Christian West and Its Singers: The First Thousand Years* (New Haven, CT: Yale University Press, 2010), pp.358–59.
11   Anna J. Reisenweaver, 'Guido of Arezzo and His Influence on Music Learning', *Musical Offerings*, 3:1 (2012), pp.37–59; Page, *Christian West*, pp.443–64.
12   Golb (trans.), 'Autograph Memoirs', Document XVIII: The Music of Obadiah, Songs 2–3 (musical version and translation), pp.22–24.

document, with each line of the stave marked with Hebrew letters representing the clef. This example of Obadiah's music writing appears to be an early illustration of Guido of Arezzo's creation of a system of lines with meaningful spaces between them, making it possible to notate plainsong so that the melody could be read at sight from the script. Again, it demonstrates that Obadiah has so far provided the first known written musical settings in Jewish liturgical poetry. Even so, there is still an unfinished discourse amongst music scholars about the degree to which the Norman was responsible for their original composition. The other side of this fragment (*verso*) begins with the words '*Va'eda mah*' (that I might know), another liturgical poem set to music, of which there are so many in this period, where only the conclusion remains:

> That I might know, that I might know
> What to speak within the gates,
> What I should say, what I should say, and Thou shouldst answer —
>   Teach me!

The final *lammdeni* (teach me) is a supplication, a mode of entreaty, a common topic of the Psalms together with praise and thanksgiving. A good example is Psalm 25:4: 'Shew me thy ways, O Lord; teach me thy paths.' Others have been tempted to discern here an autobiographical reference by Obadiah to the abandonment of his former Christian life, asking God for instruction as to what he should say. However, the supplication mode was often emphasised in the sung liturgical poems during the synagogue service as a way to beg the Lord for help and protection, and this was probably the desired meaning at the end of the verses found in this fragment of Obadiah's work. The entire tone is also reminiscent of the extract cited earlier, which lays out the reference to Elijah, the son of Obadiah, again climaxing with the same heartfelt cry of a supplicant 'teach me' (*lammdeni*), when the son begs the father for instruction.

A third and final possible example of Obadiah's work in this area was brought to light by a discovery in the Geniza made up of two additional prayer book fragments, also *piyyutim*.[13] An acrostic set out in one of the poems – a frequent feature of these works – gives the name of Obadiah the Proselyte (*Ovadyah ger*). However, this manuscript find is not in his writing, even if it appears to proclaim his name as the writer or composer. But, returning to the other two folios of the manuscript mentioned earlier, containing notations in Obadiah's own handwriting, these illustrate that he carefully had to write mirror images – in reverse – of the neumes, in accordance with the right-to-left direction rendering of his Hebrew text. The hypothesis is that this writing, assured and elegant, points to his instruction, received years earlier in a monastery, reflecting late eleventh-century practice, before his move to the Levant in 1102. Because the script in these folios is identical to the writing in the frequently mentioned colophon – found in the all-important prayer book (*siddur*) fragment that he affirms he had written himself

---

13   Cambridge University Library (CUL): T-S NS 325: Legal document.

– these two liturgical poems in his own writing represent forensic evidence of neumatic notation arising from Obadiah's Christian schooling in this musical art in the late eleventh century. By the end of this century, one or more staff lines were being drawn on pages containing the music, normally with the dry point of the stylus: this was the commencement of the modern musical staff.

Some of these details, as we mentioned, can be clearly identified on the surviving examples associated with Obadiah's poems and melodies, shown in the two folios of musical scores.

Here, on one folio, the stave is marked with a hard point but is prominently rubricated (set out in red) on the other. The neumes are above the written text, placed at various distances from an imaginary line representing a given pitch, according to their placement to that line. Each line of the stave is marked with the Hebrew letters '*Alef*' to '*He*' on the right-hand side, representing the clef. The letters are on the right-hand side as the notations are in Hebrew running from right to left. As mentioned above, the example shown here for Obadiah has the lines ruled in red, and this rubrication suggests another link with Guido of Arezzo, who had recommended that the two lines with a semitone step beneath them, for *F* and *C*, be ruled in red and yellow ink respectively. This colour-coding appeared in Europe in later centuries and may have already been reflected indirectly at this earlier date in Obadiah's music notation.

In these two *piyyutim*, Obadiah's work can be said to show echoes of compositions of western monodic chant in the Middle Ages. It is still possible that they had been composed by others coming from the West carrying this know-how and who, like him, were seeking refuge from Christendom arising from conversion and persecution. However, they could also be pieces from a Gregorian source borrowed and adapted to a Hebrew text by the Norman proselyte himself. His background and schooling in southern Italy could argue for this. Given the frequency of foreign *hazzanim* (cantors) recorded in Egypt and the demand for this eagerly sought content for synagogue services, Obadiah might be seen to have possessed a prized skill: to record and transmit such melodies by his ability to write them down. Whether Obadiah was directly influenced by Guido of Arezzo is not known, but he was certainly partly educated into this larger process associated with him, a cutting-edge new technology that Obadiah would have carried with him in some early form to the East, possibly along with other converts. These ground-breaking features for music learning were well expressed by Guido in his own words: 'you may competently sing unheard chants as soon as you see them written down, or, hearing unwritten chants, you can immediately set them down in writing as well'.[14] In other words, musicians and singers were now able to sight-read music, rather than have to laboriously memorise the song or chant. The speed at which this historic step forward was taken is not entirely clear: it may not have yet been fully established at the time of Obadiah's presence in Egypt.

---

14   Guido of Arezzo, *Epistola ad Michahelem*, p.471, in A. J. Reisenweaver, 'Guido of Arezzo and His Influence on Music Learning', *Musical Offerings*, 3:1 (2012), p.46; Page, *Christian West*, pp.396–400 and 454–58 on Guido, p.455 for red and yellow ink colouring.

Nevertheless, this was the music milestone with which Obadiah was associated, even if the precise details are full of unknowns. All this may suggest that he was energetically participating in a vibrant music market, but the few unearthed examples of music in his own hand do not necessarily prove that they were his own work, only that he noted the music down. In the original discussion about these musical compositions, some musicologists affirmed that Obadiah could not have used a melody from his Christian past for any purpose linked to his new religion. This argument became somewhat convoluted, suggesting that Obadiah would not copy, imitate or even write his own or any music that he remembered from his Italian monastic past. It was implied that, even if the Norman composed the music and notated it, such music needed to derive from his new eastern Jewish experience to accord with his new faith. On the other hand, Obadiah could have heard melodies brought to the East by converted Jewish cantors like him from western Europe. The balance of opinion must also take into account that, although Obadiah had abandoned the Christian faith and embraced that of the Torah and Moses, he had not cast aside the sensuality and appeal of this earlier music. As some see it, the experiences of the Christian training in his youth remained with him, and the diverse musical scenario of Fustāt was an incentive, even a necessity, to bring forth new content and originality in order to gain a foothold in an important and profitable market, where others must have been doing the same thing.[15] He drew those excellently formed musical neumes 20 or 30 years later, displaying the power of his memory and the pragmatism to excel and stand out in his altered religious context. There was no betrayal of his new religious convictions if he made use of his expertise in music from the past. The skills he had acquired as a Christian were not ignored: they were put to good use. Obadiah remembered and produced music in the manner in which he had been proficient, in order to fashion a new status and position for himself in a twelfth-century Jewish community in Fatimid Egypt, where he had migrated.

All this underlines what is abundantly clear, that the Norman proselyte wrote his *Autobiography* in the last part of his life as a recollection, remembering, in the 1120s or later, what had taken place years earlier. Such a perspective means that he had made a selection of experiences that had stayed with him as a strong memory. Life is always remembered retrospectively, and this looking back can constitute the kernel of this story, clarifying the emotional context of what were viewed by Obadiah as salient and life-changing moments and why these were remembered. One such recollection can be hazarded to be a mention of some verses from the Old Testament Book of Joel.

---

15   Golb, 'Music of Obadiah', pp.48–55, is an important discussion about the origin of Obadiah's music as to Western or Eastern provenance. See also Israel Adler, 'Les chants synagogaux notés au XII siècle (ca 1103–1150) par Abdias, le prosélyte normand', *Revue de Musicologie*, 51:1 (1965), pp.19–51, and Adler, 'Music Notations', pp.207–17; Alberto M. Somekh, 'Ovadiah il proselito fra poesia e liturgia', in A. De Rosa and M. Perani (eds), *Giovanni-Ovadiah da Oppido, proselito, viaggiatore e musicista dell'Età normanna. Atti del convegno internazionale Oppido Lucano 28–30 marzo 2004* (Florence: Casa Editrice Giuntina, 2005), pp.190–91.

Musical scores of Obadiah – Song 3. (Cambridge University Library)

THE SOUND OF MUSIC 127

Musical scores of Obadiah – Song 2. (Cambridge University Library)

Obadiah recalls his ordination

Obadiah takes us back to the short Old Testament Book of Joel, often cited by him as a pivotal moment in the account of his estrangement from Christianity. This work, as shown earlier, was ostensibly associated, by the young Johannes of Dreux, with the frightening events of Jewish massacres during the First Crusade of 1095–1096, moving him to question the Christian reading of the prophecies of Joel. The account of this moment in Obadiah's life quotes Joel 2:31: 'The sun shall be turned into darkness, and the moon into blood, before the great and the terrible day of the Lord come.' In his autobiographical narrative, Obadiah notably records these words in the actual Latin of the Vulgate, termed by him 'the language of the Edomites' but written out in Hebrew characters. He then gives a translation into Hebrew.

Whilst these two verses of the Book of Joel are recalled in Latin, the fearful memory of them is softened by the solace of Judaism and the certainty of the Law of the Torah and Moses, which is expressed in Hebrew. But the Latin and Hebrew are pulling in two directions. The question is why Obadiah now feels compelled to recall these lines in the Latin language of the Edomites, the old language of Christianity and of his upbringing. The Christian reading of Joel foretells the gathering on Mount Zion and the descent of the Holy Spirit: it is repeated thus in the New Testament (Acts 2:19–20) by Peter as the day of Judgement and the establishment of the heavenly Jerusalem prior to the ascension of the risen Christ. This prophecy by the apostle also citing Joel had also been preceded as was remembered earlier, by terrible portents described in the skies: an eclipse, the darkening of the sun, the blood-colour of the moon. For the Norman, however, such an explanation was not his understanding. He now actually saw the apocalyptic vision and the eclipse of 1095 as the announcement of a Jewish prophecy: Zionism and the return of Jerusalem to the nation of Israel, the in-gathering of the dispersed peoples discussed earlier. The emotional recall of these verses by the Norman proselyte is in fact associated with a hitherto unmentioned event in his early life, showing vividly the tremendous impact they had on him. His citing of the actual Latin text of Joel's prophecy retained in his Hebrew account is due to the appearance of these verses in the liturgy of the Roman Church. Joel 2:28–32 is the first of several Old Testament readings prescribed in the mass of the Saturday after Pentecost, one of the five days in the year on which ordinations can take place. These 'Ember days' (*quatuor tempora*), together with the Saturday after Lent, represented the so-called Ember Saturdays that earmarked the days of the liturgical year when priests and deacons were ordained. No doubt Obadiah is recalling the experience of his own ordination and deep familiarity with a service that, on the Saturday after Pentecost, included the passage from Joel as the first Lesson.[16] Like his memory of the Psalms and the music of chanting, the details of this service and its significance will have stayed forever imprinted in his mind. He retains the memory of these *ipsissima verba*, the very words uttered in Latin at the

---

16 A. Büchler, 'Obadiah the Proselyte and the Roman Liturgy', *Medieval Encounters*, 7:2 (2001), pp.169–70; Kedar, 'Voyages', pp.144–45, expands on Büchler's explanation.

service of his induction into the Roman Catholic Church. Now, writing his memories in Egypt some 20 years or more after his conversion, the Latin words flood the memory of Obadiah. The quoting of the Latin liturgy signifies that, at the exact moment that he entered the Roman Catholic Church, the new priest was struck by grave doubts as he began to hold fast to Judaism. Even if this happened many years earlier, it brings into focus that all the details in the *Autobiography* were written years after by a process of selecting and recalling past events that had become branded in his mind. We must now offer some final thoughts and consider how this story ends.

The scroll of Obadiah

The preservation of the story of Obadiah, only partly told from the fragments of his memoirs brought to light in the Cairo Geniza, is said to be part of a scroll – *megillah* – providing the source of the *Autobiography* that still lacks the full narrative. The survival of writing was a matter of existential concern to the Jews, for whom the written word was sacrosanct, as the story uncovered in the Cairo Geniza shows. When the bound book, or codex, was introduced in Roman times, it was also adopted by the Jews, but the scroll continued to be used for the reading of the Torah as it still is today in the synagogue, where it is displayed and carried about after the reading before being rolled together and carefully returned to the *aron hakodesh* (the holy ark). This ark recalls the Temple, but its main purpose is to protect the holiness of the Torah scroll as the primary manifestation of God's word and permanence.

Such power of the word and the scroll is carried over into the visions of the prophets that drove the Norman proselyte to undertake his final journey from Baghdad to Fustāt. This overwhelming, even psychotic, veneration for the word of the scroll is illustrated in the opening verses of the Book of Ezekiel, the words of the prophet lying at the core of the messianic predictions that also spoke to Obadiah in the years of his intensive reading and instruction in Baghdad. In an extraordinary apparition, Ezekiel, whose oracles often came to him in a state of ecstasy or trance, sees a hand appearing before him clutching a scroll, 'and there was written therein lamentations, and mourning and woe'. This forms part of Ezekiel's vision of the divine chariot bathed in fire and the four figures – one of whom, with four faces and four wings, orders Ezekiel to eat the scroll laid before him in its entirety: 'Then did I eat it; and it was in my mouth as honey for sweetness' (Ezekiel 3:3). He hears the Lord at that moment, speaking to him from above the chariot. Nothing can exceed this physical presence and potency more than the starving Ezekiel's hunger to understand and ingest the majesty and word of God and the certainty of the restoration of Jerusalem to Israel with the coming of the Messiah.

In these visions and dreams, which he saw and heard, Obadiah remained, till the end of his days, bound to the belief that his birth had been significant, that he was in some way the reincarnation of Jacob, for, as he tells us, he had not been the first-born. He, like Jacob in the biblical story, had supplanted his twin brother's birthright for a bowl of soup and a bit of bread, at a moment when Esau was tired and hungry from hunting. Jacob had then let his mother, Rebecca, dress him up in Esau's clothes so that his blind father, Isaac, would bless him. Now, he, Obadiah, was the blessed one, usurping the primogeniture that should have been accorded to Esau. This story was Obadiah's imaginative vision, a wish fulfilment of a high order, setting Johannes of Dreux on the path of the elect to tell and interpret his life. Like Jacob, Obadiah became Israel, and his sons became the children of Israel. This election was at the heart of his life story, and his father's blessing was the seal of his election. Johannes, upon becoming Obadiah and converting to Judaism, took on the persona and elect status of Jacob, becoming the new leader of Israel and set out to do battle with Christianity, to bring back Jerusalem to Israel after the loss of the city to the crusaders. During his life's journey, he became a prophet forecasting the coming of a messiah and the restoration of Zion. His journey to the East was his own crusade. In times to come, the nineteenth-century movement of a secular Zionism would advocate a mass return to Palestine to establish a national home, a Zionist state for the Jewish people that posed a direct challenge for the traditional messianic expectations of Zion proclaimed by Obadiah. These two visions, still facing each other today, have never come together, and this estrangement, with all its consequences, is a story we leave untold.

We remain unaware when Obadiah the Proselyte came to the end of his earthly travels. Any further account of his life, which must have ended in twelfth-century Egypt, forcibly remains untold but may not be over. For a biography, it has been a cornucopia equally yielding discoveries and doubts. The thrust of the account we have told has had at times some affinities with fiction; it is the unfolding storytelling of how a character got through life displaying the strengths and flaws of personality versus the power of fate. The fragments of his *Autobiography* could yet be expanded if further finds are made in the material of the Geniza or more clues are uncovered in other sources – for no biography told is ever definitive, because that is not in the nature of such journeys. But his feet certainly did walk upon Norman Italy in those ancient times and crossed the plains of the Levant, seeking to build a New Jerusalem heralding the Messiah, inspired by the words of the prophets who beheld a vision of the chariot of fire and the voice of the Lord in the firmament.

Bibliography

Abulafia, David, *Frederick II: A Medieval Emperor* (London: Oxford University Press, 1992)

Adler, E. N., 'Ovadiah le Prosélyte', *REJ*, 69 (1919), pp.129–34

Adler, Israel, 'Les chants synagogaux notés au XII siècle (ca 1103–1150) par Abdias, le prosélyte normand', *Revue de Musicologie*, 51:1 (1965), pp.19–51

Adler, Israel, 'The Music Notations by Ovadiah the Norman Proselyte and Their Significance for the Study of Jewish Music', in A. De Rosa and M. Perani (eds), *Giovanni-Ovadiah da Oppido, proselito, viaggiatore e musicista dell'Età normanna. Atti del convegno internazionale Oppido Lucano 28–30 marzo 2004* (Florence: Casa Editrice Giuntina, 2005), pp.207–17

Adler, Marcus N. (trans.), *The Itinerary of Benjamin of Tudela* (London: Oxford University Press, 1907)

Al-Muqaddasī, and Collins, Basil (trans.), *The Best Divisions for Knowledge of the Regions* (Reading: Garnet Publishing, 2001)

Alter, Robert, 'The Characteristics of Ancient Hebrew Poetry', in R. Alter and F. Kermode (eds), *The Literary Guide to the Bible* (London: Fontana Press, 1989), pp.611–24

Armstrong, Karen, *A History of Jerusalem: One City, Three Faiths* (London: Ballantine Books, 1997)

Asbridge, Thomas, *The Creation of the Principality of Antioch, 1098–1130* (Woodbridge: Boydell Press, 2000)

Asbridge, Thomas, *The Crusades: The War for the Holy Land* (London: Simon & Schuster, 2020)

Asbridge, Thomas and Edgington, Susan B. (trans), *Walter the Chancellor's The Antiochene Wars* (Aldershot: Ashgate, 1999)

Aslanov, Cyril, 'Ovadiah the Proselyte and His Linguistic Background', in A. De Rosa and M. Perani (eds), *Giovanni-Ovadiah da Oppido, proselito, viaggiatore e musicista dell'Età normanna. Atti del convegno internazionale Oppido Lucano 28–30 marzo 2004* (Florence: Casa Editrice Giuntina, 2005), pp.93–99

Astren, Fred, 'Non-Rabbinic and Non-Karaite Religious Movements', in P. I. Lieberman (ed.), *The Cambridge History of Judaism: Jews in the Medieval Islamic World* (Cambridge: Cambridge University Press, 2021), vol. 5, pp.606–33

Bareket, Elinoar, *Fustāt on the Nile: The Jewish Elite in Medieval Egypt* (Leiden: Brill, 1999)

Bartlett, Robert, *The Making of Europe: Conquest, Colonization and Cultural Change, 950–1350* (London: Allen Lane, 1993)

Barton, John, *A History of the Bible* (London: Penguin, 2020)

Ben-Sasson, Menahem, 'The Medieval Period: The Tenth to Fourteenth Centuries', in P. Lambert (ed.), *Fortifications and the Synagogue: The Fortress of Babylon and the Ben Ezra Synagogue, Cairo* (Montreal: Canadian Centre for Architecture, 1994), pp.201–23

Black, Jeremy, 'The Mediterranean as a Battleground of the European Powers: 1700–1900', in D. Abulafia (ed.), *The Mediterranean in History* (London: Thames & Hudson, 2016), pp.251–82

Blake, Robert, *Disraeli* (London: Routledge, 1969)

Bodleian Library (BoL): MS. Heb. f. 56, no. 2821

Bodleian Library (BoL): MS. Heb. f. 99, p. 36a

Bonfil, Robert, Irshai, Oded, Stroumsa, Guy G., and Talgam, Rina (eds), *Jews in Byzantium: Dialectics of Minority and Majority Cultures* (Leiden: Brill, 2012)

Booms, Dirk, 'The Normans', in D. Booms and P. Higgs (eds), *Sicily: Culture and Conquest* (London: British Museum Press, 2016), pp.173–228

Booms, Dirk, and Higgs, Peter (eds), *Sicily: Culture and Conquest* (London: British Museum Press, 2016)

Borraro, Pietro (ed.), *Antiche Civiltà Lucane. Atti del Convegno di Studi di Archeologia, Storia dell'Arte e del Folklore, Oppido Lucano, 5–8 Aprile 1970* (Galatina: Congedo, 1975)

Borst, Arno, *The Ordering of Time: From the Ancient Computus to the Modern Computer* (Cambridge: Polity Press, 1993)

Bowman, Steven B. (trans.), *Sepher Yosippon: A Tenth-Century History of Israel* (Detroit: Wayne State University Press, 2023)

Brody, Robert, *The Geonim of Babylonia and the Shaping of Medieval Jewish Culture* (New Haven, CT: Yale University Press, 1998)

Büchler, Adolf, 'Obadiah the Proselyte and the Roman Liturgy', *Medieval Encounters*, 7:2 (2001), pp.165–73

Cambridge University Library (CUL): T-S 20.160: Legal Document

Cambridge University Library (CUL): T-S J1.29: Trousseau list

Cambridge University Library (CUL): T-S NS 325: Legal document

Chajes, J. H., and Stow, Kenneth (trans), 'The Scroll or Genealogy of Ahimaaz ben Paltiel: Jewish Learning, Myth, and Ideals in an Uncertain Salentine World (1054)', in K. Jansen, J. Drell, and F. Andrews (eds), *Medieval Italy: Texts in Translation* (Philadelphia: University of Pennsylvania Press, 2009), pp.508–13

Chiesa, Bruno, and Lockwood, Wilfrid, *Ya'qub al-Qirqisānī on Jewish Sects and Christianity: A Translation of "Kitāb al-anwār". Book 1, with Two Introductory Essays* (Frankfurt: Peter Lang, 1984)

Cohen, Mark R., *Poverty and Charity in the Jewish Community of Medieval Egypt* (Princeton: Princeton University Press, 2005)

Cohen, Mark R., *Under Crescent and Cross: The Jews in the Middle Ages* (Princeton: Princeton University Press, 1994)

Cohen, Shaye J. D., 'The Rabbinic Conversion Ceremony', in *The Beginnings of Jewishness: Boundaries, Varieties, Uncertainties* (Berkeley: University of California Press, 2001), pp.198–238

Colafemmina, Cesare, 'La conversione al giudaismo di Andrea, arcivescovo di Bari: una suggestione per Giovanni-Ovadiah da Oppido', in A. De Rosa and M. Perani (eds), *Giovanni-Ovadiah da Oppido, proselito, viaggiatore e musicista dell'Età normanna. Atti del convegno internazionale Oppido Lucano 28–30 marzo 2004* (Florence: Casa Editrice Giuntina, 2005), pp.55–65

Daftary, Farhad, *A History of Shi'i Islam* (London: I. B. Tauris, 2013)

Daftary, Farhad, *The Assassin Legends: Myths of the Isma'ilis* (London: I. B. Tauris, 2011)

Daftary, Farhad, *The Ismāīlīs: Their History and Doctrines* (Cambridge: Cambridge University Press, 2007)

De Rosa, Antonio, and Perani, Mauro (eds), *Giovanni-Ovadiah da Oppido, proselito, viaggiatore e musicista dell'Età normanna. Atti del convegno internazionale Oppido Lucano 28–30 marzo 2004* (Florence: Casa Editrice Giuntina, 2005)

Dunbar, Prescott N. (trans.), and Loud, Graham A. (rev.), *The History of the Normans by Amatus of Montecassino* (Woodbridge: Boydell Press, 2004)

Eidelberg, Shlomo (trans.), 'The Narrative of the Old Persecutions, or Mainz Anonymous', in *The Jews and the Crusaders: The Hebrew Chronicles of the First and Second Crusade* (Madison: University of Wisconsin Press, 1977), pp.95–115

Erder, Yoram, 'The Doctrine of Abū 'Īsa al-Iṣfahānī and Its Sources', *Jerusalem Studies in Arabic and Islam*, 20 (1996), pp.162–99

Evans, Gillian R. (ed.), *The Medieval Theologians* (Oxford: Wiley-Blackwell, 2001)

Fleischer, Ezra, 'Piyyūṭ', in S. Safrai (ed.), *The Literature of the Sages: Second Part* (Philadelphia: Fortress Press, 2006), pp.363–73

Flusser, David, 'Josippon, a Medieval Hebrew Version of Josephus', in L. H. Feldman and G. Hata (eds), *Josephus, Judaism and Christianity* (Leiden: Brill, 1987), pp.386–97

Fonseca, C. D., 'L'apertura "trinitaria" del Concilio di Bari', in S. Palese and G. Locatelli (eds), *Il Concilio di Bari del 1098. Atti del Convegno Storico Internazionale e celebrazioni del IX Centenario del Concilio* (Bari: Edipuglia, 1999), pp.39–54

Frankopan, Peter, *The First Crusade: The Call from the East* (London: Vintage, 2013)

Friedlander, Israel, 'Jewish-Arabic Studies, I. Shiitic Elements in Jewish Sectarianism', *JQR*, 2:4 (1912), pp.481–516

Friedlander, Israel, 'Jewish-Arabic Studies, I. Shiitic Elements in Jewish Sectarianism', *JQR*, 3 (1912), pp.235–300

Ghosh, Amitav, *In an Antique Land* (London: Penguin, 2012)

Gibb, Hamilton A. R. (trans.), *The Damascus Chronicle of the Crusades: Extracted and Translated from the Chronicle of Ibn Al-Qalānisī* (Mineola, NY: Dover Publications, 2002)

Gil, Juan (ed.), *Corpus Scriptorum Mozarabicorum* (Madrid: Instituto Antonio de Nebrija, 1973), vols 1–2

Gil, Moshe, *A History of Palestine, 634–1099* (Cambridge: Cambridge University Press, 1992)

Gil, Moshe, *Jews in Islamic Countries in the Middle Ages* (Leiden: Brill, 2004)

Gil, Moshe, 'The Origins of the Karaites', in M. Polliack (ed.), *Karaite Judaism: A Guide to Its History and Literary Sources* (Leiden: Brill, 2003), pp.73–118

Goitein, Shelomo D., 'A Caliph's Decree in Favour of the Rabbinite Jews of Palestine', *JJS*, 5:3 (1954), pp.118–25

Goitein, Shelomo D., *A Mediterranean Society: The Jewish Communities of the Arab World as Portrayed in the Documents of the Cairo Geniza* (Berkeley: University of California Press, 1967–1993), vols 1–6

Goitein, Shelomo D., 'A Report on Messianic Troubles in Baghdad in 1120–21', *JQR*, 43:1 (1952), pp.57–76

Goitein, Shelomo D., *Letters of Medieval Jewish Traders* (Princeton: Princeton University Press, 1973)

Goitein, Shelomo D., 'Obadyah, a Norman Proselyte: A Propos the Discovery of a New Fragment of His "Scroll"', *JJS*, 4:2 (1953), pp.74–84

Golb, Norman, 'Dove avvenne la conversione al giudaismo del proselito Obadiah di Oppido?', in P. Borraro (ed.), *Antiche Civiltà Lucane. Atti del Convegno di Studi di Archeologia, Storia dell'Arte e del Folklore, Oppido Lucano, 5–8 Aprile 1970* (Galatina: Congedo, 1975), pp.217–25

Golb, Norman, *Jewish Proselytism – A Phenomenon in the Religious History of Early Medieval Europe* (Cincinnati: University of Cincinnati, 1988), <https://oi.uchicago.edu/sites/default/files/uploads/shared/docs/jewish_proselytism.pdf>, accessed 2024

Golb, Norman, 'Megillat Obadiah Hager', in S. Morag, I. Ben-Ami, and N. A. Stillman (eds), *Studies in Geniza and Sepharadi Heritage: Presented to Shelomo Dov Goitein on the Occasion of His Eightieth Birthday by His Students, Colleagues and Friends* (Jerusalem: Magnes Press, 1981), pp.77–107

Golb, Norman, 'Obadiah the Proselyte: Scribe of a Unique Twelfth-Century Manuscript Containing Lombardic Neumes', *Journal of Religion*, 45:2 (1965), pp.153–56

Golb, Norman (trans.), 'The Autograph Memoirs of Obadiah the Proselyte of Oppido Lucano and the Epistle of Barukh b. Isaac of Aleppo', prepared for the *Convegno internazionale di Studi Giovanni – Obadiah da Oppido: proselito, viaggiatore e musicista dell'età normanna, Oppido Lucano (Basilicata) 28-30 Marzo 2004*, <https://isac.uchicago.edu/sites/default/files/uploads/shared/docs/autograph_memoirs_obadiah.pdf>, accessed 2024 [Published in Italian as Norman Golb, 'La conversione di Giovanni-Ovadiah al giudaismo nel suo contesto storico, con particolare riferimento ai documenti della Genizah del Cairo', in A. De Rosa and M. Perani (eds), *Giovanni-Ovadiah da Oppido, proselito, viaggiatore e musicista dell'Età normanna. Atti del convegno internazionale Oppido Lucano 28–30 marzo 2004* (Florence: Casa Editrice Giuntina, 2005), pp.67–92.]

Golb, Norman, 'The Messianic Pretender Solomon Ibn al-Ruji and His Son Menachem (The So-Called "David Alroy")', *Oriental Institute, University of*

Chicago (2009), pp.1–8, <https://isac.uchicago.edu/sites/default/files/uploads/shared/docs/false_messiah-1.pdf>, accessed 2024

Golb, Norman, 'The Music of Obadiah the Proselyte and His Conversion', *JJS*, 18:1–4, (1967), pp.43–63

Goodman, Martin, *A History of Judaism* (London: Penguin, 2019)

Graham-Campbell, James (ed.), *Cultural Atlas of the Viking World* (Oxford: Checkmark Books, 1994)

Guido of Arezzo, *Epistola ad Michahelem*, in Anna J. Reisenweaver, 'Guido of Arezzo and His Influence on Music Learning', *Musical Offerings*, 3:1 (2012), p.46

Hillenbrand, Carole, *The Crusades: Islamic Perspectives* (Edinburgh: Edinburgh University Press, 2018)

Hoffman, Adina, and Cole, Peter, *Sacred Trash: The Lost and Found World of the Cairo Geniza* (New York: Schocken, 2011)

Holmes, Richard, *Sidetracks: Explorations of a Romantic Biographer* (London: Vintage, 2001)

Holo, Joshua, 'Gershom B. Judah and the Italian Roots of Early Ashkenazic Jewry', in J. L. Kraemer and M. G. Weschler (eds), *Pesher Naḥum: Texts and Studies in Jewish History and Literature from Antiquity through the Middle Ages Presented to Norman (Naḥum) Golb* (Chicago: Oriental Institute of the University of Chicago, 2012), pp.103–08

Holo, Joshua, 'Jewish Communities and Personalities within Ovadiah's Chronicle', in A. De Rosa and M. Perani (eds), *Giovanni-Ovadiah da Oppido, proselito, viaggiatore e musicista dell'Età normanna. Atti del convegno internazionale Oppido Lucano 28–30 marzo 2004* (Florence: Casa Editrice Giuntina, 2005), pp.149–64

Horace, and Svarlien, John (trans.), *Satires* (Indianapolis: Hackett, 2012)

Houben, Hubert, *Il "libro del capitolo" del monastero della SS. Trinità di Venosa (Cod. Casin. 334): Una testimonianza del Mezzogiorno normanno* (Galatina: Congedo, 1984)

Houben, Hubert, 'La Chiesa di Bari alla fine dell' XI secolo', in S. Palese and G. Locatelli (eds), *Il Concilio di Bari del 1098. Atti del Convegno Storico Internazionale e celebrazioni del IX Centenario del Concilio* (Bari: Edipuglia, 1999), pp.91–107

Irwin, Robert, 'Islam and the Crusades, 1096–1699', in J. Riley-Smith (ed.), *The Oxford Illustrated History of the Crusades* (Oxford: Oxford University Press, 1995), pp.217–59

Jamison, Evelyn (ed.), *Catalogus Baronum* (Rome: Istituto storico italiano per il Medio Evo, 1972)

Jefferson, Rebecca J. W., 'Dangerous Liaisons in Cairo: Reginald Q. Henriques and the Taylor-Schechter Geniza Manuscript Collection', *Judaica Librarianship*, 20 (2017), pp.21–51

Jefferson, Rebecca J. W., *The Cairo Geniza and the Age of Discovery in Egypt: The History and Provenance of a Jewish Archive* (London: I. B. Tauris, 2022)

Kedar, Benjamin Z., 'The Voyages of Guiàn-Ovadiah in Syria and Iraq and the Enigma of His Conversion', in A. De Rosa and M. Perani (eds), *Giovanni-Ovadiah da Oppido, proselito, viaggiatore e musicista dell'Età normanna. Atti del convegno internazionale Oppido Lucano 28–30 marzo 2004* (Florence: Casa Editrice Giuntina, 2005), pp.133–47

Kennedy, Hugh, *The Great Arab Conquests: How the Spread of Islam Changed the World We Live In* (Philadelphia: De Capo Press, 2007)

Komnene, Anna, Sewter, E. R. A. (trans.), and Frankopan, Peter (rev.), *The Alexiad* (London: Penguin, 2009)

Kramers, J. H., and Wiet, G. (trans), *Ibn Hawkal. Configuration de la Terre (Kitab Surat al-Ard)* (Paris: Editions G. P. Maisonneuve & Larose, 1964), vol. 1

Lambert, Phyllis (ed.), *Fortifications and the Synagogue: The Fortress of Babylon and the Ben Ezra Synagogue, Cairo* (Montreal: Canadian Centre for Architecture, 1994)

Lancellotti, Angelo, 'Nella cronaca di Giovanni-Abdia il proselita normanno la prima pagina di storia di Oppido della Lucania', in P. Borraro (ed.), *Antiche Civiltà Lucane. Atti del Convegno di Studi di Archeologia, Storia dell'Arte e del Folklore, Oppido Lucano, 5–8 Aprile 1970* (Galatina: Congedo, 1975), pp.251–60

Lassner, Jacob (ed.), *A Mediterranean Society: An Abridgement in One Volume* (London: University of California Press, 1999)

Le Quesne, Charles, 'Descriptions of the Ben Ezra Synagogue from the Nineteenth and Early Twentieth Centuries', in P. Lambert (ed.), *Fortifications and the Synagogue: The Fortress of Babylon and the Ben Ezra Synagogue, Cairo* (Montreal: Canadian Centre for Architecture, 1994), pp.243–51

Le Quesne, Charles, 'Legend and Tradition at the Ben Ezra Synagogue', in P. Lambert (ed.), *Fortifications and the Synagogue: The Fortress of Babylon and the Ben Ezra Synagogue, Cairo* (Montreal: Canadian Centre for Architecture, 1994), pp.197–99

Le Quesne, Charles, 'The Geniza and the Scholarly Community', in P. Lambert (ed.), *Fortifications and the Synagogue: The Fortress of Babylon and the Ben Ezra Synagogue, Cairo* (Montreal: Canadian Centre for Architecture, 1994), pp.237–42

Le Quesne, Charles, 'The Synagogue', in P. Lambert (ed.), *Fortifications and the Synagogue: The Fortress of Babylon and the Ben Ezra Synagogue, Cairo* (Montreal: Canadian Centre for Architecture, 1994), pp.79–98

Le Strange, Guy, *Baghdad during the Abbasid Caliphate* (New York: Cosimo Classics, 2011)

Le Strange, Guy, *Palestine under the Moslems: A Description of Syria and the Holy Land from A.D. 650 to 1500* (London: Alexander P. Watt, 1890)

Le Strange, Guy, *The Lands of the Eastern Caliphate* (Cambridge: Cambridge University Press, 1905)

Levin, Gabriel (trans.), *Yehuda Halevi: Poems from the Diwan* (Manchester: Anvil Press Poetry, 2002)

Lewis, Bernard, 'The Ismāʿīlites and the Assassins', in M. W. Baldwin (ed.), *A History of the Crusades: The First Hundred Years* (Madison: University of Wisconsin Press, 1969), vol. 1, pp.99–134

Lieberman, Phillip I., 'Demography and Migrations', in P. I. Lieberman (ed.), *The Cambridge History of Judaism: Jews in the Medieval Islamic World* (Cambridge: Cambridge University Press, 2021), vol. 5, pp.371–411

Lieberman, Phillip I. (ed.), *The Cambridge History of Judaism: Jews in the Medieval Islamic World* (Cambridge: Cambridge University Press, 2021), vol. 5

Lunde, Paul, and Stone, Caroline (trans), *Ibn Fadlān and the Land of Darkness: Arab Travellers in the Far North* (London: Penguin, 2012)

Maalouf, Amin, *The Crusades through Arab Eyes* (London: Al Saqi, 2006)

Madoz, José (ed.), *El Epistolario de Álvaro de Córdoba. Edición Crítica* (Madrid: Consejo Superior de Investigaciones Cientificas, 1947)

Maimonides, 'The Epistle to Yemen', in A. Halkin (trans.), *Crisis and Leadership: Epistles of Maimonides* (New York: Jewish Publication Society of America, 1985), pp.91–131

Mann, Jacob, 'Obadya le Prosélyte', *REJ*, 71 (1921), pp.88–93 [Also to be found in Jacob Mann, *The Collected Articles of Jacob Mann* (Israel: M. Shalom, 1971), vol. 1, pp.113–17.]

Mann, Jacob, 'Obadya, Prosélyte Normand converti au Judaïsme, et sa Meguilla, décrivant des événements survenus en Orient au temps des Croisades', *REJ*, 89 (1930), pp.245–59 [Also to be found in Jacob Mann, *The Collected Articles of Jacob Mann* (Israel: M. Shalom, 1971), vol. 1, pp.118–32.]

Marcus, Jacob R., *The Jew in the Medieval World: A Sourcebook, 315–1791* (Cincinnati: Hebrew Union College Press, 1938)

Marozzi, Justin, *Baghdad: City of Peace, City of Blood* (London: Penguin, 2015)

Martin, Jean-Marie, *La Pouille du VIe au XIIe siècle* (Rome: Ecole française de Rome, 1993)

McCormick, Michael, *Origins of the European Economy: Communications and Commerce AD 300–900* (Cambridge: Cambridge University Press, 2001)

Miller, Philip E., 'Rabbi Shemaria's Commentary on Proverbs 19:14', *JQR*, 73:2 (1982), pp.146–51

Moore, Robert I., *The Formation of a Persecuting Society* (Oxford: Wiley, 1990)

Moorehead, Alan, *The White Nile* (London: Penguin, 1963)

Morton, Nicholas, *The Field of Blood: The Battle for Aleppo and the Remaking of the Medieval Middle East* (New York: Basic Books, 2018)

Muratori, Ludovico A., *Rerum Italicarum Scriptores* (Mediolani: Typographia Societatis Palatinae in Regia Curia, 1724), vol. 5

Musca, Giosuè, and Tateo, Francesco, 'La comunità ebraica', in F. Tateo (ed.), *Storia di Bari. Dalla Prehistoria al Mille* (Bari: Editori Laterza, 1989), vol. 1, pp.305–11

Nelson, Janet L., *King and Emperor: A New Life of Charlemagne* (London: University of California Press, 2019)

Nelson, Janet L., 'The Frankish Empire', in P. Sawyer (ed.), *The Oxford Illustrated History of the Vikings* (Oxford: Oxford University Press, 1999), pp.19–47

Nemoy, Leon, *Karaite Anthology: Excerpts from the Early Literature* (New Haven, CT: Yale University Press, 1963)

Norwich, John J., *The Normans in the South, 1016–1130* (London: Faber & Faber, 2018)

Olszowy-Schlanger, Judith, 'The Anatomy of Non-Biblical Scrolls from the Cairo Geniza', in I. Wardrey (ed.), *Jewish Manuscripts: New Cultures* (Berlin: De Gruyter, 2017), pp.49–88

Page, Christopher, *The Christian West and Its Singers: The First Thousand Years* (New Haven, CT: Yale University Press, 2010)

Palese, Salvatore, and Locatelli, Giancarlo (eds), *Il Concilio di Bari del 1098. Atti del Convegno Storico Internazionale e celebrazioni del IX Centenario del Concilio* (Bari: Edipuglia, 1999)

Perani, Mauro, 'Una menzione di Obadiah il Proselito da Oppido Lucano in un commento a Proverbi 19,14 di Shemariah ben Elijah ben Jacob Ikriti', *Sefer Yuhasin: Rivista per la storia degli Ebrei nell'Italia Meridionale*, 7 (1991), pp.3–15

Perlmann, Moshe D. (ed. and trans.), *Silencing the Jews* (New York: American Academy for Jewish Research, 1964)

Pine-Coffin, R. S. (trans.), *Saint Augustine Confessions* (London: Penguin, 1961)

Prawer, Joshua, 'The Autobiography of Obadyah the Norman, a Convert to Judaism at the Time of the First Crusade', in I. Twersky (ed.), *Studies in Medieval Jewish History and Literature* (Cambridge: Harvard University Press, 1979), pp.110–34

Pryor, John H., 'The Voyages of Saewulf', in R. Huygens (ed.), *Peregrinationes Tres* (Turnhout: Brepols, 1994), pp.34–57

Rankin, Susan, *Writing Sounds in Carolingian Europe: The Invention of Musical Notation* (Cambridge: Cambridge University Press, 2018)

Reif, Stefan C., *A Jewish Archive from Old Cairo: The History of Cambridge University's Genizah Collection* (Richmond: Curzon, 2000)

Reisenweaver, Anna J., 'Guido of Arezzo and His Influence on Music Learning', *Musical Offerings*, 3:1 (2012), pp.37–59

Rendsburg, Gary A., *How the Bible is Written* (Peabody, MA: Hendrickson Publishers, 2019)

Rendsburg, Gary A., 'The Psalms as Hymns in the Temple of Jerusalem', in J. H. Charlesworth (ed.), *Jesus and Temple: Textual and Archaeological Explorations* (Minneapolis: Fortress Press, 2014), pp.95–122

Rendsburg, Gary A., and Shamah, Peter M., *Johannes of Oppido = Obadiah the Proselyte* (2018), <https://johannes-obadiah.org>, accessed 2024

Richards, D. S. (trans.), *The Chronicle of Ibn al-Athir for the Crusading Period from al-Kamil fi'l-Ta'rikh. Part 1* (Abingdon: Routledge, 2010)

Riess, Frank, *The Journey of Deacon Bodo from the Rhine to the Guadalquivir: Apostasy and Conversion to Judaism in Early Medieval Europe* (London: Routledge, 2019)

Rosenblatt, Samuel (trans.), *Saadia Gaon: The Book of Beliefs and Opinions* (New Haven, CT: Yale University Press, 1955)

Rotman, Youval, 'Converts in Byzantine Italy: Local Representation of Jewish-Christian Rivalry', in R. Bonfil, O. Irshai, G. G. Stroumsa, and R. Talgam (eds), *Jews in Byzantium: Dialectics of Minority and Majority Cultures* (Leiden: Brill, 2012), pp.893–921

'Rule of St. Benedict', *Christian Classics Ethereal Library*, <https://ccel.org/ccel/benedict/rule/rule.toc.html>, accessed 2024

Runciman, Steven, *A History of the Crusades* (London: Penguin, 1980–1981), vols 1–2

Rustow, Marina, *Heresy and the Politics of Community: The Jews of the Fatimid Caliphate* (Ithaca, NY: Cornell University Press, 2008)

Rustow, Marina, 'The Qaraites as Sect: The Tyranny of a Construct', in S. Stern (ed.), *Sects and Sectarianism in Jewish History* (Leiden: Brill, 2011), pp.149–86

Savy, Pierre, 'Autour de la conversion d'Obadiah et de quelques autres (vers 1100)', *Archives de sciences sociales des religions*, 182 (2018), pp.207–26

Sawyer, Peter, 'The Age of the Vikings, and Before', in P. Sawyer (ed.), *The Oxford Illustrated History of the Vikings* (Oxford: Oxford University Press, 1999), pp.1–18

Sawyer, Peter (ed.), *The Oxford Illustrated History of the Vikings* (Oxford: Oxford University Press, 1999)

Sæwulf, 'The Travels of Sæwulf, A.D. 1102 and 1103', in T. Wright (ed.), *Early Travels in Palestine* (London: Henry G. Bohn, 1848), pp.31–50

Schama, Simon, *The Story of the Jews: Finding the Words 1000 BCE–1492 CE* (London: The Bodley Head, 2013)

Scheiber, Alexander, 'Der normannische Proselyt Obadja, der Aufzeichner der erstern hebräischen Melodie', *Studia Musicologica Academiae Scientiarum Hungaricae*, 8:1/4 (1966), pp.173–87

Scheiber, Alexander, 'Fragment from the Chronicle of Obadyah, the Norman Proselyte: From the Kaufmann Geniza', *Acta Orientalia Academiae Scientarium Hungaricae*, 4:1/3 (1954), pp.271–96

Scheiber, Alexander, 'Der lebenslauf des Johannes-Obadja aus Oppido', in P. Borraro (ed.), *Antiche Civiltà Lucane. Atti del Convegno di Studi di Archeologia, Storia dell'Arte e del Folklore, Oppido Lucano, 5–8 Aprile 1970* (Galatina: Congedo, 1975), pp.227–48

Scheiber, Alexander, 'Obadiah the Norman Proselyte Notator of the First Known Hebrew Melody', *Tarbiz*, 34 (1965), pp.366–71 [Written in Hebrew.]

Scheindlin, Raymond P., *The Song of the Distant Dove: Judah Halevi's Pilgrimage* (Oxford: Oxford University Press, 2008)

Schmierer-Lee, Melonie, and Rendsburg, Gary, 'Q&A Wednesday: From Monk to Jew in 1102 – Obadiah the Proselyte, with Gary Rendsburg', *Geniza Fragments* (2021), <https://www.lib.cam.ac.uk/genizah-fragments/posts/qa-wednesday-monk-jew-1102-obadiah-proselyte-gary-rendsburg>, accessed 2024

Sheehan, Peter, 'The Roman Fortifications', in P. Lambert (ed.), *Fortifications and the Synagogue: The Fortress of Babylon and the Ben Ezra Synagogue, Cairo* (Montreal: Canadian Centre for Architecture, 1994), pp.49–64

Simonsohn, Shlomo, *The Jews of Italy: Antiquity* (Leiden: Brill, 2014)

Smith, John A., *Music in Ancient Judaism and Early Christianity* (Burlington: Ashgate, 2011)

Somekh, Alberto M., 'Ovadiah il prosélito fra poesia e liturgia', in A. De Rosa and M. Perani (eds), *Giovanni-Ovadiah da Oppido, proselito, viaggiatore e musicista dell'Età normanna. Atti del convegno internazionale Oppido Lucano 28–30 marzo 2004* (Florence: Casa Editrice Giuntina, 2005), pp.175–94

Stillman, Norman A., *The Jews of Arab Lands: A History and Source Book* (Philadelphia: Jewish Publication Society of America, 1979)

Tyerman, Christopher, *God's War: A New History of the Crusades* (London: Penguin, 2007)

Von Falkenhausen, Vera, 'Identità religiose in una società multiculturale: l'Italia meridionale nell'epoca di Giovanni-Ovadiah', in A. De Rosa and M. Perani (eds), *Giovanni-Ovadiah da Oppido, proselito, viaggiatore e musicista dell'Età normanna. Atti del convegno internazionale Oppido Lucano 28–30 marzo 2004* (Florence: Casa Editrice Giuntina, 2005), pp.25–44

Von Falkenhausen, Vera, 'The Jews in Byzantine Southern Italy', in R. Bonfil, O. Irshai, G. G. Stroumsa, and R. Talgam (eds), *Jews in Byzantium: Dialectics of Minority and Majority Cultures* (Leiden: Brill, 2012), pp.271–96

Waugh, Teresa (trans.), *The Travels of Marco Polo: A Modern Translation* (London: Sidgwick and Jackson, 1984)

Werner, Eric, *The Sacred Bridge: The Interdependence of Liturgy and Music in Synagogue and Church during the First Millennium* (New York: Columbia University Press, 1959)

Wertheimer, Solomon A., *Ginze Yerushalem* (Jerusalem: Publisher unknown, 1901), vols 1–2

Wickham, Chris, *Medieval Europe* (New Haven, CT: Yale University Press, 2016)

Wickham, Chris, *The Inheritance of Rome: A History of Europe from 400 to 1000* (London: Penguin, 2009)

Wolf, Kenneth B. (trans.), *The Deeds of Count Roger of Calabria and Sicily and of His Brother Duke Robert Guiscard* (Ann Arbor: University of Michigan Press, 2005)

Yagur, Moshe, 'The Donor and the Gravedigger: Converts to Judaism in the Cairo Geniza Documents', in Y. Fox and Y. Yisraeli (eds), *Contesting Inter-Religious Conversion in the Medieval World* (New York: Routledge, 2017), pp.115–34

'Yevamot, Talmud: The William Davidson Edition', *Sefaria*, <www.sefaria.org/yevamot>, accessed 2024

Index

Abraham 35, 63, 64, 80, 81
Academy: in Aleppo 47, 63, 65; in Baghdad 76, 77; like *yeshiva* 78; session of 79; head of 101; Pumbedita academy 111
Adler, Hermann 13, 15
Adler, Nathan Elkan 13, 19, 20, 84
Al-Muqaddasī, 69, 71, 74, 75, 108, 109
Alamut, 89, 90, 93, 106
Alexandria 34, 35, 46, 60, 61, 108
Alexios Komnenos 39, 54
Al-Isfahānī 84, 85, 101
Al-Karkh 69, 75, 76
Al-Maghribī, Samuel 91, 92, 101, 120
Al-Mas'udi 66, 67
Al-Qirqisānī 83, 84, 85
Amadiya 87, 90, 92
Andreas of Bari 30, 31, 32, 33, 35, 36, 38, 50
Anna Komnene 66, 67
Antioch; Holy Lance in 56; ownership of 56; principality of 57; St Symeon port of 58; Bohemond's power base 61; Obadiah passes through 61: Roger of 93; Walter chancellor of 94
Aramaic 13, 63, 79, 85, 114, 117
Ark, *aron hakodesh* 12, 77, 115, 129
Assassins 89, 91, 93, 98
Augustine of Hippo 48, 118
Autograph Memoirs 23
Azerbaijan 87, 91

Babylonia 33, 70, 71, 79, 110, 111
Baghdad: Obadiah in 21; image and care of Obadiah in 67; Obadiah arrival in 68; description of by Benjamin of Tudela 71; power of Seljuks in 72; Jewish people in 72; rioting and dress restrictions in 73; prosperity of Jewish community in 75; synagogues and exilarch wealth in 75; floods and fires 76; synagogue life in 77; academies Sura and Pumbedita relocated to 78; description of academy in 79; messianic moment in 81

Baniyas 97, 98, Obadiah arrival in 98, Karaite priest in 98, exchange with Obadiah 99
Bari: Byzantine capital 25; recalled by Obadiah 28; Andreas of *see Andreas of Bari*; confrontation over dogma with Byzantine religion 32; persecution of Jews and book burning in 34; siege of 37-38; Council of 45; crusaders sail from 46; Obadiah sails from 61
Baring, Evelyn 11, 15
Barukh of Aleppo, Rabbi 19, 47, 63, 64, 65, 66, 67
Ben Ezra synagogue 12, 13, 14, 110, 112, 115, 116
Ben Sira, Jesus 15, 119
Benjamin of Tudela 36, 62, 67, 71, 76, 89, 90, 91, 109
Bible 23, 41, 45, 49, 52, 70, 71, 77, 101
Bima, reading table 77, 115
Bohemond 46, 47, 53, 53, 55, 56, 58, 61, 66
Byzantine 25, 31, 32, 34, 35, 36, 37, 38, 39, 42, 46, 54, 55, 66, 83, 95, 98, 107

Cairo: British seize 11; synagogue in old 12; manuscripts in old 13; geniza in 14; Schechter in 14; manuscripts taken from old 17; Urso ends in 33; poor relief in 67; foundation of by Fatimids 108; grows to join Fustāt 109; Jews leave old city for 112; music scores found in old 129
Cambridge 13, 14, 16, 17, 18, 19, 20, 22
Clermont 42, 45
Constantinople 25, 31, 32, 36, 37, 38, 42, 45, 46, 54, 61
Conversion: date of Johannes 21; Andrea's 31; certainty of Andrea's 33; Jews seek candidates for 39; pressure for Jews to 43; date of Johannes/Obadiah's 47;letter of from Italy 47; Johannes describes his 52; a new name Obadiah after 53; departs for Levant after 60; Rabbi Barukh certifies in Aleppo 63; Talmudic Law and 64;

Ceremony described as in Yevamot 64; recalls his in Aleppo 99; writing Christian music after 124

Damascus 69, 82, 97, 98, 100, 101
David Alroy 90
Dhimmi 71, 73, 75
Disraeli, Benjamin 11, 90
Dress restrictions 73, 82
Dreux 24, 27, 28, 30, 38, 43, 49, 66, 128, 130

Edom: kingdom of 31; region in Palestine 49; contest with Israel 50; link with Rome 51; Obadiah a convert from 53; exile in 81; end of 104
Egypt: Viceroy of 11; and Cairo 13; and Geniza 13; Andreas and 31; Fatimid government in 33; Eliphaz in 51; Al-Afdal vizier in 87; Obadiah travels from Baniyas to 100; Tustari brothers in 103; *miṣr* term for 107; Fustāt capital of 108; Amalric invades 109; Jews in 110; Obadiah in 112; foreign cantors in 124
Elijah the son of Obadiah 113, 114, 115, 116, 123
End Time 81, 103, 104, 106
Esau 48, 49, 50, 51, 52, 129
Exilarch 71, 72, 74, 75, 78, 83, 91, 101, 102, 115
Ezekiel 81, 105, 106, 129

Field of Blood, battle 94, 95, 96
First Crusade 19, 35, 36, 42, 43, 44, 45, 52, 55, 56, 80, 103, 106, 128
Franks 44, 54, 55, 56, 57, 61, 63, 66, 90, 93, 94, 95, 96, 97, 98, 103
Fustāt: Letters in 67; wedding in 74; founding of 107; name of 107; panorama of 108; Nilometer in 109; decline of 109; Jews in 110; commerce in 111; synagogue 112; Obadiah's marriage in 113; scribes and cantors in 114, music in 120

Geniza: definition of 13; in Cairo synagogue 14; Schechter visits 14; contents removed to Cambridge 16; fragments of studied 19; Barukh's letter in 63; charity records in 67; poems set to music found in 121; compositions by Obadiah from 123
ger tsedek/ger toshav 19, *64*, 123
Godfrey of Bouillon 44, 56, 58
Gog 105

Goitein, Shelomo 19, 20, 21
Golb, Norman 21, 22, 23, 38, 73
Greek 11, 15, 26, 28, 31, 32, 37, 38, 39, 45, 71, 107, 119, 120
Guido of Arezzo 122, 124
Guiscard, Robert 26, 27, 33, 34, 37, 39, 40, 46, 58, 66

Halevi, Judah 60, 86
Ḥasan-i Sabbaḥ 89, 90, 93
Hauteville 26, 27, 28, 39, 46, 66
Hebrew: considered language of God 14; Ecclesiasticus in original 14; manuscripts in Geniza 16; prayer book in 19; appearance of codex in 20; original of Obadiah memoir 23; Persecution in Bari of communities 34; Venosa inscriptions in 39; Jacob name in 49; Sepher Yosippon written in 51; month of Elul in 60; milk word in 63; meaning of 'sar' in 65; language of Tanakh in 73; word 'academy' in 78; text in by Elijah 114; musical score of Obadiah in 124

Ilghazi/Ghazi bin Urtuq 94, 95, 96
In-gathering in Jerusalem 81, 86, 99, 128
Iraq 24, 58, 62, 69, 70, 74, 83, 111
Islam 20, 33, 43, 57, 69, 70, 71, 82, 83, 84, 86, 90, 91, 101, 106, 108, 120
Israel 45, 49, 50, 51, 52, 63, 64, 65, 70, 71, 72, 81, 82, 87, 89, 90, 98, 99, 100, 102, 103, 104, 105, 119, 128, 129, 130
Italy 21, 24, 25, 26, 27, 28, 31, 33, 35, 36, 37, 39, 40, 41, 42, 46, 47, 51, 52, 57, 59, 63, 64, 65, 80, 81, 113, 116, 117, 121.124, 130

Jacob: story of in Genesis 48; name of 49; is the younger son 49; Esau and brother 49; story of linked to Johannes's identity 49; story of leads to new name for Johannes 54; the blessing of to his sons 104
Jerusalem: destruction of and First Temple12; destruction in 70 CE 35; journey to 43; First Crusade and 44; Zion and restoration of 45; patriarchal city 46; desecration of 49; capture of and massacre 57; contested place of three faiths 57; Kingdom of 58; pilgrims visit 59; Barukh describes 63; exile from and return 70; expectation of Messiah restoring 80; in-gathering and 81; Halevi and 86; Jews flown to 89; Kingdom of attacks Aleppo

94; Zechariah and 99; Obadiah to go to 100; Mount Zion and 105;Ezekiel and 106; Christian heavenly 128
Joel book of 45, 54, 81, 103, 125
Johannes: (*early life*) discovery of 18; scholars unravel life of 19; experience of dream 22; birth of 24; parents of 27; Norman background of 28; place of birth 28; recollects Andreas 30; enters a monastery 38; studies of music 41; experience of violence against Jews 43; visions of 45; conversion of 47; identity with Jacob 50; takes a new name 52 (*see Obadiah*)
Judaism 31, 32, 33, 39, 41, 43, 45, 47, 48, 49, 50, 51, 53, 54, 57, 63, 64, 78, 80, 81, 83, 84, 91, 101, 102, 103, 104, 119, 128, 129, 130

Karaite 83, 84, 98, 99, 100, 101, 102, 103, 105, 110

Levant 46, 51, 52, 54, 61, 63, 66, 68, 87, 95, 114, 123, 130
Lucania/Basilicata 24, 28, 30

Mahdī 90, 92, 105, 106
Maimonides 85, 104, 115, 120
Mann, Jacob 19, 53
Messiah: coming of 53; resurrection 56; the anointed one 80; announced by prophets 81; establishes a Jewish kingdom 82;; Maimonides names a false 85; flight to Holy Land by 86; Solomon b. Ruji seen as the 87; *qā'im* prophet/announcer of 92; Obadiah meets false 99; Obadiah seen as 100; date for coming of 103; Maimonides sets date for 104; Ezekiel and the arrival of 129

Nizari Ismaili state 89, 90, 92, 93

Obadiah (*see Johannes*); a cleric took the name 18; born with the name Johannes 19; change of religion and drawn to the book of that gave him his name 53; journey of to Antioch 61; meeting in Aleppo 63; conversion of confirmed by Barukh 64; appearance of 66, 67; arrives in Baghdad 70; lives and studies in Baghdad, describes dress restrictions 73; resides in the synagogue 77; records a messianic sect in Hakkari region 87; in Aleppo 94; recounts battle of Field of Blood 96, 97; encounters false Messiah in Baniyas 99; resides in Fustāt 111; marriage of 113; Elijah his son 114; work as scribe and cantor 117
Oppido 21, 24, 27, 28, 30, 38, 47, 118

Persia 62, 70, 71, 79, 83, 84, 85, 89, 90, 91, 116, 120
Psalms: and Benedictine rule 40; golden letters of in Baghdad synagogue 75; chanted in Baghdad 115; Augustine account of 118; singing and memory of by Johannes in Benedictine monastery 118; definition of 119; song of ascents 119

Schechter, Solomon 14, 15, 16, 17, 19
Scheiber, Alexander 20, 21, 22, 117
Sepher Yosippon 35, 51, 52
Shi'i 76, 90, 91, 92, 101, 102, 106, 110
Siddur, Sabbath prayer book 19, 53, 113, 123
Solomon ha-Kohen 98, 99, 100, 101, 102, 103, 110
Suez Canal 11, 14, 107
Syria 24, 47, 54, 58, 62, 74, 89, 93

Talmud 47, 50, 53, 64, 78, 79, 101, 104, 117
Torah 12, 20, 31, 64, 77, 115, 117, 122, 125, 128, 129

Venosa: given to Drogo 27; abbey in, also centre of Jewish community 39; Home of Horace 39; shrine of the Norman dynasty 40; Johannes linked to abbey at 40

Yevamot: Talmudic tractate that depicts conversion 64; cited in Obadiah conversion 64

Zoroastrianism 83